SHELTER
From The Storm

D1603820

SHELTER
From The Storm

Bob Dylan's
Rolling Thunder Years

by SID GRIFFIN

SHELTER FROM THE STORM

Bob Dylan's Rolling Thunder Years

Sid Griffin

A GENUINE JAWBONE BOOK
First Edition 2010
Published in the UK and the USA by Jawbone Press
2a Union Court,
20–22 Union Road,
London SW4 6JP,
England

www.jawbonepress.com

ISBN 978-1-906002-27-5

DESIGN Paul Cooper Design
EDITOR David Sheppard

Printed by Wai Man Book Binding (China) Ltd

1 2 3 4 5 14 13 12 11 10

Contents

THIS PAGE, CLOCKWISE FROM TOP: **The Rolling Thunder Revue map; the tour curtain, designed by Bob Neuwirth with Dylan's input; the flyer handed out on New England street corners.** OPPOSITE PAGE: **Dylan, in whiteface, on the tour.**

LEFT TO RIGHT: **Roger McGuinn, Arlo Guthrie, Ramblin' Jack Elliott, cameraman David Myers, Joan Baez, Dylan, Mick Ronson, Rob Stoner, Ronee Blakley, Bob Neuwirth, and Steve Soles perform the show-ending 'This Land Is Your Land' at the Civic Center, Springfield, Massachusetts, November 6 1975.**

The view from behind the Rolling Thunder Revue
stage. Note the presence of Allen Ginsberg,
standing on the right, beside the piano.

OPPOSITE PAGE: **Dylan on stage in Boston.**
ABOVE: **Dylan and Allen Ginsberg, who produced the Rolling Thunder tour newsletter.**
RIGHT: **Scarlet Rivera, Roger McGuinn, Dylan, and T Bone Burnett at the Boston Music Hall.**

RENALDO & CLARA

NOW SHOWING! NOW SHOWING!

Starring

BOB DYLAN & JOAN BAEZ

Written and Directed By Bob Dylan Produced by Lombard Street Films, Inc.
Distributed Worldwide by Circuit Films Metrocolor R RESTRICTED

THE PLAYERS

Renaldo	**BOB DYLAN**
Clara	**SARA DYLAN**
The Woman In White	**JOAN BAEZ**
Bob Dylan	**RONNIE HAWKINS**
Mrs. Dylan	**RONEE BLAKLEY**
Longheno de Castro	**JACK ELLIOTT**
Lafkezio	**HARRY DEAN STANTON**
The Masked Tortilla	**BOB NEUWIRTH**
The Father	**ALLEN GINSBERG**
Mandolin Player	**ARLO GUTHRIE**
Guest Artist	**ROBERTA FLACK**
Musicians	**ROLLING THUNDER REVIEW**

Exclusive Engagement

Galeria Cinema
57 Boylston St.
Harvard Sq.
661-3737

SHOWN AT 1:30 & 7:30

THIS PAGE, CLOCKWISE FROM TOP: **Roger McGuinn, Joni Mitchell, Richie Havens, Joan Baez, Dylan, Rob Stoner, Ronee Blakley, and Bob Neuwirth on stage at the Boston Music Hall, November 21 1975; the 'Hurricane' 45; a poster for** *Renaldo & Clara*.
OPPOSITE PAGE: **Another Dylan solo spot.**

A.S. Griffin
12A Fitzjohns House
46 Fitzjohns Avenue
London
NW3 5LU
United Kingdom

March 3 2009

Dear Pentagon

I am in a discussion group on military history over here in London. We were talking about the Blitz of 1940. Somehow, the subject of the Rolling Thunder air campaign in Vietnam came up.

When I heard the phrase 'Rolling Thunder' I thought two things: that it is the Native American term for 'speaking the truth' and that Bob Dylan, of all people, once had a rock tour called the Rolling Thunder Revue.

Could someone there please tell me the origins of the Rolling Thunder name with regard to the Vietnam War? Why was that name chosen? What did it represent? Is there some apparent significance which I and my learned colleagues might have missed? It was obviously not a name picked at random, so I assume there's an explanation which, after all these years, would not have any security implications.

Any information you could pass my way about Rolling Thunder would be greatly appreciated.

With all good wishes from England,

A.S. Griffin

OPPOSITE PAGE: **Joan Baez duets with Dylan at the Boston Music Hall, November 21 1975. Their dynamic was a major focus of both Rolling Thunder Revue tours.**
ABOVE: **The author's letter to the Pentagon concerning the origins of the phrase 'Rolling Thunder.'**

Introduction

"A hero is anyone who walks to his own drummer."
(BOB DYLAN)

As the 20th century drew to a close, *Time* magazine published its list of the 100 Most Important People of the Century. The great and the good were divided into sections; Bob Dylan was listed in the Artists & Entertainers category. Writer Jay Cocks referred to him as a "Master poet, caustic social critic, and intrepid, guiding spirit of the counterculture generation," which, while accurate, accounts for only a portion of Dylan's act, a portion of his art. It isn't difficult to imagine Bob Dylan being included among the other categories in the *Time* 100 – Leaders & Revolutionaries, Builders & Titans, and Heroes & Icons – for he is all of those.

This book also focuses on a portion of Dylan's act and art, the period of time roughly from summer 1975, and the beginnings of the Rolling Thunder Revue, to summer 1976, when Dylan retreated to edit *Renaldo & Clara* with Howard Alk. Although the book backs up a bit before summer 1975 at times, in order to present the necessary back-story, and occasionally slides past summer 1976, to complete the narrative, it is ostensibly the tale of a little over a year in a still-young man's life. It was a year in which the still-young man appeared on American television honoring an old friend, recorded a Number One studio album of groundbreaking music, toured his native land, twice, filmed and began editing his first motion picture as director, campaigned proudly for the release of a man who he felt was wrongly incarcerated, filmed a television special, junked it, then filmed and edited a second one, and released a live album of performances captured on the second leg of his gypsy-circus tour. It was a hell of a year.

There are several texts on the first Rolling Thunder Revue tour, two books on *Desire*, chapter after chapter discussing *Renaldo & Clara* in miscellaneous Dylan tomes, and a number of volumes on the Hurricane Carter legal case. However, there is only one book which shifts through *all* the art, digests much of the criticism of years hence, and puts both tours, the television specials, the music, the personalities, the wild movie, the social campaigning, and the live album, on equal footing and under one roof.

And that is the book you are holding.

Sid Griffin

Camden Town, London, England,
Summer 2010

CHAPTER 1
THE WORLD OF JOHN HAMMOND

WTTW are the call letters of a distinguished Chicago television station, a nonprofit broadcasting outlet of the US Public Broadcasting System (PBS) network. Located at 5400 North St. Louis Avenue, near the campus of Northeastern University, you'll find the station, poetically enough, just east of Bohemian National Cemetery and a short drive along West Foster Avenue from the windy shores of Lake Michigan.

The studios of WTTW were the location of the PBS live performance series *Soundstage*, which had broadcast a memorable Chicago special featuring many of the city's South Side blues greats – one of the rare occasions that Willie Dixon had been seen on US television. On September 10 1975, *Soundstage* hosted a tribute to legendary Columbia Records executive John Hammond, Sr, the man whose skills gave careers to Bessie Smith, Count Basie, Billie Holiday, Aretha Franklin, Pete Seeger, Bruce Springsteen, and a young scruff from northern Minnesota called Bob Dylan. *Soundstage* gave over an entire episode to celebrate Hammond's career. The great man was feted by many peers and colleagues and a not quite so young scruff from Malibu via New York City called Bob Dylan.

In an extremely rare television appearance, his first since a 1969 performance of 'Living The Blues' on *The Johnny Cash Show*, Bob Dylan took the stage at the midpoint of the broadcast, clutching his beloved and worn Martin 00-21 guitar. Watched today, it seems a curious, yet significant performance. After a rambling, if sincere, intro from Lieberson, the camera shifts right, revealing a small, brightly lit stage. Dylan's puzzled face is that of a man who has suddenly awoken from a deep sleep and is trying to figure out what it was that roused him. The television cameras must be burning hot; Dylan wipes his eyes and you can see the sweat on this temples and neck. He's wearing striped, flared trousers, a tuxedo shirt with ruffles, and a leather blazer. He looks good, his hair full and misshapen on top, like Kramer's in *Seinfeld*. With him is an almost completely obscured drummer, the late Howie Wyeth. The drummer's pal, Rob Stoner, on bass, is right behind Dylan and looking every inch the confident, professional backing musician with his cowboy shirt and expressionless countenance. On the left, to Dylan's right, is dark-haired violinist Scarlet Rivera. She is wearing a long, white, Laura Ashley dress of the kind that any self-respecting lady of the canyon, circa 1975, would have died for.

Their three-song performance was shown nationally on December 13 1975, just after the first Rolling Thunder Revue tour had concluded and with

'Hurricane,' Dylan's protest paean to contentiously imprisoned heavyweight boxer Rubin 'Hurricane' Carter, newly released as a single. In September 1975, all this was still ahead; but that didn't stop the then newly assembled quartet playing 'Hurricane' twice during their performance. Dylan expert Clinton Heylin suggests the two versions were edited together for the broadcast. This, of course, means they had to deliver the song at exactly the same tempo, twice. However the smoke and mirrors were placed, Wyeth is audibly holding back, perhaps responding to Dylan's curious intro; his initial strumming is uncertain until he turns to the band so that they hear his tempo better. Stoner remains as if made of, well, stone; he is not yet the animated bassist of the Rolling Thunder Revue's 1976 *Hard Rain* television special, and not yet the onstage ringmaster, interpreting Dylan's visual cues for the remainder of the band. This is the musicians' first big onstage test with Dylan, and they're on national television, so there is a chance they are all, consciously or not, playing it safe.

Dylan and caution have never been synonyms. Scarlet Rivera says this show was no exception. "When we did the John Hammond special, a live TV show, we'd just finished the album [*Desire*] and everything was in the key of that album. I was really quite nervous that night because I had never performed on a live TV show before. Just before going out, Bob changed the key of the song and that made me concentrate like crazy. I think, in retrospect, maybe he did it to be tricky, but also, maybe, to help me concentrate and not be totally freaked out."[1]

Rivera fiddles almost constantly during 'Hurricane,' playing what bluegrass musicians call *long notes*; in other words, sustained twin notes or double stops. These are less explicit when it comes to essaying a melody but are harmonically pleasing within the broader musical picture; pedal-steel players or organists hit similar sustained notes to suggest poignancy or pathos. If Rivera were a lead guitarist, playing fills with this frequency, she'd be out of a job right after the show; somehow, the violin is less obtrusive. She's on key, too, although her fiddle frequently clashes with Dylan's harmonica. If the band had tuned to Dylan's harp they'd all be in pitch, period, but they did not; they have audibly tuned to something else. So, while the band's stringed instruments are well tempered with one another, they are a tad flat to the harmonica, which makes Dylan's wheezing sound harsh. Unlike his vocal: indeed, Dylan is not spitting out the 'Hurricane' verses with any righteous venom; instead he is *stating* the case, setting the stage like a playwright giving directions to reluctant actors during a rehearsal.

Next up is 'Simple Twist Of Fate,' from Dylan's widely lauded, January 1975 album, *Blood On The Tracks*. The audience will know this one. Dylan is dripping with sweat but never loses the leather jacket. There are obviously two kinds of cool in Bob's world. The lyrics to the song have been changed. By this time, Dylan had been writing with playwright Jacques Levy; the smart money says the stage-setting quality of the rewritten verses is attributable to Levy's influence. The performance is neither better nor less interesting than the *Blood On The Tracks* cut, but it *is* different. It might be another song entirely, yet it still sounds like it would have belonged on the album.

"I want to dedicate this song to someone out there tonight," says Dylan, before the third song, "she knows who she is." In those 16 short words there is enough fodder for Dylan freaks to feast on for weeks. Was this a dedication to his wife Sara (perhaps heralding a version of the eponymous song from *Desire*)? If so, why not say it? Perhaps Dylan knew his mother would be watching the show.

He didn't take the stage until just after 2am, and some punters had actually gone home, but many thought Dylan was about to dedicate the tune to the evening's man of the hour, John Hammond; before, that is, Dylan used the pronoun "she." Afterward, there was allegedly some criticism from other performers on the *World Of John Hammond* show who were disappointed that Dylan hadn't said a few words about the man who'd signed him to Columbia. For Dylan, and his real fans, his attendance said all that was necessary.

The evening's third song is 'Oh Sister.' Taken at a slower tempo than on the then unreleased *Desire*, it sounds, in places, like a doppelganger for an older Dylan song, *Girl From The North Country*. Bob squints in concentration as he sings the second verse. On the bridge, Stoner sings a fine harmony. It is astonishing how every Dylanologist and his brother missed the song's Christian overtones. Certainly, no one commented on it at the time, although its lyrics seem unambiguous: "Oh, sister, am I not a brother to you / And one deserving of affection? / And is our purpose not the same on this earth / To love and follow His direction? / We grew up together from the cradle to the grave / We died and were reborn and then mysteriously saved."

The show was as well-received at the time as it was under-promoted. Most Americans avoid commercial-free, relatively highbrow public broadcasting as if it were train transportation or a diet; but those tree-hugging, tofu-eating, bearded types who did watch PBS back then saw a fascinating, if mystifying, performance and a clear glimpse into two of Dylan's future artistic periods.

CHAPTER 2
DESIRE AND ROLLING THUNDER, FALL 1975

"Memory is the father of tears."
(DANNIE ABSE)

I n 1975, Bob Dylan was at the mercy of fate, his own heart, and changing musical taste. The big news was, he wanted to do something about it; he felt rejuvenated, in some ways at least, and wanted to show the world he still had it. His 1974 tour with The Band had been considered a great success but, as Dylan would confess to *Rolling Stone's* Larry 'Ratso' Sloman, it had not been enjoyable for him.

Dylan had no formal manager in 1975, his only career guidance was provided by attorney David Braun and those charged with looking after his day-to-day affairs, such as secretary/*aide de camp* Naomi Saltzman. His previous manager, Albert Grossman, was long out of the picture (although still financially interested, thanks to his owning a sizeable portion of Dylan's song publishing), and Hollywood player Jerry Weintraub's stewardship of Dylan's affairs wouldn't commence for another two years. At this point, perhaps more so than at any time in his career, Dylan was making all the primary moves himself.

The year had begun well. *Blood On The Tracks* was released in January; it proved to be one of the greatest artistic and commercial successes of Dylan's career. There was no tour to promote the album, however. On March 23, Dylan performed at the S.N.A.C.K. benefit concert in San Francisco, backed by several members of The Band and Neil Young. This was a Bill Graham organized event designed to promote the extracurricular activities of local high school students (the full campaign title was Students Need Athletic and Cultural Kicks, hence the acronym) which was broadcast live on K101 FM radio. Alas, Dylan's vocal mic was not functioning properly, so, despite the stellar line-up, as a musical document it is less than valuable.

Earlier in March, Dylan was a guest on his friend Mary Travers's KNX FM radio show, in Los Angeles. The interview was broadcast via a hodgepodge of radio networks in April and May. Travers had been one third of Peter Paul & Mary, another act managed by Albert Grossman, who'd split at the turn of the 70s. KNX had once been a middle-of-the-road station playing Frank Sinatra, Tony Bennett, Johnny Mathis, and their ilk. However, in 1970 it got hip, seemingly overnight, thanks to the arrival of new program director, Steve Marshall, who hired a fresh crop of DJs, including Mary Travers.

In the broadcast interview, Dylan seemed only marginally more forthcoming than he would have been with anyone else, which was surprising considering how long he had known Travers and how much they had in common as performers. At no point did Dylan refer to his host as "Mary," nor was he particularly warm. He was articulate, however, and quite animated when a question or subject piqued his interest. He described their mutual friend, the singer Richie Havens, being "like a king" before Travers played Havens's startlingly tender version of Dylan's 'Just Like A Woman.' Typically, Dylan dodged some questions, disputed others, and memorably replied to Travers's comment about the honest simplicity of *Blood On The Tracks*: "A lot of people tell me they enjoyed that album ... it is hard for me to relate to that; I mean, people enjoying that type of pain, you know?" By the end of the interview, Dylan was asking a few muffled questions and Travers was doing most of the talking.

In May, Dylan took a vacation in the South of France with his friend David Oppenheim, the painter whose work had adorned the sleeve of *Blood On The Tracks*. They would spend over a month there, the two men celebrating Dylan's midlife crisis a few years early, perhaps. Dylan was most impressed by time spent in the forests of La Camargue, in Provence, where he stayed with a gypsy king who allegedly had 12 wives. Dylan claims he wrote the song 'One More Cup Of Coffee' in late May, shortly after his 34th birthday; a day he'd spent with the king, presumably some, or all, of the wives, and possibly Oppenheim, at a gypsy festival.

On return from Europe, Dylan visited the New Jersey prison in which prizefighter Rubin 'Hurricane' Carter was controversially incarcerated. Carter had sent Dylan a copy of his autobiography, *The Sixteenth Round*, which detailed his arrest on a never conclusively proven double-murder charge. That month, Robbie Robertson's rather more polished version of *The Basement Tapes* was released. Dylan did nothing to promote it but it proved to be a Top Ten album in both the USA and the UK, nonetheless. *Rolling Stone* alleged that Dylan had expressed surprise when *The Basement Tapes* proved such a rapid seller, apparently commenting of the much-bootlegged home recordings: "I thought everybody had 'em already!"

By late June, although still married to Sara, his wife of ten years, Dylan was living alone in Greenwich Village. He would spend much of the summer revisiting familiar Manhattan haunts and jamming with musical acquaintances, old and new. He was particularly impressed by two very different artists then cutting a swathe through the city: Patti Smith, a newcomer to music, although she had been publicly reading her poetry since 1970, and Bette Midler, a singer known for her onstage sass and verve. On June 26, Dylan saw Patti Smith perform at the Other End, a venue which would become something of a second home for Bob and his cronies throughout the summer of 1975.

There is some confusion amongst Dylanologists about the names the Other End and the Bitter End; the two are often used interchangeably. In operation since 1961, and located at 147 Bleeker Street, in Greenwich Village, the famous, and actually surprisingly small, club has hosted many a comic on their way up, including Bill Cosby, George Carlin, and Woody Allen. It's been equally famous as a friendly gig for folk singers such as Pete Seeger, Arlo Guthrie, Tom Paxton, Peter Paul & Mary, and, of course, the young Bob Dylan. Jazz and rhythm & blues acts played there, too. The hard-to-please Nina Simone liked the intimacy of the club's bohemian environs, while Stevie Wonder somehow squeezed a 13-piece band on stage with him during a late-60s residency there. The Bitter End has also been the recording location for several live albums by such names as Randy Newman, Curtis Mayfield, and The Isley Brothers. A 1963 concert album by folk group The Chad Mitchell Trio was even called *At The Bitter End*. The album jacket photograph features a picture of a young, grinning Roger (then known as Jim) McGuinn; he was the trio's banjo-playing accompanist (which ought to have made them the Chad Mitchell *Quartet*). McGuinn would have a propitious meeting with Dylan at the same venue in the late summer of 1975.

The Bitter End was jointly owned by Fred Weintraub and Paul Colby, until, that is, Weintraub's East Coast television and motion picture concerns determined that he move to California and sell his share of the business to Colby. Weintraub, part of the production team for the movie *Woodstock*, was involved in innumerable music shows, including ABC television's original *Hootenanny* program, ironically the very show which blacklisted one-time Bitter End performer Pete Seeger. Weintraub would subsequently work on the *Dukes Of Hazzard* television series, as well as a number of low budget, lowbrow, martial arts films. Lest he be portrayed as a cultural lightweight, however, it should be noted that Weintraub was also once arrested on an obscenity charge alongside taboo-busting, provocateur-comedian Lenny Bruce, and stood beside Bruce during subsequent legal proceedings.

A devotee of good food, good music, and good friendships, Paul Colby was a quite different character. Many in Dylan's circle have stated that Bob was genuinely close to him. Breaking into the entertainment business by becoming a radio plugger (pitching new records to broadcast DJs), Colby had worked his way up until he was employed to promote the latest songs by the likes of Benny Goodman, Frank Sinatra, and Tony Bennett, with all of whom he became friends. He knew his wines, too, and hand built furniture in his spare time.

Although Weintraub had sold his share of the club to Colby, he retained the rights to the name the Bitter End. Thus, Colby, while continuing to run the venue as it was, had to find another designation. He chose the Other End. Years later, Colby secured the rights to the name the Bitter End and changed it back to this original moniker (which it still bears today). When Dylan, Ramblin' Jack Elliott, Bob Neuwirth, and their entourage were cavorting there, in summer 1975, the sign over the door read the Other End. Nonetheless, old habits die hard, and in the memories, and in the interviews, of many ex-folkies, the club is often referred to as the Bitter End, even in the post-Weintraub period.

During his June 26 visit, Dylan was pleased to hang with his friend Colby and thrilled by the performance of Patti Smith, an artist Dylan's confidant and longtime cohort Bob Neuwirth had been championing for some time. Smith offered several facets which chimed with Dylan. Firstly, the use of poetry in her act, as inspiration, recited or read from a book, or as improvised lyrics in her songs. Secondly, Dylan noticed that Smith and her band's extemporized songs eschewed the default settings of orthodox rock'n'roll jamming. Rather than the usual chord progressions overlaid with blues scales, these were true improvisations, closer to Ornette Coleman than Cream. Smith's musicians followed her lyrical flights intuitively, playing with a kind of harsh beauty. Dylan's various backing bands, as talented and unrehearsed as they had often been, and inventive as his songs undoubtedly were, had always stuck to formal musical structures. Indeed, even when Dylan and the indisputably gifted Hawks tried jamming, at London's Royal Albert Hall, on the final song of the 1966 world tour, it proved something of a damp squib. Even with virtuoso Garth Hudson on keyboards, their two-minute improvisation at the end of 'Like A Rolling Stone' amounted to little more than a sloppily repeated chord progression. It was not so much free jazz as the sound of a garage band rehearsing 'Hang On Sloopy.'

Another reason for Dylan to be enamored of Patti Smith was that she was audibly and visibly influenced by him and worked identifiably, as did he, in the tradition of the Beats. Indeed, she was a strong new link in that particular chain, somehow making a connection between Lawrence Ferlinghetti's City Lights bookstore in North Beach, San Francisco, the infamous Beat Hotel, at 9 Rue Gît-le-Cœur, Paris, and the recently opened CBGB's, a dingy basement club at the fag end of the Bowery that was HQ to Smith and a febrile yet cerebral new generation of rockers. For Dylan to stumble upon Patti Smith and her band on stage at the Other End, must have been akin to Ramblin' Jack Elliott witnessing the young Dylan in Greenwich Village for the first time in 1961. Dylan was so impressed with Smith's performance that he insisted on being photographed with the newcomer.

Bette Midler had already tasted fame and had two albums to her name by the time she started running with the Dylan crowd, that summer. She had enjoyed a hit single as far back as 1972 with a cover of The Andrews Sisters' 'Boogie Woogie Bugle Boy' and been the cover story in *Newsweek's* December 17 1973 issue, its headline blaring: "Here Comes Bette! The Divine Miss Midler." Dylan's fascination with Midler was evidence of his regard for the Great American Songbook, something which would play out, here and there, during the first Rolling Thunder tour, later that fall. Dylan and Midler quickly hit it off, warming to each other on the common ground of New York City, audience expectations, and the pressures of the business.

Both Bette Midler and Patti Smith would become members of an exclusive, after-hours party cabal, based around Dylan and the Other End. Future Rolling Thunder musician David Mansfield was among their number and remembers the clubhouse feel of the venue. "Back in '75, the Other End bar was next door [to the stage] and it was basically a bar [without music]; there was an interior door between them, so you could walk into the bar after the show was over ... That [Dylan-related social] scene was all about drinking at the bar afterward."[1]

On June 30, Dylan was being driven in a friend's car when he spied a woman with extremely long hair, carrying a violin case; it was Scarlet Rivera. "I was walking down the [Lower] East Side on, 13th Street ... this was purely a fateful event," Rivera later recalled. "I had my violin in my hand and I was going across the street to a basement apartment, to do a rehearsal. Within those few seconds, his [Dylan's] car cut me off. He said, 'Hey, can you play that thing?' He insisted on hearing me play, so I agreed and went to his studio, on the [Lower] East Side. It was like a loft, really, not a recording studio; just an upright piano and an acoustic guitar in the room ... and that's when he played all of the songs that would be on *Desire*. He did little bits of 'Mozambique' and bits of 'One More Cup Of Coffee' … eventually [he] moved over to the piano and a small smile came over his face at some point."[2]

In other accounts, Rivera says it was Dylan's female companion who spoke to her and asked about her musical abilities, but no matter. The first all-important piece in the Rolling Thunder Revue puzzle was now set in place. That evening, they met again and jammed. Afterward, Dylan took Rivera to the Bottom Line club, where he played harmonica behind Muddy Waters and then introduced Rivera to the audience, bringing her up to fiddle behind the great bluesman as the audience gaped in astonishment.

On July 2, Dylan saw his old friend Ramblin' Jack Elliott in concert at the Other End, the singing cowboy having been booked for a run of evening shows there. Greatly enjoying the performance, Dylan returned the following night during which he jumped on stage to play guitar with Elliott on a version of Woody Guthrie's 'Pretty Boy Floyd,' allegedly the first Guthrie song Dylan had ever learned to play. The duo followed this with pianist Meade Lux Lewis's immortal 'How Long Blues.' Elliott then left the stage and Dylan performed a staggering version of a brand new composition, 'Abandoned Love.' How staggering? Musician and archivist Tom Stevens later described the performance. "The effect is like a bomb going off, and it's arguably among the very finest Dylan acoustic performances ever, up there with, say, '(It's All Over Now) Baby Blue' from Newport '65."[3] Typically, Dylan would record 'Abandoned Love' but not release it on his next album, *Desire*. (It was a willful habit that would see 'The Groom's Still Waiting At The Altar' omitted from 1981's *Shot Of Love*, 'Blind Willie McTell' being left off 1983's *Infidels*, and 'Red River Shore' not making the final cut of *Time Out Of Mind* in 1997; all of them songs that would have been album highlights. 'Abandoned Love,' in a version cut at the *Desire* sessions, was finally released on the boxed set, *Biograph*, in 1985.)

To Ramblin' Jack Elliott, July 3 1975 might as well have been yesterday. "Yeah, Bob was there and a whole bunch of the gang were around. Bob got up and played a song. Patti Smith came as Bob's date. At the end of the evening, when I was in the back room with the owner [Paul Colby], Bob walked in, handed me a glass of wine, and said, 'Jack, we've been talking, Bobby Neuwirth and I. We've been making plans and thinking about doing a little tour where we would get a bus, and get Joan Baez, and you and me, and Bobby Neuwirth, and play some little gigs around New England. What do you think about it?' I said,

'Count me in, I'd love to do that,' and I took a sip of wine and nothing more was said."

Later that summer, Elliott was back at the Other End, where Bob Neuwirth caught his show. Afterward, the two of them adjourned to Neuwirth's nearby apartment where they phoned Dylan, who was temporarily stationed at his house in California. By this time, plans for Rolling Thunder were advanced. "Neuwirth put me on the phone [to Dylan]," Elliott recalls. "Bob said, 'Hey, Jack, so you remember that thing we were talking about? We are going to do it in November, starting in New York.' I said, 'OK, I'll see you in New York on into November,' and that was all we said. In October, I showed up in NYC at my favorite hotel, the Gramercy Park, and we all got together there and spent three weeks rehearsing, and then got in the bus, and about ten other vehicles, and headed up to New England to start the tour."[4]

It could well be stated that July 3 1975 marks the beginning of the Rolling Thunder Revue; not the official start of any physical tour, but the date on which serendipitous events and changing musical tastes coalesced to present Dylan with the daylight he needed to run toward. Most importantly, the dictates of his heart convinced Dylan that his idea of an acoustic gypsy caravan would be just the thing, the best career move for him and his soul, and a welcome antidote to the successful but stressful 1974 stadium tour with The Band.

Independence Day 1975 was another significant date in the genesis of Rolling Thunder. All that week at the Other End, Bob Neuwirth had been ringmaster of what amounted to an old-style hootenanny, with all kinds of folk artists dropping by to perform. On July 4, Neuwirth was to play a set himself. It must strike many Dylan followers as auspicious that on July 3 one of Bob's original inspirations was playing the Other End and the following day his most trusted lieutenant was performing at the same venue. Bob Neuwirth: "My friend Aviva booked the club [the Other End] at the time ... Bob and I happened to go see Jack [Elliott], and in Jack's inimitable way [we] ended up on stage during his show. It was so much fun that I talked Paul Colby into letting me on the bill the next week. [During that following week,] we all played together, along with whoever happened to walk in."[5]

Neuwirth's eponymous solo album had come and gone the previous year on the Asylum label. While it had left the charts untroubled, Neuwirth's standing among his peers can be judged by the album's stellar roll call of guest musicians, which included Rita Coolidge, Cass Elliot, Don Everly, Richie Furay,

Chris Hillman, Booker T. Jones, Kris Kristofferson, and Dusty Springfield (among many others).

The week of Other End shows which followed Ramblin' Jack's mid-summer performance was unlike any formal record company showcase and equally unlike an orthodox club residency (even if that was supposed to be the idea). Spontaneity was afoot; July 4 turned into a full-on Independence Day folkie hoot, with Dylan leaping up on stage, this time to perform with his old friend Neuwirth.

The following night, Neuwirth's set was interrupted by Dylan once again performing an impromptu song. This time, he stayed put to play piano alongside Rob Stoner (real name Robert Rothstein) on bass, English guitarist Mick Ronson, and nominal headliner Neuwirth on guitar and mandolin. These four hoarse men of the Apocalypse would then back Patti Smith on over a dozen folk chestnuts from the *Fireside Book Of Folk Songs*. It is hard to imagine Smith, a firebrand poetess, steeped in Rimbaud, Jim Morrison, and the redemptive power of electrified rock'n'roll, happily singing the likes of 'Goodnight Irene,' 'I've Been Working On The Railroad,' 'Erie Canal,' and 'Bring Me A Little Water, Sylvie,' but that is exactly what she did. For Dylan, it must have been a double thrill, love at first sight and joy in discovering that his brand of Beat Americana had another torchbearer. Here was a woman who could sing Leadbelly songs, recite Arthur Rimbaud verbatim, or burst into a Little Anthony & The Imperials' hit, with equal alacrity. No wonder he was smitten.

Rob Stoner had met bluegrass fan Bob Neuwirth two-and-a-half years earlier, in San Francisco, where Stoner was performing with John Herald, the ex-Greenbriar Boy who Dylan once called "the country Stevie Wonder." Herald was still using the Greenbriar Boys name but the line-up was now fluid – even The Grateful Dead's Jerry Garcia had been a band-member for a spell. Herald's West Coast sojourn would provide the opportunity for some future Rolling Thunder Revue musicians to work together for the first time. In addition to Stoner, the jacket of the 1973 Paramount album *John Herald* would credit Howie Wyeth on keyboards and Steve Soles on guitar. It would also list a 'thank you' to Bob Neuwirth, who had recorded several Herald live concerts in order to provide B-sides for singles culled from the album. When all these East Coast characters found themselves back in the bosom of New York City, in mid 1975, they naturally started thinking about working together.

On July 5, another Rolling Thunder stalwart arrived: David Mansfield. Just 19, Mansfield had been playing in Eric Anderson's band and was, despite his tender years, fast becoming a professional sideman of note. He'd arrived at the Other End after word had spread of the fun being had there. "Actually, a girlfriend of mine dragged me down there … she basically thought it was a free-for-all," Mansfield recalls. "She said, 'You'd fit in perfectly, since there is nobody playing violin.' Neuwirth had a big commitment. He had to play maybe five days, not just one evening, so I think he liked to cover himself with a whole lot of other musicians and singer-songwriters; I think it made him feel more comfortable. He had this phalanx of people between him and this terrifying audience. I just brought my violin … there were 500 guitar players on stage already."

Mansfield was soon mingling with what would soon become his Rolling Thunder Revue colleagues. "I didn't bump into *everybody* during that Other End thing, although T Bone [Burnett] was there and Steven Soles was there. As soon as Bobby [Neuwirth] got the gig, he sent those guys tickets and said, 'Back me up,' but I don't think Roger McGuinn sat in and played with them then, although they [McGuinn and Neuwirth] were hanging out after hours."[6]

Mansfield mentions T Bone Burnett's presence at Neuwirth's Other End residency; it was another piece of the Rolling Thunder mosaic falling into place. Burnett had been recording in his own Fort Worth, Texas, studio since the late 60s and had worked with The Legendary Stardust Cowboy (and plays on the Cowboy's classic *Paralyzed*). Circa 1971, Burnett was in Los Angeles "writing songs and sleeping on couches." His Texas buddy, Lindsay Holland, had gone to school back east and was roommates at Princeton with Jonathan Taplin, who later looked after The Band for Albert Grossman. Holland was invited by Taplin to join one leg of the 1974 Dylan/Band tour, whereupon Holland gave Dylan a tape of some of Burnett's material. In the meantime, Burnett had met Neuwirth and soon found himself invited by Grossman to come to the manager's Bearsville, New York headquarters to audition for a revamped version of The Full Tilt Boogie Band, effectively to see if he could replace their former (now deceased) singer, Janis Joplin. So, Burnett was now part of the periphery of Dylan's circle, another distant ring revolving around Bob's Saturn.

Burnett finally met Dylan, face to face, at Jonathan Taplin's wedding. They got along well. Sometime in the summer of '75, Burnett received a call from Dylan asking him if he was free to come on the road. Burnett readily agreed, thinking he would probably be Neuwirth's guitarist. That night, at the Other End, would mark Burnett's first meeting with David Mansfield and the rest of what would become known, for delightfully vague reasons, as Guam, the Rolling Thunder Revue backing band.

Dylanologists have a number of theories why Guam was chosen as the name of the tour backing band. It was the name of the island from which bombers took off during the North Vietnam bombing campaign called Rolling Thunder by the Pentagon; it was the westernmost postmark for a US stamp; it was chosen because no one on the tour had ever been there. McGuinn believes this last reason. "I was there when they named [the band]. Bob Neuwirth said, 'Let's name the band for a place none of us have been to!' Guam was the only place we could think of, as the guys were a well-traveled band." [7] T Bone Burnett has another theory. "Neuwirth got that name right out of thin air. [It means] absolutely nothing! Then you would reverse-engineer it. It's the westernmost United States postal stop, whatever ... it was just funny. I remember very well Neuwirth saying, 'Why ... it is Guam!' and everybody laughing. The point was that it was a Dadaist point." [8]

One night at the Other End, Dylan bumped into Woody Guthrie's old pal, Logan English, a former MC at the nearby Gerde's Folk City. English had been one of Guthrie's regular visitors when the folk icon was bedridden with Huntington's disease, at New Jersey's Greystone Psychiatric Hospital. Ramblin' Jack Elliott and the young Bob Dylan were also regulars at Guthrie's bedside in the early 60s. Although fame had taken the youthful Bobby Dylan away from the folk clubs of New York City, he had not forgotten those who were kind to him when he'd started out. That fateful night, in the Other End's small barroom, Dylan thought he saw a face from the past, and the face from the past thought he saw Dylan. *Rolling Stone*'s Lucian K. Truscott IV reported the following exchange taking place. "'That you, Logan?' Dylan asked sleepily. 'Yeah Bobby, it's me,' said Logan English. 'Hey man, I thought you were dead,' said Dylan. 'I've heard the same about you a few times,' English replied. They both laughed." [9]

Roger McGuinn was in on the ground floor of Rolling Thunder. Earlier on that year, he'd had an inkling of what Dylan was planning while relaxing between tours at his home in Malibu, California. Dylan had property nearby and he was a frequent visitor to the McGuinn homestead. "He and I were hanging out in Malibu, playing basketball in the backyard ... about the only time we ever did this," McGuinn recalls. "Bob had wanted to shoot hoops, so I got out the basketball and we were shooting at the goal over the garage. Then

Bob said, 'I wanna do something different,' and I said, 'Whaddya mean, man?' Bob thought about it and said, 'I don't know ... something like a circus.' And that was it; that was about all the conversation there was about it and we went back to shooting baskets."

Some six months later, McGuinn, on the road with his band, had a day off in New York City. "I decided to go to the Village and hang out. I ran into Larry Sloman at Folk City and we went to Chinatown to get something to eat. Over dinner, he mentioned that Dylan was probably at the Other End. We walked into the backroom [of the club] and there were Jacques Levy and Dylan sitting at a table. Those two stood up really fast when they saw me walk in, and the brandies they were enjoying went flying off the table. 'Roger,' they both exclaimed, 'we were just talking about you. We are going off on tour and we want you to come along with us.' I said, 'Well, I am about to tour and I have all these commitments with my band, I can't do it.'"

The next day, McGuinn received a call from Sloman, urging him to change his mind. "So I thought about it and I called my agent and said that I wanted to postpone these dates so I could go out with Dylan. They arranged to do that and worked out a deal where I got a fee for the whole tour ... but let me tell you, this was *not* about the money!"[10]

While out on the West Coast, and contemplating "something like a circus," Dylan popped into Elektra Sound Recorders, on LA's La Cienega Boulevard, where he recorded some harmonica on a David Blue song, 'Who Love,' a track destined for Blue's album *Com'n Back For More*, released on Asylum in the fall of 1975. Future Eagle Don Felder was part of the David Blue band, a group that would become frustrated during their own autumn 1975 tour in support of the album as, whenever there was a day or two off, Blue would suddenly fly out to be with the Rolling Thunder Revue, leaving his band to twiddle their thumbs in Podunk or Nowhere Ville.

Slowly, Rolling Thunder was taking shape. As he had with Scarlet Rivera, Dylan had first met the aforementioned Larry 'Ratso' Sloman, another future mainstay of the RTR posse, while sitting in a car. Their paths had crossed the previous fall. "I'm walking down Fifth Avenue, and I am going right by that fancy salon, Elizabeth Arden, where all the high society women go," Sloman remembers. "Outside the salon is Dylan, sitting in a car. I guess he was waiting for Sara or something. I introduced myself and said, 'Hey, I hear you are doing a new album' and he goes, 'How do you know?' I say, 'I write for *Rolling Stone* and I am a roommate of Phil Ochs.' He *immediately* lightened up and said, 'How's Phil? Give him my best.' That is how I made the contact and was able to write the preview piece on *Blood On The Tracks* for *Rolling Stone*."[11]

Sloman confirms Roger McGuinn's story about his timely appearance at the Other End. "I had heard from the grapevine that Dylan was in town, was recording [*Desire*], and was hanging out in the Village again. One night, I went to see McGuinn at Mike Porco's place, [Gerde's] Folk City. I remember they called him up on stage to do a song and he decided to do it from the audience using his giant cell phone. Anyway, we decide to leave Folk City, and I said, 'Hey, let's go by the Other End, maybe Bob is still in town. We walked in there and immediately saw Dylan, Ronee Blakley, and Bob Neuwirth. They were all hanging out. Dylan was extremely pleased to see Roger. Then I reintroduced myself. We were hanging out that whole night; it was a lot of fun. We went to all Dylan's old haunts and he was just so excited to be back in New York. He [Dylan] said to Roger, 'We are going to do this tour and you have got to come on it.' Dylan said to me, 'Why don't you cover it?' I said, 'Yeah.' I approached *Rolling Stone* and they were, of course, more than pleased to have me cover it."[12]

There is no historical plaque outside Jacques and Claudia Levy's LaGuardia Place home, but there should be. Jacques Levy had a PhD in clinical psychology but was equally at home working in the theater. As far back as 1965, he had directed a one-act play, *Red Cross*, written by an aspiring musician and playwright by the name of Sam Shepard. Greater fame came to Levy in 1969 when his direction of Kenneth Tynan's theatrical revue *Oh! Calcutta!* had become a cause célèbre among the chattering classes. That same year, he approached Roger McGuinn to help him write a modern, country-rock version of Henrik Ibsen's play *Peer Gynt*. The pair began work on what became known as *Gene Tryp* (an anagram of the original title), and although they would drop the project after two years, several of its songs entered The Byrds' repertoire, most notably 'Chestnut Mare', a sizeable hit in the UK and a song whose lyrics had impressed Bob Dylan so much that, several years later, he thought writing with its co-author might be a good idea.

Having met briefly in California, and again in New York, in the spring of 1974, Levy and Dylan crossed paths again in July 1975. "The third time we met, it was complete serendipity," Levy later recalled. "I walked out of my house, on LaGuardia Place, and Bob walked passed me, by himself, on his way somewhere. I didn't know where he was going. I said, 'Bob!' and he turned and looked at me, and said, 'Oh, hi' and we chatted and I asked where he was going, and it turned out that he was going to a place that I often hung out, a little bar on Bleeker Street called the Other End. ... So, I went with him and we had a drink together and that is how the two of us connected."

Dylan expressed his fondness for 'Chestnut Mare.' "I think he liked the idea that I could tell a story; there was a story in that song. Bob is not really that good at telling stories; he doesn't go from A to B to C to D. He has got a lot of good stuff in his songs, but they don't usually add up to a story. Once in a while it does, and I think he liked that."[13]

Dylan may have had a new muse somewhere in this Greenwich Village scene; he definitely had his mojo working again, yet he had few new songs to show for it. From his adventures with David Oppenheim, in France, he had 'One More Cup Of Coffee,' and from somewhere, possibly the depths of his soul, he had 'Abandoned Love.' As Scarlet Rivera recalled, when she met Dylan he also had early drafts of songs destined for *Desire*, such as 'Isis' and 'Mozambique.' Jacques Levy's storytelling and directorial skills would impact heavily on Dylan. Levy's art was all about going "from A to B to C to D," as the lyrics to 'Chestnut Mare' bore testament.

One night, Dylan suggested to Levy that they retire to his LaGuardia Place loft to listen to and analyze some of Bob's new songs, which he would play on Claudia Levy's piano. The first song they worked on was 'Isis.' They revised it drastically. At about 3am, they raced around the block to the Other End, arriving not long before the club closed for the night. Although those assembled were under the grip of the grape, Dylan announced he had a new song and asked if anyone wanted to hear it. A chorus of huzzahs arose and instead of singing it, Dylan surprised even Levy by reading the new 'Isis' lyric off a piece of paper as if it were a poem. The tipsy punters responded enthusiastically and both Levy and Dylan were greatly encouraged. The influence of Levy's cinematic storytelling technique, like that of the Manhattan painting classes which he had attended under the tutelage of Norman Raeben the previous year, would help Dylan revitalize his approach to the craft of song. What a relief this must have been to a songwriter who had tried for so long to get his artistic vision back; a songwriter who, according to Roger McGuinn, had only recently discovered the existence of both the rhyming dictionary and the thesaurus.

Levy explained to interviewer Derek Barker how important 'Isis' was to his collaboration with Dylan. "That was the first song we wrote. We knew that song was important and that it really worked. We are very happy with it but we had no idea that it would have the sort of power that it wound up having on the Rolling Thunder Revue. When that song was sung [at Rolling Thunder shows] and that rock band played it, it had a fantastic impact and the song took on a whole new character."[14]

For all the truth of Levy's statement about 'Isis', perhaps the biggest leap forward for Dylan, and the most obvious evidence of Levy's fingerprints, was in the song 'Hurricane.' Although Dylan had read Rubin Carter's autobiography, *The Sixteenth Round*, in France, while carousing with David Oppenheim, it had inspired no immediate bursting forth of song. His most renowned political songwriting was a decade distant by 1975, although in late 1971 he had released the single 'George Jackson,' a tribute to the eponymous Black Panther activist, shot and killed by prison guards in San Quentin Jail earlier that summer. With the high-profile furor surrounding Carter and his plight, it would, perhaps, have been more surprising if an artist of Dylan's stature and track record *hadn't* come up with a song protesting the dimming of the New Jersey light for the dubiously imprisoned prizefighter.

The story of Rubin 'Hurricane' Carter could not be made up; no publisher would find it believable as a work of fiction. Carter's life has been the subject of at least eight lengthy non-fiction books, including his own, however, as well as a major motion picture starring Denzel Washington, and not to mention dozens of websites. At least four of these are wildly anti-Carter and claim that the boxer was not only guilty of murder but that he was a first class liar and a charlatan whose tall tales took in the naïve Bob Dylan as well as other supporters such as Muhammed Ali and film director Norman Jewison, whose movie *The Hurricane* championed Carter no less explicitly than Dylan's nobly intended song.

There isn't enough space here to thoroughly discuss the Carter story – indeed, if three, full-blown trials could not uncover every pertinent fact about his case then a few paragraphs in a book about Bob Dylan are hardly likely to shed any new light. However, without knowing some of the background to Carter's story, its profound subsequent impact on Dylan will never be fully understood.

Rubin 'Hurricane' Carter was a very good, but not great, middleweight prizefighter. He was born May 6 1937, in Delawanna, New Jersey. His father had suffered from the attentions of the Ku Klux Klan in Georgia and had moved the family north to New Jersey, hoping for a better life. He taught his son that African-Americans had to stand their ground. Alas, the young Rubin took this concept rather too literally and joined a street gang called The Apaches. By the age of 14, he was on first-name terms with the local police and was sent, after miscellaneous misdemeanors, to Jamesburg State Home For Boys (now the New Jersey Training School For Boys) in southern New Jersey for a term of two years. He escaped, but was subsequently arrested for attacking a man with a bottle and stealing his wristwatch and money. Sent back to the State Home, he escaped again and joined the US Army, aged 17, where he served his country as a paratrooper and, more significantly, learned to box. As soon as he was discharged, however, he was re-arrested and forced to serve out his remaining sentence.

When finally released, Carter was not at liberty for long. He was arrested yet again after committing two robberies and an unprovoked assault, all on the same day. He was duly sent to prison where he was diagnosed, according to official records, reprinted on several Carter websites, as "Aggressive, hostile, negativistic, hedonistic, sadistic, unproductive, and useless." Those may have been his good points. It is a tribute to Dylan's tender soul that he could empathize with such a life story and locate the positive parts of this troubled man's spirit. Yet, prison did one thing for Rubin Carter; the military had been right, he could make use of his anger and aggression in the ring. Within a month of his 1961 release, he had won his first professional bout, dispatching a longtime palooka called Pike Reed inside four rounds.

Carter would go on to win ten of his first 11 fights, most victories coming in the early rounds. The average prizefighter throws punches in combinations of four to eight blows but Stratton Hammon, of *The Ring* magazine, confirms that Carter earned the nickname 'Hurricane' thanks to his ability to throw up to 75 punches in a single minute. This was proven when Hammon ran archive fight footage through a computer program. It revealed that Carter's combinations delivered as many as a dozen hard punches in the space of a mere four seconds. Carter was what ring experts call a *brawler* or a *mauler*, the kind of fighter who wants the bout over early and is eager to overwhelm his opponent quickly. The adversary's strategy is to wait and tire the overly vigorous pugilist, draining his energy so that by end of a nine or 15-round bout, a fighter like Rubin Carter is fatigued enough to begin literally letting his guard down. Hammon maintains that this is exactly what started to happen to Carter later in his career, when his losses began to mount. In his early ring days, however, Carter was truly something. At his peak, in December 1964, he fought the defending middleweight champion, Joey Giardello, in a World Boxing Association title match, in Philadelphia. Carter started strongly and landed a few solid rights to Giardello's head in the early rounds, but by the fifth the defending champion had taken control. Carter, having exerted so much energy in the early rounds trying to a land a knockout punch, was weary and increasingly besieged by Giardello. When the final bell sounded, Giardello had won on points – the unanimous decision of the judges. Boxing experts believed it was a fair result and there was no report of skullduggery (contrary to Norman Jewison's screenplay, which portrayed the bout as unfair and tainted by racism – an allegation which caused Giardello to file a lawsuit against the director).

Something in Rubin Carter was broken that night, possibly his heart and certainly his fighting spirit. He lost eight of his next 14 fights and began to hit the bottle when not in training. He became involved in several barroom brawls, usually started by men who had imbibed so much alcohol that they had no qualms about challenging a well built, obviously aggressive, visibly angry, bald man in a razor-creased, sharkskin suit.

Fate, however, would not allow Carter to limp off into obscurity, another of boxing's forgotten could-have-beens. At around 2:30am on June 17 1966, two African-Americans, carrying a shotgun and pistol, entered the Lafayette Bar & Grill on East 18th Street, in Paterson, New Jersey. They opened fire on bartender James Oliver, drinkers William Marins and Fred Nauyaks, and waitress Hazel Tanis. Oliver and Nauyaks died instantly; Marins was hit in the skull but miraculously survived. Tanis survived horrific, close-range handgun shots, but later died from a blood clot on her lung. Witness Patricia Valentine looked out of her apartment window, above the Lafayette, and saw two African-Americans escape in a white car with out-of-state license plates. Valentine raced downstairs to discover the carnage. Although shocked, she managed to call the police.

A bulletin was issued within five minutes. At 2:40am, Sgt Theodore Capter, a police officer with the local Paterson force, pulled over a white car with Rubin Carter, John Artis, and a third man inside. Capter, a boxing fan, recognized Carter and let them drive away. Carter later claimed he was giving Artis a ride home, yet when they were stopped, Artis was actually at the wheel while Carter was lying down on the backseat.

Back at the murder scene, two petty criminals had shown up, Alfred Bello and Arthur Dexter Bradley, one of whom called the police (not knowing they had already been contacted). Bello was such a noble citizen that he leapt over the bar and rifled the cash register of $62. He told the police that he'd seen two African-Americans jump into a white car with out-of-state plates. Rubin Carter had rented just such a car and now the police were specifically looking for him.

The second time the police spotted the car, only Carter and Artis were in it; the third man had vanished. They were told to drive back to the Lafayette Bar & Grill and once there, both Valentine and Bello confirmed that Carter's white rental car was similar to the getaway vehicle, although neither could positively identify Carter and Artis as the killers. A police search of the car produced one live .32 bullet and one live shotgun shell, both of which matched the calibers used in the killings. After being taken to a local hospital, the wounded Marins could not positively identify the two men as the killers. Carter and Artis were taken to a police station to make a statement, given lie detector tests, and then released. And so begins one of the most confusing, twisted, and lengthy legal sagas in New Jersey's history.

In October 1966, Carter was arrested and charged with murder for the shootings at the Lafayette Bar & Grill. In May 1967, he and Artis were found guilty of all charges by an all-white jury and given life sentences. As each man had loudly and repeatedly protested their innocence, and there were almost immediate accusations of racism tainting the trial, a campaign to free them soon gained momentum. To add to the hue and cry, in September 1974, Carter's gripping autobiography *The Sixteenth Round* was published. He'd mailed a copy to Dylan because, while he was no real fan of his music, he respected Dylan's strong stand on civil rights, and even claimed to have witnessed his performance at the 1963 March on Washington for Jobs and Freedom. The publication date of Carter's book was timely; that same month, Bello and Bradley recanted their testimony, both admitting that they had lied to the police in the hope of gaining reward money.

A 'Hurricane' trust fund was soon up and running, launched by supporters hoping to finance lawyers for a retrial. Dylan visited Carter in jail in June and was impressed by his face-to-face meeting with the erstwhile boxer. Dylan's response was made evident in a now famous quote: "The first time I saw him I left knowing one thing ... I realized that the man's philosophy and my philosophy were running down the same road and you don't meet too many people like that."[15]

A retrial was duly granted, and on March 17 1976, the convictions of Carter and Artis were overturned, not thanks to any specific feat of Dylan's, or that of other celebrity Carter supporters, but because two witnesses for the prosecution admitted that they had been economical with the truth during their testimony. At the second trial, Bello changed his story *again*, stating that he had previously been offered money by Carter's supporters to join their side.

Six weeks after being released, Carter, still an angry man, struck 63-year-old Carolyn Kelley, a member of his defense fund team, knocking her to the floor of his hotel room where he then kicked her. (He claimed she was so upset at his rejection of her romantic advances that she had been threatening him.) At a second retrial that December, the convictions of Carter and Artis were reinstated, this time by a jury containing two African-Americans, all 12 jurors having heard the closing argument for the prosecution presented by a black lawyer. In 1985, their second convictions were overturned after a Federal District Court hearing. The prosecution did not press for a third trial, sadly noting that a number of witnesses were deceased. Carter had been in jail for 19 years. Despite this, he had never started a lawsuit for damages or false imprisonment, as might have been expected in the litigious USA.

As the many anti-Carter websites repeat ad nauseum, Rubin 'Hurricane' Carter was never found innocent. His convictions were overturned due to the apparent racial prejudice of the first jury, and because key evidence was withheld from the later trial, a direct violation of the Constitution of the United States.

Rubin Carter now readily admits he was an angry man who wore a pistol back in 1966. He was known to the police as a hothead, and known to friends as an advocate of African-American rights. He had warned that Black Americans might have to turn to violence to get what they deserved; a view reflecting the civil rights movement's growing edginess.

His attitude, his outlandishness, and his outspoken political frankness *may* have made him a target of the authorities in New Jersey in the 60s. While it's true that many of Carter's assertions have been completely discredited over the years, and some believe him to be a liar – moreover, a liar with a wild temper – that is no basis for thinking him a murderer. Carter has often reiterated the fact that he was making around $100,000 a year from boxing, a substantial sum in the mid 60s; why would he risk it all on cold-blooded murder in his own neighborhood, where, sooner or later, he was bound to be recognized? It's a question that remains unanswered. The only thing certain about Rubin Carter is that he was no angel and is not quite the role model he apparently feels himself to be. If nothing else, Carter's activities made him the subject of a great song and a great performance by its composer, even if said composer got most of the facts wrong.

Indeed, Dylan and Levy did not let the truth get in the way of a good story. While Carter really could have been "champion of the world," if he'd defeated Joey Giardello, much of the remainder of the lyric to 'Hurricane' is hallmarked by factual errors. For one thing, Carter was not "number one contender" for the middleweight crown, as the song declares, having never been better than number three in the weight division – his status when he fought Joey Giardello for the title.

Patti Valentine did not, as the song claims, see Bello, or exchange words with him, at the crime scene. By the same token, victim Willie Marins was never reported to have said, "He ain't the guy," when Carter and Artis were brought before him by the police; nor did this occur at 4am, as the song posits. Marins actually said "I don't know," when asked to identify the two men.

The song also paints an idyll of escape for which Carter is supposed to be yearning, a rural paradise "Where the trout streams flow and the air is nice." It's a poetic image but one that doesn't quite square with Carter's real character. He was not known as an outdoorsman and more typically left his wife alone at home while he went out drinking in Paterson, spending so much time at a bar called the Nite Spot that he had his own 'private' chair there.

It was at the Nite Spot that Carter was to be found shortly before his arrest. The club was located only a few blocks from the Lafayette Bar & Grill, however, and so Carter was almost certainly not "in another part of town" when the killings occurred, as Dylan's song suggests. In addition, the lyric originally had Bello and Bradley robbing the victim's dead bodies, when in fact Bello had helped himself to $62 cash from the bar's register and nothing more. Dylan had initially confused Bradley and Bello's roles, too, a mistake that would mean an initial recording of 'Hurricane' had to be scrapped, on the advice of Columbia's lawyers. They didn't blanch at other inaccuracies, however, such as Dylan having Bello say, at the scene of the crime, "I was only robbing the register" – something he actually only admitted to the police four months later.

Desire producer Don DeVito used Don Meehan as engineer for the album sessions at Columbia's Manhattan studios in the summer of 1975. In his unpublished memoir, *Dancing With Pigs*, Meehan remembered the commotion surrounding the legally questionable version of 'Hurricane.' "I got a frantic call from Don DeVito at the studio. [He said Columbia chief Walter] Yetnikoff 'just called me from downtown and said that you have to get up the Dylan tapes and erase everything we did on the first version of 'Hurricane." There was a special cage within the vault area [of the studio] that contained all of Bob Dylan's tapes, which you had to have special permission to enter. I took the tapes to a mixing room and proceeded with the destruct order. I thought to myself, 'This is history, man. How can they do this?' There I was, all alone, with an order and a decision like this that I knew must be followed. I did the next best thing I could think of; I erased all of the vocal tracks of Bob and Emmylou [Harris, who had sung harmony on the original take]. Don said he was at a club downtown when he got an emergency phone call from Walter Yetnikoff to go over to the studio immediately and drag out the tapes in question and erase them, *now!* Don said it was a very serious situation and that it had to be done forthwith."[16]

Readers will be relived to be reminded that this is a book concerned with a specific period of Bob Dylan's career and not a study of New Jersey jurisprudence, nor a biography of a middleweight pugilist. A boxer, coincidently, who once blew away an orange-feathered robin with a .22 caliber rifle, just as the unfortunate bird flew outside his training camp window, while a writer from *Sports Illustrated* magazine looked on aghast. Bob Dylan certainly picked an odd choice for a philosophical soul mate when he sided with Rubin Carter after that first, fateful conversation in June 1975. Rubin Carter later recalled his meetings with Dylan, perhaps exaggerating the extent of their discussions. "We talked the first day ... eight, nine, ten hours. We talked about everything and I thought that was the end of it. I didn't know Bob Dylan was going to write a song; *he* didn't know he was going to write a song. The next day, Bob was back and we talked another eight, nine, ten hours. The next day, Bob was back again and we talked *another* eight, nine, ten hours. ..."[17]

The Rubin 'Hurricane' Carter story would have been a great play for Jacques Levy to stage for the theater; as it was, he helped stage it as a song. Claudia Levy later described how the Dylan-Levy collaboration developed. "Bob wanted do a song about Hurricane; that was very much on his mind, and Jacques knew all about that, knew the whole case. ... [It was originally] done noticeably like a dirge; it was very slow and there was a back up of black singers. One of the things Jacques use to say is that you could *never* know how Bob would frame something."

In Larry Sloman's book, *On The Road With Bob Dylan*, Jacques Levy describes how Dylan wrestled with his subject, noting his facility for the cinematic. "He

[Dylan] was just filled with all these feelings about Hurricane. He couldn't make the first step. I think the first step was putting the song in a total storytelling mode. I don't remember whose idea it was to do that. But really, the beginning of the song is like stage directions, like what you would read in a script: 'Pistol shots ring out in a barroom night' … 'Here comes the story of the Hurricane.' Boom! Titles. You know, Bob loves movies, and he can write these movies that take place in eight to ten minutes, yet seem as full, or fuller, than regular movies."[18]

'Hurricane' was released as a single in November 1975, a sign of just how much Dylan wanted to get the message out. A song with the so-called 'n-word' nestling among its lyrics was unlikely to get much mainstream radio play in the USA, but it nonetheless rose to Number 33 on the *Billboard* Hot 100, and to the edge of the Top 40 in the UK. It was an impressive showing for so controversial a statement. And for such a 'single issue' protest, it has remained remarkably enduring. Since its release, 'Hurricane' has featured on four major motion picture soundtracks and has been covered no less than 16 times, including a version by Vanilla Ice which, once heard, is truly never forgotten.

In mid July 1975, Dylan and Levy had dinner at the New York City apartment of Martam and Jerry Orbach, the latter an actor most famous for his role in US television show *Law & Order*. Martam Orbach was then researching a book about the mafia hoodlum Joey Gallo. Jerry Orbach had played a prominent role in a popular 1971 movie, *The Gang Who Couldn't Shoot Straight*, a light-hearted take on two rival Mafia clans. His character was allegedly based on Gallo. The gangster had been so upset by the actor's portrayal of an underworld big shot that he had contacted the Orbachs and invited them to dinner specifically to put them straight about the reality of his life.

Impressed and seduced by the cultivated Mafioso who painted watercolors and had read Machiavelli, Kafka, and Sartre during long stretches in prison, it was apparently all too easy to forget that 'Crazy Joe' Gallo was also a violent gangster and racketeer; in much the same way that Dylan could conveniently ignore the miscreant elements of Rubin Carter's life story. Certainly, the dark, brutal side of Joey Gallo was not what inspired Dylan and Levy to pen a song about him. However, when that song, 'Joey,' was later unveiled in all it's romanticized glory, there were many understandably aghast observers who reasoned that Joey Gallo was not worthy of tribute in any way, shape, or form.

In truth, 'Crazy Joe' was exactly that, *crazy*, even if he was also articulate, well-dressed, scholarly, and charming when he needed to be. He was a member of the Profaci family, part of New York City's Colombo crime syndicate, as were his brothers, Lawrence and Albert. Joey Gallo owned nightclubs and sweatshops, neither of which featured overpaid employees or bothered with inconveniences like union rights.

Such activity was expediently ignored by the many Manhattan theatrical types who enjoyed Gallo's erudite company and sense of style – his seductive Mafia chic. They were also impressed by his relatively enlightened views about race. However, Gallo was hardly a champion of civil rights. Ever the pragmatic business man, he actually sought to unite the crime gangs of Little Italy and Harlem by building bridges between the Profaci family and the African-American underworld. Gallo was ambitious, too, so much so that in 1957 he instigated efforts to overthrow Mafia boss Joseph Profaci and take control of the family, aided by his two brothers. As the blood flowed in the streets of New York and the Gallo-Profaci War body count mounted, the New York Police Department sat back and enjoyed the show. In 1961, after a conviction for extortion, Gallo was sent to New York State's Greenhaven prison and the bloodshed duly slowed to a trickle.

None of this would stop Dylan and Levy idealizing Gallo in 'Joey.' Their only reference to the bloody Mafia turf wars being the ambiguous line: "There was talk they killed their rivals but the truth was far from that." In fact "the truth" of this intra-Mob carnage was contained in innumerable NYPD records, not to mention page after page of explicit *New York Times* articles. Dylan apparently chose not to consult any such source. Is this the same Bob Dylan who would visit the New York Public Library to read up historical accounts in order to lend historical veracity to his song "Cross The Green Mountain,' written for the soundtrack of the 2003 American Civil War movie *Gods And Generals*?

While in prison, Gallo continued to befriend black criminals with the aim of uniting the Italian and African-American gangs to create an unassailable underworld force. With perhaps inadvertent irony, his fellow Italian-American inmates gave him the nickname 'The Criminal' for supposedly turning his back on his own kind and reaching out to the black gangsters. Some crime writers allege that Crazy Joe's nickname was given by the many Italian gangland contemporaries who considered his plan to amalgamate with the African-Americans insane. Whatever the case, prison did nothing to quell Gallo's violent streak; he even attempted to poison any fellow inmate who angered him by offering them drinks (and even antipasto) laced with strychnine.

In a thought-provoking article in the April 1976 edition of *Creem* magazine, provocateur journalist Lester Bangs would haul Dylan and *Desire* over the critical coals, focusing his censure on 'Joey' in particular. Although many Dylan diehards loathed the journalist's piece, it was an undisputedly well-written and unusually passionate essay from the habitually glib Bangs. In it, the journalist correctly pointed out that while Joey Gallo may have been accepted by the likes of actors Joan Hackett and Ben Gazzara, playwright Neil Simon, comedian David Steinberg, and writer Peter Stone, he was also "a psychopath" who, towards the end of his life, was routinely fed Thorazine by his wife: "... which he docilely took, even though it still didn't stop Gallo beating the shit out of her."[19]

It seems incredible that the protest singer who wrote so movingly about persecuted souls like Emmett Till, Davey Moore, Donald White, Medgar Evers, Hattie Carroll, George Jackson, and, yes, Rubin Carter, could also sing so benignly about a malevolent hood like Joey Gallo. Dylan later reflected on the Orbach's dinner-party comments about Gallo which had so inspired him and Jacques Levy to pen a biographical song. "As soon as I walked in the door, Marty was talking about Joey. She was a good friend of Joey's. They were real tight. I just listened for a few hours ... he [Gallo] left a certain impression on me, I never considered him a gangster. I always thought of him as some kind of hero in some kind of way. An underdog fighting against the elements. He retained a certain amount of his freedom and he went out the way he had to ... it was like listening to a story about Billy The Kid. So we went ahead and wrote that up in one night."[20]

It is worth pointing out that Billy The Kid may be worth his weight in metaphors for both late 19th century dime-store novelists and modern-day screenwriters, but the real outlaw Billy The Kid (born Henry McCarty but fond of the alias William Bonney) killed at least ten men, probably twice that number, and not always in self-defense. However, the lack of formal public records for New Mexico and most of the Old West in which The Kid was at large in the 1880s has allowed a romantic myth to grow up around him. In contrast, Gallo's past is enshrined in factual police and New York State records and is available in grim detail on the archived pages of the *New York Times*. There is little excuse for making Joey Gallo out to be anything but the violent gangster he really was.

Perhaps Levy, a man of the theater who was close to Jerry Orbach, had simply been seduced by Joey Gallo's dramatic possibilities, and Dylan just went along for the ride. Whoever seized on the subject, it is difficult to see how either man could mistake for a latter-day Robin Hood a man who after his 1971 release from jail bragged at Manhattan cocktail parties about his part in the homosexual gang rape of a young prison inmate, who beat his wife so hard her ribs broke, and whose own children hated him so much they demanded their mother divorce this beast of a father.

There were layers of irony to this story, too. Gallo's second wife would celebrate her husband's 1971 liberty by purchasing him some LPs, thinking he might enjoy listening to some contemporary rock music. Among the albums Mrs Gallo brought home was one called *Untitled* by a Californian band hot on the comeback trail: The Byrds. The family loved the record and one evening played the song 'Chestnut Mare' (co-written, of course, by 'Joey' collaborator Jacques Levy) for the head of the household. Gallo's reaction, as described by his wife, was quoted in Lester Bangs's *Creem* article. "He [Joey] got especially mad over a Byrds song called 'Chestnut Mare' that I wanted him to hear ... 'Listen to the lyrics,' I said, 'they're so pretty and so well done.' 'I don't want to hear any fags singing about any fucking horse,' she reports her husband as saying, 'It's not about a horse ... if you'll listen, it's about life.'"[21] Gallo's answer was to jump out of the bathtub, from where he'd been listening, grab the record off the turntable, and throw it down the building's incinerator.

In an extraordinarily frank 2009 interview with Bill Flanagan, Dylan actually denied writing the lyrics to Joey. When Flanagan suggested to him that 'Joey' had taken liberties with the truth, Dylan replied: "Really? I wouldn't know. Jacques Levy wrote the words. Jacques had a theatrical mind and he wrote a lot of plays. So the song might have been theatre of the mind. Some say Davy Crockett takes a lot of liberties with the truth and Billy The Kid does, too ... [the calypso song] 'FDR In Trinidad.' Have you ever heard that?[22]

April 7 1972 found Gallo celebrating his 43rd birthday with his bodyguard and some friends at a favorite restaurant, Umberto's Clam House, in Little Italy. Thinking they were safe inside Mafia home turf, Gallo and his defender foolishly sat with their backs to the restaurant's front entrance. Two gunmen entered and opened fire with a pair of revolvers. Gallo was hit five times and stumbled to the street where he died.

Desire engineer Don Meehan remembers the recording of 'Joey' and the effect it had on certain parties gathered in Columbia's studio E. "Don DeVito told me an interesting story about Joey's brother who, unbeknownst to me, was sitting behind me in the control room of the studio when we were recording the song. Don said he [Joey's brother] was in tears the entire time during the seven-minute long recording. This was indeed my favorite cut and I also felt some emotional tinge as it went down."[23]

The question begs to be asked: who in Dylan's party knew the Gallo clan well enough to invite Joey's brother into the control booth? One possible connection is this: *Desire* producer Don DeVito's brother was Richard DeVito, who at the time of the recording was a high ranking officer in the NYPD's street crime division, and a man who would frequently liaise with the so-called 'pizza squad' (the NYPD unit specifically created to combat Mafia activity). Perhaps some information was exchanged for an invite to Columbia's studios? Another possibility is that Levy had passed on information about 'Joey' and the recording sessions to his friends the Orbachs, who were still on sociable terms with Gallo's surviving brothers.

'Joey' wouldn't be the only song on *Desire* to suffer from the "inverted, benevolent prejudice known to the liberal mentality," as Lester Bangs put it. Another was 'Mozambique,' one of the songs that Dylan had played to Scarlet Rivera on the day he'd met her. It was an apparently ingenuous celebration of the sun-kissed African country washed by the Indian Ocean: "I like to spend some time in Mozambique / The sunny sky is aqua blue / And all the couples dancing cheek to cheek / It's very nice to stay a week or two." In fact, Mozambique had only gained independence from its colonial master, Portugal, in June 1975, becoming the People's Republic of Mozambique. It suffered from an exceptionally high infant mortality rate and a correspondingly low standard of living, which sank ever lower as the colonial middle and upper classes fled, emptying their bank accounts in the process. It was a curious choice of locale to paint as an idyllic holiday escape, but Mozambique does lend itself to rhyme and, perhaps, in the country's new-found independence Dylan saw an optimistic metaphor. Although found in august musical company on *Desire*, 'Mozambique' remains, to use Michael Gray's dismissive phrase, "a featherweight pop song."

'Mozambique' was apparently one of a number of songs completed at Jacques Levy's weekend home on Long Island later that July. Others included 'Black Diamond Bay,' 'Romance In Durango,' 'Oh Sister,' and 'Sara' (although the latter, like the previously completed 'One More Cup Of Coffee,' was actually a solo Dylan composition).

Before the Long Island hiatus, however, Dylan wanted to record two of the songs he'd already penned with Levy, 'Joey' and 'Rita Mae,' the latter a paean to lesbian novelist Rita Mae Brown. On July 14, Dylan entered Columbia's studio E, in New York City, with guitarist Dave Mason and his band backing him up. Session veterans Vince Bell, on mandolin, and Dominic Cortese, on accordion, were also there, as was James 'Sugar Blue' Whiting, along with his trusty Hohner Marine Band harmonicas. Both songs were attempted but neither was considered to have the sound that Dylan was looking for. They discussed recording 'Abandoned Love' but did not attempt a take.

Shortly after the July 14 session, Dylan and Levy split for the latter's aforementioned weekend retreat in East Hampton. There, according to Levy, they wrote 14 songs together, including a clutch best known to bootleg purchasers and Dylan completists, among them 'Catfish,' 'Money Blues,' 'Town,' 'Golden Loom,' and a real obscurity, 'Wiretappin.' Perhaps one of the most memorable Long Island compositions was 'Oh Sister.' Joan Baez was one of those who found the song's attempt to come to grips with modern feminism awkward, however – so much so that she came up with a witty parody called, wait for it, 'Oh Brother.'

In the mid 70s, this reaching out to feminists was the only aspect of the song that Dylan's critics, advocates, and camp followers considered. Yet, as noted in the opening chapter of this book, there is little doubt that, here, Dylan was less interested in feminist principles than he was in religious ones. 'Oh Sister' is not so much a statement about New Woman as a signpost, a station of Dylan's cross, as he moves ever closer to conversion to Christianity.

Another of the Long Island compositions was 'Romance In Durango.' The version that would be recorded for *Desire* is impossible to hear without thinking of Sam Peckinpah's Westerns and country music star Marty Robbins's Texan cowboy classic, 'El Paso.' Durango, Mexico, was the location for much of the *Pat Garrett & Billy The Kid* shoot, which had occupied Dylan for much of the winter of 1972–73. The song is laced with Mexican imagery, from its gripping opening line, "Hot chili peppers in the blistering sun," to its cantina, hacienda, and corrida-set action concerning the cowboy narrator's love for one Magdalena, and their hurried flight from some unnamed foe, which ends with the narrator being gunned down. Sam Peckinpah and Bob Dylan had had their differences on location in Mexico, but on the 1975 Rolling Thunder tour, the Peckinpah homage 'Romance In Durango' would be performed 30 times out of 31 shows, with Dylan bestowing more onstage dedications to its director than he did to anyone else.

The plot of 'Romance In Durango' echoes the narrative of Marty Robbins' 'El Paso' so closely that it seems Dylan was making a conscious parody (something he'd done before, with the song 'Fourth Time Around,' for example, written a decade earlier and based unapologetically on The Beatles' 'Norwegian Wood'). Like the opening lines of 'Hurricane,' the song bears Jacques Levy's stage-setting hallmarks, and, again like 'Hurricane,' it's another Dylan story-song punctuated by uncharacteristic narrative-propelling specificity.

The final Dylan-Levy collaboration included on *Desire* would be the song 'Black Diamond Bay.' Standard practice on the vinyl LP format was to reserve the penultimate song on the second side for the album's weakest cut; it was the point at which record industry veterans considered most listeners grew fatigued and were possibly no longer paying attention. At the turn of the 60s, this spot was even referred to by US music industry insiders as 'the graveyard.' 'Black Diamond Bay' would occupy this slot on Dylan's new album – potentially the most undesirable place on *Desire*. However, this song was far from being 'graveyard' fodder and is, in fact, one of the hidden gems of Dylan's career. It's a song that sounds promising at first and keeps rewarding with repeated listens. As in a Robert Altman film, it offers various seemingly unconnected characters and events that appear then disappear before the disparate parts are eventually woven together into a single, coherent narrative.

Long before they'd gleefully discovered that 1985's *Empire Burlesque* was riddled with lines from old Humphrey Bogart movies, Dylanologists had noted that 'Black Diamond Bay' seemed to be based, at least partially, on Joseph Conrad's *Victory*, a 1915 novel about a man who renounces the world, only to reengage with it after falling in love with a strange, beautiful woman. A similar figure appears in Dylan and Levy's song, which shares with Conrad's novel references to a hotel, a volcano, and the titular Black Diamond Bay location.

Proving that the lessons learned from Norman Raeben, used to such great effect on *Blood On The Tracks*, were enduring ones, 'Black Diamond Bay' is also a song which stops time and contains variable narrative points of view. It concludes with a major temporal/perspective shift in which the narrator reveals that the entirety of events detailed previously in the song have taken place not in 'real life' but in a television news broadcast.

Dylan was doing more than recycling the contents of Conrad's novel in 'Black Diamond Bay.' One of the miracles of Bob Dylan's music is that you can enjoy a song like this on the most superficial level, while driving to work or jogging while it plays on your iPod, say, and it *sounds* terrific. Yet, you can also examine the song as if it were one of Dalton Trumbo's blacklisted scripts, or a newly discovered Dead Sea Scroll, knowing all the while that, even having completely unpicked the song, at any moment it can be enjoyed as terrific pop music while still holding up as art.

T.S. Eliot said that one of the surest tests of the superiority or inferiority of a poet is in the way in which he or she borrows. "Immature poets imitate; mature poets steal; bad poets deface what they take, and good poets make it into something better, or at least something different … A good poet will usually borrow from authors remote in time, or alien in language, or diverse in interest."[24] The latter certainly sounds like a description of the Bob Dylan who penned 'Black Diamond Bay.'

'Sara' was the final song on *Desire*, one of the album's two songs written without any input from Levy. Being the most personal of essays, there is little any outside collaborator could have contributed. Here, Dylan sings, unambiguously, about his wife and the apparently parlous state of their marriage. He is held firmly in a classic emotional trap, between the need to be free and the need to belong. This is identifiably the work of the man who would make *Renaldo & Clara*, with it's intimations of broken relationships and complex love triangles. Both the movie and 'Sara' are examples of a notoriously private artist, one who would routinely castigate anyone, friend or foe, for attempting to examine his private life through his lyrics, suddenly and openly admitting his most tender feelings and his most private thoughts. Here was the great evader abruptly revealing for posterity the contents of his heart in public statements of unequivocal candor. It is astonishing to hear such frankness from so private and obfuscating a personality, but this naked plea for his wife's forgiveness, and for her acceptance of the love he is offering, is an example of what great artists do, and what we, knowingly or unwittingly, ask them to do: open their minds, souls, and hearts so as to articulate the things we cannot say and to thus provide us with inspiration and hope.

In 'Sara,' Dylan uses the metaphor of a beach to describe the state of his marital relationship. At the beginning, he paints a sunny, bucolic scene, with children at play, but by the close he is picturing a shoreline deserted but for seaweed and ship wreckage. This evocation of warm love grown cold was easy enough to comprehend. However, 'Sara' is a song dense with references, from the autobiographical ("Stayin' up for days in the Chelsea Hotel / Writin' 'Sad-

Eyed Lady Of The Lowlands' for you"), to the allegorical ("Scorpio Sphinx in a calico dress" … "Glamorous nymph with an arrow and bow"). While it was both intimate and personal, it was also oddly lofty and contained some lines which Dylan followers immediately admired and quoted, and others that were pored over, their meaning much debated. Not every critic was taken by the song's smattering of grand, mythological allusions, but Dylan's many interpreters, whether they were academician, poetry lover, or rock fan, seemed to each have a robust opinion. Ultimately, Sara didn't forgive her husband's frankly confessed "unworthiness," as they were to separate permanently, divorcing in 1977.

For all their brutal candor and vaunting poetry on the page, Dylan's lyrics have always been invested with further layers of meaning when he sings them; and for all their nods to the French symbolist poets Dylan admired so much these are first and foremost song lyrics. His singing, untutored and often the focus of criticism from non-aficionados, is, for others, Dylan's greatest gift. Rolling Thunder tourist T Bone Burnett is obviously in the latter camp. "You know, Bob is an incredibly great singer. He is just better than anybody. As a guy who writes and sings rock'n'roll songs in his own inventive way, just period, he is really the Homer of our times. He did exactly what Homer did, collecting and creating all the greatest songs of the culture."[25]

On July 28, Dylan returned to Columbia's studio E to record, this time with the largest band he had ever assembled around him. Besides bassist Rob Stoner, violinist Scarlet Rivera, and harmonist Emmylou Harris, there were no less than five guitarists, including a visiting Eric Clapton, three additional backing singers, two horns, two percussionists, not including drummer John Sessewell, Sugar Blue on harmonica, an accordionist, a second bass player, and, conceivably, Adolf Hitler on vibes. Session engineer Don Meehan recalls a party atmosphere, with a spread of cordon bleu catering and fine wines flowing, and the chaos which resulted. "Bob's basic band showed up … but then more musicians kept coming and I'd continue to go out and set up more microphones. I think I wound up with about 30 microphones and as many musicians! Before it was over, the entire studio was lined up with musicians, wall to wall, and I was even running out of tape tracks to put them [all] on. It was almost like a Hall of Fame night, a Tribute to Bob Dylan. The difficulty was that, with so many star players and everyone playing on top of each other, and soloing and playing fills over one another, there was almost too much music to sort and come up with any kind of decent mix. At 4am, we were still at it." [26]

Only one song, 'Romance In Durango,' was successfully captured during this fiesta-like Monday night session, with all the guest artists playing. On July 29, they reassembled, this time with two drummers but without the backing singers and three of the guitarists. Clapton was a no show. It was another night of chaos, so much so that at one point Don Meehan ran into the live room to play bass (on 'Money Blues') while Rob Stoner helped run the recording console.

By now, even Dylan had got the message; this was no way to record. Producer Don DeVito should have – must have – advised Dylan about the unwieldiness of the setup. Bob's former recording stewards Tom Wilson and John Hammond would surely never have let things get this out of hand, while producer Bob Johnston had famously strode into a Nashville studio live room in the middle of a Dylan session to announce, loudly: "Gentlemen, we have *too many* men on the floor." Was everyone in Columbia's studio E afraid of offending Bob Dylan back in the summer '75?

Some guidance was surely needed. It would come from an unlikely source: bassist Rob Stoner. "DeVito called me up and said Bob had asked for me to come down to the studio," Stoner recalls. "They were having trouble recording the songs for *Desire* because there was just too large an ensemble to get the result that Bob liked, which was more of a spontaneous type thing. So, I hung out for a couple of nights watching them not getting results and eventually Bob took me aside, 'cause he knew me previously, and he asked me what would I do if I were in his situation. I told him that I thought it would be better if he sent everybody home and just came in with a small new group and started afresh. He took me up on my dare and said, 'We'll do that and you call the musicians.' He asked who I would like to get and I suggested my drummer, Howie Wyeth … I thought that we would just do it as a trio. He mentioned this gypsy violinist he had met, Scarlet Rivera, and he thought she would be an interesting element, so we did it, really, as a quartet: the drummer, Scarlet, Bob, and I. We went in and tried it and it clicked, and we ended up doing the album, and in very short order."[27]

Dylan was hardly intimate with Stoner, but he did know him through John Herald, Bob Neuwirth, and from the Other End folk jams at which Stoner had backed up Ramblin' Jack Elliott. Nonetheless, and (almost) true to his word, the next night at studio E, Dylan invited along only Emmylou Harris, Howie Wyeth, Rob Stoner, Scarlet Rivera and percussionist Sheena Seidenberg. With a leaner band, the session shifted into overdrive and definitive takes of 'Oh Sister,' 'One

More Cup Of Coffee,' 'Black Diamond Bay,' 'Mozambique,' and 'Joey' were all completed during this productive day, each a version that would grace the released *Desire*. In addition, they re-cut 'Rita May,' which would be issued as the B-side to a live recording single, 'Stuck Inside Of Mobile With The Memphis Blues Again' (from the 1976 live album *Hard Rain*), and 'Golden Loom,' a song that would lie dormant until being released in 1991 on *The Bootleg Series Volumes 1–3 (Rare & Unreleased) 1961–1991*. Also committed to tape during this session was the ill-fated first version of 'Hurricane.' July 30 1975 had proved to be Dylan's most productive recording date since the whole of 1964's *Another Side Of Bob Dylan* was cut in a single evening (although that had involved a much simpler setup: voice, guitar, harmonica, and lashings of red wine).

Don Meehan makes this productive evening seem even more incredible when he describes exactly how Dylan recorded. "Although I maintained control, I found myself wondering what he [Dylan] was thinking. He didn't talk much. I had to keep my eye on him constantly because he would wonder all around the studio and want to start a take wherever he was. Whether he was next to the bass amp, or the guitar amp, or the drums, I had to run out and follow him as well as follow Emmylou Harris [who was following Dylan] with microphones. And then he would turn his head back and forth away from the mic. Finally, I put two mics on him and followed him with those and one on his acoustic guitar. And then, without saying anything, he sits down at the piano and starts playing and singing. We would always put up baffling behind a singer, especially on a live session. But no one ever recorded live anymore, and here was Bob Dylan moving around in a small studio with bass and electric guitars; and even though we had Howie [Wyeth] in a booth, the drums were blasting. There was no telling him [Dylan] that he had to go in the vocal booth, or overdub [the vocals, later]. So I guess you could say he was inventive, recording live like no one else would do at the time, *and* exasperating, and trying and testing me to the fullest."[28]

On July 31, this same, stripped-down ensemble reconvened. They warmed up on 'Golden Loom,' recorded 'Abandoned Love,' and got nowhere with a song called 'Town' (which remains unreleased). They then cut the emotional 'Sara,' with its subject, Mrs Dylan, standing in the control booth beside Don DeVito. They also captured the version of 'Isis' heard on *Desire*. At the end of the session, there was talk of recutting the previously recorded, large ensemble version of 'Romance In Durango' with the smaller group, but Dylan was allegedly talked out of it by producer DeVito.

They should have been done and dusted. However, even before the October 24 re-recording of 'Hurricane,' with Ronee Blakley replacing Emmylou Harris, there would be yet another session – and not in New York City. In fact, the *Desire* multi-track tapes were shipped to Minneapolis, at Dylan's behest. There, he and his brother David Zimmerman planned to mix the album. This came as a bitter blow to both DeVito and Meehan, who remained in New York City. They needn't have fretted; whatever the Zimmerman brothers may have mixed, nothing ever saw the light of day; nor did the results of further recording sessions in Minneapolis in mid August, with Dylan backed by a local band called Willie Murphy & the Bees, whom his brother had recommended.

Don Meehan remembers how well the stripped-down *Desire* band suited Dylan's needs and how naturally they gelled as a unit. "Howie [Wyeth] just played his ass off the way he felt, and he was a powerhouse. I just loved recording him. And Rob [Stoner] really took charge. He was the leader and called the shots. If you listen close, you will hear that Dylan added beats and skipped beats, and to a bass player, or a drummer, this is a total nightmare because you never know exactly where the count is, or, as a musician would say, 'where the one is.' But Rob and Howie followed him to a tee. I recorded some demos for Rob later and when I remarked about how great I thought the album [*Desire*] came out, he would just say, 'Aww, man, it just sounds like a demo.'"[29]

Meehan also believes that he, as much as Don DeVito, was *Desire's* de facto producer. "One night, I was mixing 'Joey' all by myself and I wanted to hear accordion and Italian-flavored guitar, or mandolin, on it. So, I called DeVito, who called Dylan. A few minutes later, Don called back with the OK. He asked me if I knew who to call. I did … so I had Vinnie Bell and Dominic Cortese there in a half-hour, about the same time that DeVito came over. The song was over seven minutes long and they laid it down in one take."[30]

As we know, on September 10, Dylan, Stoner, Wyeth, and Rivera taped the *World Of John Hammond* television special – the first evidence of the *Desire* sound being translated into a live experience. Early the following month, Dylan was back, briefly, in a Manhattan studio, this time in the company of Bette Midler during sessions for her *Songs For The New Depression* album. Midler was a veteran of Dylan's summer 1975 Village carousing scene and encouraged her producer and longtime friend Mark Klingman to invite Dylan to contribute to her new album. Dylan agreed and even offered Midler a song, an updated version of 'Buckets Of Rain' from *Blood On The Tracks*.

Inspired by his collaborations with Jacques Levy, Dylan had begun re-working the lyrics to several of his extant songs; 'Tangled Up In Blue' and 'Shelter From The Storm' were others that received substantially modified words. Dylan and Midler delivered 'Buckets Of Rain' as a wry duet. On the finished track, Dylan's background vocal was mixed up every bit as loudly as it was on 'Wallflower,' the song he'd given to Doug Sahm in 1973, for the album *Doug Sahm And Band*.

Despite the ill auguries of 'Sara,' Dylan then took some time off with his wife and children and attended to various family matters in both Malibu and Minnesota. He returned to New York City in mid October and checked into the Gramercy Park Hotel on Lexington Avenue. He was soon hanging out at the Other End, again, with Roger McGuinn, David Blue, and Jacques Levy. They were joined by Louis Kemp, one of Dylan's boyhood friends from Hibbing.

Almost immediately on his return to the city, Dylan's office booked rehearsal time at Studio Instrument Rentals (SIR) studios in Manhattan. A number of musicians began to receive invites to come and play with Dylan. At no point was it formally announced that these were rehearsals for a tour, however. Stoner, Wyeth, and Rivera were, naturally enough, first to be asked, with McGuinn also requested, as was ace harmony singer Steven Soles. Neuwirth, Ramblin' Jack, and Joan Baez were in from the start, as per Dylan's conversation with Ramblin' Jack back in July. Versatile multi-instrumentalist David Mansfield and guitarist T Bone Burnett also joined in, as did percussionist Luther Rix, who moved to drums whenever Wyeth shifted to his second instrument, the piano. Mick Ronson, invited by Neuwirth ever since Ronson showed up at Neuwirth's Other End residency in July, took about a half-second to notice tape decks recording the ensemble's initially chaotic jams. Dylan veterans McGuinn and Baez knew what was up; the rookie players did not. Dylan had tapes so he could listen to which musicians fit in best and decide on arrangements.

Rob Stoner had an inkling of what was to come. "Rick Danko told me that Bob had been kicking around the idea of a traveling carnival for years, even when he was still working with The Band. He had just come off working with The Band, live ... and he needed to have something that was really different. So, he figured this was that time to pull the carnival idea out of the hat."[31]

The troops were not yet completely assembled, however. Ronee Blakley came into the fold after meeting Dylan at a David Blue show at, where else, the Other End. Afterward, she and Dylan jammed together and they got along so famously that an invitation to the SIR rehearsals was duly extended. Whether or not Bette Midler and Emmylou Harris had previous commitments or were simply not asked isn't clear. Also notable by her absence was Patti Smith, who would have been otherwise engaged with the imminent release of her debut album, the epochal *Horses*.

More pieces began to fall into place. Playwright Sam Shepard, an ex-beau of Smith's and admired as a playwright by Jacques Levy, arrived by train from California. (Shepard loathed air travel; ironically, since he went on to star as ace test pilot Chuck Yeager in Philip Kaufman's 1983 movie *The Right Stuff*.) Dylan now had screenplays as much as music and "something like a circus" on his mind.

Perhaps his scattershot focus was one reason why the SIR rehearsals remained chaotic, so much so that the multi-talented David Mansfield found them bordering on being unprofessional. "With Dylan, it was like he would just start a song and you sort of join in. There was never any discussion about who played what instrument, much less what note! He would pick up a guitar with his back toward you and everybody would sort of lurch towards their equipment and, after about ten bars, everybody would know what instrument they were playing. After 11 bars they would know what chord they were playing. Scarlet was playing violin most of the time, so I usually picked up a mandolin or steel guitar, or something else."

Mansfield remembers that Dylan's original plan was to play with the core band from *Desire*, namely the Stoner, Wyeth, Rivera trio (an idea backed up by the line-up at the *World Of John Hammond* television show). "He did a lot of material with them [the core band] but then it just sort of morphed into this larger ensemble during the process of rehearsal. So, we'd do certain songs, like 'Isis,' and everybody played on it, kitchen sink style. Other songs, like 'Sara,' he would just do with the trio, as he had done it in the studio, with maybe [Steven] Soles on second acoustic or singing harmony."[32]

Despite this, the pervading quality of the SIR rehearsals was one of noisy disorder. Two of the interviewees for this book have confessed that Bob Dylan did not, by fall 1975 at any rate, know how to signal a band to stop at the end of a song. If a coherent ensemble, capable of playing a gig, let alone a tour, was going to evolve out of these rehearsals, they would need some sense of structure. At the rate they were going, the shows would be no more than large-scale versions of Bob Neuwirth's spontaneous Other End concerts-cum-hootenannies. Someone had to take the reins.

That someone was, once again, Rob Stoner. "I saw that it was a very confused situation, which was due to dissolve into chaos very rapidly unless somebody stepped in." Stoner later recalled. "It wasn't like it was my place to step in, but somebody had to ... so, by default, I just went ahead and did it. ... I had experienced as a bandleader – not that Mick Ronson didn't have experience as a bandleader, or T Bone, or any of these other people; but I just happened to be the guy that took to do it and everybody just accepted my role."[33]

Being the leader of this ungainly troupe wasn't a position anyone at SIR seemed to particularly lust after. All the principals remember Dylan's side of rehearsals being fairly loose, although T Bone Burnett puts that into perspective. "Dylan doesn't give you an arrangement; you busk along. A song would just start and then we would play. Most of the rehearsal was done with the other people besides Bob. We had to work out the whole Guam part of the show; we had to work out a set with Joan Baez and a set with Jack Elliott, with Roger McGuinn and with whomever else might happen along. That's what we were doing most of the time, rehearsing with the other singers. Bob [Dylan] never rehearsed that much. He was there all the time, hanging out and listening, and then he would rehearse a little bit. Even on stage, he would change things. He wasn't one for getting everything all bolted down."[34]

Whether or not Dylan's disdain for formally rehearsing his own material reflected the fatigue he'd felt during the more structured Tour '74, with The Band, or was a desire to mimic the improvisations of Patti Smith's group, is not known. Either way, Dylan seemed to relish the spontaneity, and the good company of the musicians. In New York City, he was quite the social animal and the musical community could provide any number of distractions. In October, there was yet another Village party to attend, the 61st birthday celebration of Gerde's Folk City owner, Mike Porco, one of Dylan's earliest Greenwich Village supporters.

By now, Dylan already had the cameras rolling on his largely improvised tour-documentary-cum-mysterioso-movie, *Renaldo & Clara*, and the troupe, who would be its stars and bit players (their musicianly numbers swollen by an extensive road and film crew and by the likes of Jacques Levy, who would direct the stage show and lighting, and the tour's Beat poet-in-residence Allen Ginsberg) hadn't even left town on the great road adventure that would provide the cinematic background. Ginsberg had received a 4am phone call from Dylan in September asking him to join the tour to set up scenes for the film they would shoot. Dylan asked him who else should be invited, and Ginsberg roped in his partner Peter Orlovsky, Denise Mercedes (given the job of taking care of Dylan's *Desire* chapeau), and fellow poet Anne Waldman.

A week's rehearsals at SIR had not been enough to knock the show into shape, which meant they were obliged to rehearse some more at the first tour stop, Plymouth, Massachusetts, where the original Pilgrims had landed in 1620. How Ginsberg, Neuwirth, and Dylan must have loved that. They would no doubt discuss the subject on the drive north from New York City.

It was now time to pack their bags, they had a bus to catch; specifically, an old Greyhound vehicle which been converted into a tour-bus called Phydeaux (pronounced *Fido*) by Frank Zappa to transport The Mothers Of Invention, and rented to Dylan. While Phydeaux would be a traveling home to McGuinn, Baez, Burnett, Ronson, Stoner, et al, Dylan himself preferred to cruise in either a red Cadillac Eldorado convertible or a green motorhome, often co-piloted by Ramblin' Jack Elliott.

Early on, the Rolling Thunder Revue was as spontaneously informal as Dylan had originally planned; a clear reaction to the military-style planning behind Tour '74. Dylan fan Hunt Helm recalls the Revue's typically covert manifestation in Boston. "I was working a summer job in the Graduate Admissions office at Harvard University, as a clerk/typist ... there was not a whole lot going on. Then, one weekday morning, the Rolling Thunder Revue advance team showed up out of nowhere. I came up those old, wooden escalators in Harvard Square and saw a few people who looked like me, handing out these little tan flyers that said Bob Dylan and the Rolling Thunder Revue would be playing at the Harvard Square Theater that night. Tickets were on sale that very moment. That was the only publicity, about 10 minutes of handing out a few flyers; the rest was word-of-mouth. I went back to the house for some money, came back, bought my tickets and got to work about two hours late. That night, I was close enough to see Bob Dylan wearing a great big wrist watch, but not close enough to see what time it was."[35]

It takes a lot of care, ironically, to get away with spontaneity on so grand a scale. While away in Minnesota, back in the summer, Dylan had hooked up with his old friend Louis Kemp. He had followed Dylan to Manhattan where he'd happily mixed with the throng at the Other End. Kemp was an affable, no-nonsense businessman who'd taken a small, family fisheries business and turned it into a large and extremely successful family fisheries business which had – like seemingly all extremely successful family concerns – latterly been gobbled up by a multinational corporation. Kemp was an experienced hand at planning and organization, and had witnessed the Bob Dylan touring phenomenon at close range, having traveled with the Tour '74 party.

Dylan trusted Kemp, and, in a way, hiring his old chum would be as important a move for Rolling Thunder as using Jacques Levy to direct the show. Kemp recalls Dylan broaching the idea of the tour. "I came back from my Alaska Salmon season, in July of '75, and hung out with Bob in Minnesota. Bob had come back from New York, where he had recorded *Desire*. Bob said he had this idea for a tour, not a big money tour, but a fun, party-like experience, like a traveling musical circus, mostly in small places. Bob said to me, 'Louie, you were on the whole Tour '74 with me, you saw how it works. You're a business guy; you can put it together and run it the way I want.' I asked Bob, 'What is it that you want this tour to be like?' He said, 'I want to travel in buses and campers like the country & western people do, not airplanes, and invite good musicians to join us and go from town to town in mostly small halls. I want it to be fun with great music; I don't care if I make money, just make sure we cover the expenses.' To make a long story short, I said, 'Yes ... it sounds fun; I will produce it for you. What do you want to call it?' Bob thought for a little while and then said, 'Lets call it the Rolling Thunder Revue.' Bob said he would take care of the music side, and the show, I would take care of the rest."[36]

Several books exist on the Rolling Thunder fall 1975 tour. They tend to discuss the many personalities involved and focus on the backstage machinations; at their best (Larry Sloman, take a bow) they make for excellent, engaging reading. Put them together with the multiplicity of books and articles on *Renaldo & Clara*, and a strong image emerges of the traveling and the behind-the-scenes camaraderie and intrigue. The only area that fails to get a mention is the stage. Some of what happened, musically, on Rolling Thunder has been heard in live recordings, some of the musical performances have been seen in *Renaldo & Clara* and other footage, but the show itself remains something of a mystery. If you weren't at the gigs, you have relatively little to go on.

Live recordings exist of every Rolling Thunder concert from fall '75. There isn't room to discuss and digest them here at the length Dylanphiles may, understandably, feel each show deserves (that is another book, just wait). However, a show at Toronto's Maple Leaf Gardens, on December 2 1975, was particularly powerful, with the band in fine form and Dylan inspired like seldom before. The tapes were rolling, and examining them reveals the magic of Rolling Thunder at its most potent. Here follows, in sequence, just what happened, on that cold Ontario evening. This is what the punters heard and saw in a four-hour show they would never forget.

At Rolling Thunder's more discreet shows, the circus-like painted curtain, as seen on the jacket of *The Bootleg Series Vol. 5: Bob Dylan Live 1975, The Rolling Thunder Revue*, would rise and fall under Jacques Levy's direction, signaling the start of the show, the intermission, and the beginning of the second half. At larger arenas, such as Maple Leaf Gardens, it was usually deployed as a backdrop. First to stroll out in front of it is MC Bob Neuwirth. Typically, he would get things, well, rolling with a friendly greeting and an intimation of the unusual fare to come. "Welcome to our living room; this is the Rolling Thunder living room and you are all welcome to our living room ... do whatever it takes to get your head together. This show is a little bit different than some you've seen before, so keep your eyes open! You won't miss a damn thing."

The backing band then pick up their instruments and break into the opening number, 'Good Love Is Hard To Find,' a song by Ned Albright, the musical partner of Rolling Thunder tourist Steven Soles and a noted Los Angeles producer, songwriter, and keyboardist who'd worked with everyone from Don McLean to The Banana Splits. They'd begun with a relative obscurity; it was an approach the audience would have to get used to. As Neuwirth had promised, this show really was "a little bit different ..."

As if to reiterate the point, the band then perform Neuwirth's song 'I Love My Music' (mistakenly called 'Sleazy' by most bootleggers), after which Neuwirth introduces his friend, T Bone Burnett. Today a major industry player thanks to his many impressive production credits, collaborations, movie soundtracks, and, ahem, his Academy Award, on this tour, Burnett was almost an unknown. Curiously, he treats the audience to a version of Warren Zevon's 'Werewolves Of London,' a song that wouldn't become a hit, for its author, for three further years. "Zevon and I were old friends," Burnett explains. "We had been writing together and he played me that tune one day – I heard it the day after he wrote it, I think, and I always remembered it. I loved the tune and it seemed like a good tune to do for a crowd who had never heard me, or it, before. Whatever I was gonna do, nobody would have ever heard before."[37] Burnett was also fond of performing 'Hula Hoop' during his Rolling Thunder spot. Eventually recorded for his 1983 album, *Proof Through The Night*, it was a song he'd written with John Fleming and his old Texas pal, Roscoe West. For Guam's portion of the set, Jacques Levy would arrange for a spotlight to fall on whoever was singing centre stage, while the remainder of the troupe would be swathed in primary colors. This worked well as it gave each singer pride of place in the audience's eyes for their particular spot and thereby bolstered the relatively democratic feeling of the Revue. At this point in the show, the spotlight falls on Steven Soles. He would frequently perform, as he does tonight, 'Laissez-Faire,' a song by David Ackles, from the singer's self-titled 1968 album. At times, Soles's smooth vocal performance could make the song sound astonishingly like a Graham Nash solo track. David Mansfield appears stage left to accompany Soles on mandolin.

Rob Stoner then steps forward to sing Dylan's 'Catfish,' a song he, along with the rest of Dylan's musicians, had attempted to record on July 29, at Columbia's studio E. Stoner had a strong, bluesy voice, perfect for arenas and not immediately associable with the rockabilly which was his true love. In his memoirs, *Chronicles, Volume One*, Dylan denies knowing much about baseball, although that same book mentions several of the sport's vintage stars, long forgotten by most modern fans. 'Catfish' is a song about New York Yankees' great Jim 'Catfish' Hunter, so His Bobness obviously had at least some passing interest in the National Pastime. Guam's version is the most rocking tune to come from the stage thus far.

Next, Neuwirth introduces Mick Ronson – a name which would always attract a fine hand on tour. Ronson's usual song of choice was 'Is Their Life On Mars?' with Burnett singing a close harmony on the choruses. Although its title suggested the British guitarist's past association with David Bowie, this was not *that* 'Life On Mars' but, in fact, another song by Roscoe West, which Burnett had suggested. In a 1976 *Melody Maker* interview, Ronson explained how much he'd had to adapt to the band and to Dylan's music. "I'd never even heard half of these numbers [of Dylan's], so I was having to listen and watch. I wasn't used to the sequence of songs, or how they developed. At first I was completely baffled by them all. Really baffled and confused. All I could do was try and play, just try to fit in with what was happening. I thought I was terrible at first. I was getting a bit frustrated. I wasn't playing well. But as the rehearsals went on, I started pulling myself into it a bit more. They took a bit of time with me, which I appreciated. Not many people would have had that kind of patience in that sort of situation. There was no great pressure on me to get it right, or to get out."[38]

After the first leg of Rolling Thunder was over, Ronson, backed by members of Guam, would book into New York City's Sundragon Studios to record 'Is Their Life On Mars' (which would eventually be released, among the extra tracks, on a CD reissue of Ronson's 1976 album, *Play Don't Worry*).

At this point, MC Bob Neuwirth introduces the members of the band to the audience. Then he talks about the movie *Nashville*, Robert Altman's biting satire of American politics which had premiered that June, by way of introducing one of its stars, Ronee Blakley. She takes the stage to sing 'Alabama Dark,' a song about a particular hero of Neuwirth's (and Dylan's for that matter), Hank Williams. The song was performed in a Cajun style, with David Mansfield on fiddle (his jaunty approach quite distinct from the long, lyrical lines played by Scarlet Rivera), a marked contrast with the succeeding torch ballad, 'Need A New Sun Rising Everyday,' which Blakley sang at nearly every show on the fall tour. Then it's back to Cajun-flavored country & western, with Neuwirth singing 'Cindy's Saddle,' his own composition possibly inspired by his friend Cindy Bullens (who was briefly along for the Rolling Thunder ride) and which was a favorite song of T Bone Burnett's.

'Mercedes Benz' is Neuwirth's most famous composition. On Rolling Thunder he performed it as a Cajun waltz, in three-part harmony with Soles and Burnett and with a prominent part for Mansfield's dobro. A co-write with no less than Janis Joplin and Beat poet Michael McClure, at Maple Leaf Gardens it is the most enthusiastically applauded song of the evening so far. It's the first song the audience could reasonably be expected to recognize, thanks to the well-known a cappella version Joplin recorded for her final album, *Pearl*, a chart topper in 1971.

At this point in the show, Guam would have generally played anywhere from a dozen to 16 songs. If there is a special guest artist in the house, then it would be around this time that they would be invited on stage. In Toronto, Ronnie 'The Hawk' Hawkins takes the podium, with most of his band in tow, to perform two songs. First up is 'Forty Days,' his first chart hit, back in 1959. The transplanted Arkansan then sings a lengthy medley of 'Bo Diddley'/'Who Do You Love?,' the latter half of which morphs rather magically into a melodic, Allman Brothers-style guitar duet, followed by a slide solo worthy of Brother Duane at his best. Ronnie Hawkins: "These folks all jammed [on stage] that night in Toronto. Hell, I think I had about 20 people playing with me! It looked like *everybody* was on that stage!"[39] Hawkins was a perfect cameo guest for

Toronto, just as another hometown hero, Gordon Lightfoot, would be later in the set (and like Leonard Cohen might have been in Montreal, had he not chosen to remain off stage).

Amateur footage taken of the Toronto show illustrates how Jacques Levy then has the stage lights dim, ratcheting up the sense of anticipation. As the lights came up again, they reveal Joni Mitchell – another, very different, Canadian music star. Never part of the SIR rehearsal scene, she'd first joined the tour on November 13, in New Haven, Connecticut. Understandably, there is huge applause for Mitchell; many of the audience would have undoubtedly heard that she had attached herself to the tour. She performs 'Woman Of Heart And Mind' from her album *For The Roses*; the audience responding effusively to so familiar a tune. Although her song 'Coyote' would later be immortalized in Martin Scorsese's concert film *The Last Waltz*, it was still brand new when she played it at Maple Leaf Gardens; yet it, too, is rapturously received. She ends her guest slot by performing 'Edith And The Kingpin' and 'Don't Interrupt The Sorrow,' brave choices considering the album from which they were taken, *The Hissing Of Summer Lawns*, would not be released until later in the fall.

Mitchell was absolutely unafraid to play material with which the audience was entirely unfamiliar (as was Dylan, who would also deliver old songs in radical new arrangements). With the Guam-backed solo slots offering generally unfamiliar material and with showcased artists such as Ramblin' Jack Elliott known to the Maple Leaf Gardens crowd primarily by reputation, it would be left to the likes of Joan Baez, Roger McGuinn, and, of course, Dylan, later in the set, to reward the audience's patience with songs they could immediately recognize.

Before that, however, Bob Neuwirth combines his MC chores and performance skills to introduce Ramblin' Jack Elliott's set, singing a tribute song to the singing cowboy written by Kris Kristofferson called, naturally enough, 'Ramblin' Jack' ("I got a friend named Ramblin' Jack / He's got a face like a tumbled down shack"). Elliott would frequently start his set with a cover of Jesse Fuller's 'San Francisco Bay Blues' followed by a very accurate replication of Woody Guthrie's 'Talking Fisherman Blues,' a song in the style which influenced tonight's headliner no less than it did Ramblin' Jack.

After performing his first two songs solo, Elliott is joined by Roger McGuinn and most of Guam for versions of Louis Jordan & His Tympany Five's 'Salt Pork, West Virginia' and transatlantic folk hero Derroll Adams's 'I'm A Rich And Ramblin' Boy' (Adams is another Dylan satellite, having been seen and heard in *Dont Look Back*, at the hotel party scene during which the management accuse one of Dylan's guests of throwing a bottle from a window). The latter song was recorded by Elliott and Adams in 1957 on their album, *The Ramblin' Boys*, while they were, well, ramblin' around the British Isles, and is basically their rewrite of A.P. Carter's 'Rich And Ramblin' Boys.' On the Rolling Thunder tour, Adams's original vocal parts were sung by Neuwirth.

Dylan and McGuinn were big fans of Jack Elliott, and there was no pressure on him to play specific songs, even though his performance was the nightly precursor to Dylan's first appearance. Elliott certainly recalls there being no obligation to formally 'introduce' the headliner. "First it was the band playing to get the audience warmed up; they would play about five, six, or seven songs and then I would come out and play four or five tunes. Then I'd leave the stage and Bob would come out; he would usually swat me on the shoulder and say, 'Good set, Jack,' and then he'd run out. So, I was the one who introduced him, but I didn't *say* anything; I just played and left."

At the tour's initial shows, Elliott performed his mini-set completely solo. Then, one night early on in the tour, he remarked to his fellow Phydeaux passengers how everyone else seemed to be backing each and that he was the only act playing alone. McGuinn immediately volunteered his services on his beloved and unique Vega five-string banjo, with T Bone Burnett the next to raise his hand. "You know, the funny thing was, at the time ... nobody played with him [Elliott] because everybody thought that Ramblin' Jack was a solo guy and he didn't really necessarily play in time, or he played his own way," recalls Burnett. "The rhythm section didn't play with him 'cause, maybe, they didn't feel they would know how to accompany him."[40] Curiously, Elliott recalls the conclusion of his set being the first time he had ever played an electric guitar on stage; having handed his Martin acoustic to a crew member, he would be given Burnett's Fender Telecaster to play.

It was no coincidence that Jacques Levy had Ramblin' Jack Elliott on stage directly before Bob Dylan. Levy was making a musicological connection plain for all to see; it was the handing over of folk music's brightest burning torch. Elliott had been of huge importance to the young Robert Zimmerman. While everyone knew that Dylan's debut album had been a young Hibbing boy's version of Woody Guthrie, it was actually no less a young Hibbing boy's version of Ramblin' Jack Elliott. During Dylan's early, scuffling days in New York City, Elliott used to preface his version of a Dylan cover with the introduction: "This here's a song written by my son, Bob Dylan." It was an in-joke which drew laughs but which, in terms of musical style, was an undoubtedly accurate description. No wonder Dylan wrote so favorably of Jack in *Chronicles*.

After that the lights go down and then up again, signaling that it is time for Dylan. There would be no MC introduction from Neuwirth but instead the Two Bobs (as the crew called them), would begin with a duet on Dylan's 'When I Paint My Masterpiece,' perhaps a nod to Neuwirth, who was (and remains) a very fine painter and a serious student of art. With its nostalgic lyrics, the song was also a nod to the duo's shared past – Dylan and Neuwirth had been friends since 1961. Buddies they may have been, but close harmony singers à la Don and Phil Everly, they were not. At Maple Leaf Gardens, the Two Bobs shout most of the lyrics to the song as if in a competition to be heard outside the hall. Thankfully, this was not their approach every night.

'It Ain't Me, Babe' is up next, as it was on every date of the fall tour. It was a song so dear to Dylan at this point that he nearly always delivered a spellbinding rendition. Several Rolling Thunder versions were recorded, and one appears on the promo EP *4 Songs From Renaldo And Clara* (the same version is on the 2001 album, *Live 1961-2000*) while a different version is on *The Bootleg Series Vol. 5: Bob Dylan Live 1975, The Rolling Thunder Revue*.

In Toronto, 'The Lonesome Death Of Hattie Carroll' was next, although 'A Hard Rain's A-Gonna Fall' was the usual third selection on the fall tour. Dylan's audience had never heard these acoustic songs from his so-called 'protest period' sung against a full electric backing (with the exception of 'It Ain't Me, Babe,' which had been performed by the Dylan/Band ensemble on Tour '74, in an arrangement that was not so dissimilar to the Rolling Thunder take). Nonetheless, the full-on cavalry charge which was Dylan and Guam performing 'A Hard Rain's A-Gonna Fall,' with amps on eleven, was still a very novel sound in 1975. It must have been an unbelievably difficult emotional stretch for any old folkies in the audience.

The sound of the Rolling Thunder songs wasn't the only novel thing for veteran Bob Dylan fans who witnessed the tour. For one thing, Bob was uncharacteristically warm and relatively communicative on stage, regularly addressing the audience between songs. He would often dedicate a song to Sam Peckinpah, Mexican revolutionary Pancho Villa, or, perhaps, some celebrity friend backstage. He would also introduce some Guam members to the audience by name.

The other main well from which Dylan was now drawing material was *Desire*. Although the album had not yet been released, he was anxious to perform its songs. Indeed, with a caprice that is pure Dylan, he performed more selections from *Desire* on the fall 1975 portion of Rolling Thunder, when the album was still under wraps, than he did on the spring 1976 leg, by which time it had proved to be a Number One hit in the USA.

One of the *Desire* songs which came alive in its live version that fall was 'Romance In Durango,' Guam relishing the opportunity to throw various Mexican musical shapes, in turn driving Dylan to some often vertiginous vocal acrobatics. However, no *Desire* song, not even the impassioned 'Hurricane,' was played more dynamically and forcefully than 'Isis.' T Bone Burnett was particularly impressed both by Dylan's vocal prowess and by the repertoire he was able to draw upon. "He was singing the best he sang in his whole life. It was incredible, and the material we were playing was mostly from *Blood On The Tracks* and *Desire* ... a great period for him as a writer and singer. We would occasionally pull out one of the old ones, but most of the material was from those two albums."[41]

In Toronto, with the applause from 'Isis' still ringing throughout the auditorium, Bob Neuwirth takes the microphone and states, in matter-of-fact fashion: "We'll be back in about 15 minutes." Levy then dims the stage lights for a half-minute before the house lights come up brightly on an audience trying to emotionally digest all that they've seen and heard.

After the interval, the second set begins with a series of duets by Dylan and Joan Baez. At the smaller venues, earlier on in the tour, this dynamic duo would begin their performance while still *behind* the Rolling Thunder Revue tour curtain. After they'd sung a couple of lines the curtain would be slowly raised. This was Jacques Levy at his theatrical best; it was a simple device that nonetheless created an incredible sense of drama.

Often, Baez would be dressed similarly to Dylan and at times, such as the Night Of The Hurricane benefit show at Madison Square Garden later in December, they were turned out identically. On such occasions, people in the first few rows could not tell which figure was Dylan and which was Baez, so similar in stature were they.

Baez would harmonize with the unpredictable Dylan as best she could, basically by staring intently at his mouth. In Toronto, they perform 'Blowin' In The Wind,' 'Wild Mountain Thyme,' 'Mama, You Been On My Mind,' and a version, Merle Travis's 'Dark As A Dungeon,' before finishing with 'I Shall Be Released.' Other venues heard Dylan-Baez duets on 'I Dreamed I Saw St. Augustine,' 'The Times They Are A-Changin',' 'The Lonesome Death Of Hattie Carroll,' and the old Johnny Ace hit, 'Never Let Me Go.' For the folkies in the audience, these duets were akin to the Second Coming. It was the first time the two folk icons had performed together in public since 1964.

'Blowin' In The Wind' would prove to be particularly glorious, both musically and dynamically; their stirring version of Dylan's most unequivocal anthem regularly bringing punters to their feet, as it did in Toronto (Baez would release a fine 'Blowin' In The Wind' duet with Dylan, recorded on the spring 1976 Rolling Thunder tour, on her 1993 boxed set, *Rare, Live & Classic*).

Their version of 'Wild Mountain Thyme' is rather less stirring, it being the kind of over-familiar folk standard too often mauled by would-be Woody Guthries in folk clubs worldwide. Dylan fans will remember a very young Bob recording it back in Minneapolis in May 1961, in Bonnie Beecher's apartment, and that an older, wiser Bob sang it quite tenderly at the Isle Of Wight Festival, in 1969. Baez had recorded the song back in 1965, on her Vanguard album *Farewell, Angelina*.

The then unreleased Dylan rarity, 'Mama, You Been On My Mind,' by contrast, proved to be a lovely surprise, with Guam joining in more audibly and effectively than on 'Wild Mountain Thyme,' during which they'd just tapped along, demurely. Lively bass and drums make the song swing to the point where it loses any hint of sentimentality and became more of a barroom lament, an exotic cross between Bertolt Brecht and the then popular New Riders Of The Purple Sage. Baez's harmony parallels Dylan, up and down, across, back again, and then over and out; never letting him get away. It is an astonishing display on her part.

Their penultimate duet in Toronto is 'Dark As A Dungeon,' a song almost as worn out as 'Wild Mountain Thyme,' but performed here as the proud but desperate plea for the dignity of a Kentucky miner (the profession avoided by the song's Kentucky-born author, Merle Travis). If singing is acting, then Dylan and Baez should share an Oscar. How many times could either of them have possibly been down a dusty, claustrophobic coal mine? Yet, when you hear their voices, you don't question their travails, their pain, or their sincerity. Dylan must have felt close to the song as he performed it here and there for years after Rolling Thunder. He even cut a version of it for *Infidels*, in 1983.

The final duet between the folk world's Queen and its abdicated King is a lovely reading of 'I Shall Be Released.' Despite being taped at Big Pink back in 1967 (and The Band subsequently releasing a memorable version on their debut album, the following year), the song hadn't appeared on CBS's *The Basement Tapes* double LP, released the previous June, and only existed in a somewhat throwaway acoustic version, recorded with Happy Traum, on Dylan's *Greatest Hits, Vol 2*, back in 1971. Only those Dylan fans with a copy of the *Great White Wonder* bootleg, or its many offspring, had previously heard Dylan sing this anthemic prisoner's lament with a full band behind him. Its nightly performance would prove to be one of the highlights of Rolling Thunder.

Back at Maple Leaf Gardens, Levy now takes the center spotlight down momentarily, allowing Dylan to quit the stage and Baez to put a capo on her guitar. She then plays 'Diamonds And Rust,' arguably her finest original song, and one received by the audience like a love letter from a long-lost paramour. Her a cappella version of 'Swing Low, Sweet Chariot' follows. It hovers uncertainly between Southern spiritual, Anglican Church solo, vocal warm-up exercise, and supper club torch ballad, and suffers for it. Although it's a dazzling display of her vocal chops, it never sounds like heartfelt spirituality, or a genuine plea for salvation, but instead like an undoubtedly talented performer showing off.

Baez is back on firmer ground with her next selection, Woody Guthrie's 'Pastures Of Plenty.' The song is prefaced by a rallying cry for Canada's United Farm Workers Union; indeed, there is genuine sentiment palpable in every syllable she sings. She follows this with Canadian bard Leonard Cohen's most famous song, 'Suzanne.' It's a wise choice as it's instantly recognized by the Toronto crowd; even the opening lines receive considerable applause. Dylan, a fan of Cohen, would invite the Canadian troubadour to join the tour when the party reached his hometown, Montreal, a couple of days later.

The Guam musicians now crawl back on stage in near darkness and Baez introduces Kris Kristofferson's 'Help Me Make It Through The Night.' A huge hit for Gladys Knight & The Pips back in 1972, and practically a standard by late 1975, it is given the full Guam-meets-Nashville treatment with drums, bass, dobro, piano, and T Bone Burnett's harmony vocals all much in evidence.

Baez then sings Dave Loggins's schmaltzy 'Please Come To Boston' and, despite Mansfield's violin sweetly echoing and reflecting the melody, the song's *Wuthering Heights* lyrics and Baez's pure soprano voice only emphasize its saccharine flavor. Perhaps surprisingly for an audience who so enjoy the headliner's notably rougher approach to his own material, the inherent sweetness of 'Please Come To Boston' provokes a warm round of applause.

Baez completes her set with a version of Robbie Robertson's 'The Night They Drove Old Dixie Down,' a song with which she'd had a hit back in 1971 – Roger McGuinn strolls on stage unannounced to help out with the chorus. He stays on for a surprisingly short, two-song set. Earlier in the tour, he would come on before Baez and play just *one* song, a curious decision, presumably made by set director and erstwhile collaborator Jacques Levy, and with Dylan's full knowledge. It was, of course, the head Byrd's work with Levy on 'Chestnut Mare' which had alerted Dylan to the director's talents as a lyricist in the first place. Why had Dylan and Levy been so eager to encourage McGuinn to join the tour at their Other End meeting if he was only to be granted one or two songs per night? Was McGuinn's presence designed to help fulfill some kind of hip quotient? With The Byrds, he'd undoubtedly played a huge role in making Dylan's music palatable for a wider public and would subsequently go on to enjoy a career worthy of his Rock & Roll Hall Of Fame investiture. In contrast, Baez got a six-song set every night, Ramblin' Jack did four or five songs, and guest artists such as Joni Mitchell or Gordon Lightfoot would generally be given four-song sets. Bob Neuwirth, hardly a star like McGuinn, regularly played two songs in his set, occasionally three.

Baez introduces McGuinn with a noticeable dryness; as we shall see, her opinion of the ensuing 'Eight Miles High' was not very, well, high. Nonetheless, at the conclusion of its Maple Leaf Gardens airing, the paying customers are ecstatic. They had just heard a fine, dynamic, full-band version of The Byrds' classic, with Mansfield's pedal steel doing amazing swoops and slides around McGuinn's vocal and modal, 12-string Rickenbacker lead work, evoking the jet plane ride which is the song's subject.

McGuinn then plays 'Chestnut Mare.' This is, presumably, more to Joan Baez's taste, as she sings a beautiful harmony part at the chorus. In a version captured for *Renaldo & Clara*, the song was essayed too fast, but Toronto hears a gorgeous version of the Jacques Levy co-write, with David Mansfield's pedal steel and Mick Ronson's lead guitar intertwined to poignant effect. It's is one of the highlights of the show so far, giving 'I Shall Be Released' a run for its money.

At its conclusion, McGuinn leaves the stage to make way for local boy made good, Gordon Lightfoot. Baez remembered the occasion in the second part of a *Rock Around The World* radio show Rolling Thunder special, broadcast May 2 1976. "The emphasis was on keeping the egos down ... and inviting guests when we could, in various places. Obviously people like Gordon Lightfoot in Toronto were naturals and people would show up and we would try to fit them in. The show probably went from three-and-a-half hours to ending up five hours long. ... [It] started off with 50 or 60 [in the tour party] and the number of people ended up at over 100."

Gordon Lightfoot was a major star of the mid 70s. Famed in Canada much earlier, he was primarily known in the USA as a songwriter before his 1970 hit single 'If You Could Read My Mind' got him on the airwaves as a performer. The Ontario native would subsequently enjoy a string of US hits. That night at Maple Leaf Gardens, there would have been few ticket holders unfamiliar with 'Sundown,' 'Carefree Highway,' or 'Rainy Day People,' each a chart smash. Lightfoot and Dylan once shared Albert Grossman as a manager and Dylan had once said of Lightfoot: "Every time I hear a song of his, it's like I wish it would last for ever." Fellow Canadian Robbie Robertson called Lightfoot "absolutely a national treasure."[42]

Starting with the then unreleased 'Race Among The Ruins' (which he would record for his 1976 album *Summertime Dream*), Lightfoot is the epitome of musical confidence and measured masculinity. Backed by his own band, he seems effortless as a performer, completely at ease with the hometown crowd and incapable of breaking a sweat. He has the Ontario crowd in his palm from the very first chord. His second song of four is 'Cherokee Bend,' a cut from his *Cold On The Shoulder* album which had been released the previous February. In many ways, Lightfoot is the male equivalent of Joni Mitchell, the two Canadians then at the top of their game, penning cerebral anthems for their generation, both of whom fought feelings of insecurity on stage while nonetheless appearing born to be in the spotlight.

If Lightfoot has a weakness it is an over-reliance on a particular mid-tempo which lends much of his original material a homogenous quality. His third song at Maple Leaf Gardens is 'Long Way Back Home,' from the album *Back Here On Earth*, released on United Artists in 1968. It is essayed at the exact same pedestrian tempo, and with the same rhythm, as his first two selections. No one seems to mind, however. Neuwirth then calls him back for another song and Lightfoot duly obliges, slaying the locals by performing 'Sundown,' his hit single of the previous year. Amateur footage of this evening's show records

Dylan, who rematerializes next, beginning 'Mr. Tambourine Man' alone in near darkness, the spotlight coming up slowly as he begins to sing. Compared with his version of the same song recorded at the first of two shows in Boston, on November 21 (as heard on the album *The Bootleg Series Vol. 5: Bob Dylan Live 1975, The Rolling Thunder Revue* album), the most noticeable feature was the silent reverence with which the song was received. That is, until the relatively reserved Toronto crowd whoop it up for Dylan's shimmering harmonica solo.

He follows this with 'Tangled Up In Blue,' a song not yet fully rewritten into its post-Levy version, and featuring only minor lyric changes from the familiar *Blood On The Tracks* original. It is delivered a tad slower and more deliberately than the more urgent versions captured for *Renaldo & Clara* and one documented on *The Bootleg Series Vol. 5*, which originates from the second Boston show.

'Oh Sister' follows. It is a version laden with sorrow; slower than on *Desire*, with Dylan almost speaking the lyrics at times. Gordon Lightfoot, backed by the adept Guam musicians, could have delivered a wonderful version of this song. Alas, at the chorus, Dylan and what sounds like Neuwirth continue with their earlier shouting contest. Then the ensemble suddenly stops on a dime (proving that some rehearsal had taken place, after all) – band and punters waiting in deadly silence for a moment before the song kicks into life again. It is an offbeat move, but an undeniably dramatic one. During the brief silence, not a dropping pin, still less a discouraging word, is heard.

"Here's a song about a man who was framed," is Dylan's laconic introduction to 'Hurricane,' which follows. Recordings evince Guam commencing in surprisingly calm fashion, only picking up the dynamics when Dylan arrives at the rousing chorus. Scarlet Rivera's violin also makes its unmistakable mark, her notes gliding sinuously around Dylan's vocal melody; no other violinist sounded quite like her, as David Mansfield notes. "Scarlet had certain notes that were a little sharp or a little flat, compared to perfectly even-tempered scale; but I think they were her choices. The most obvious [comparison] would be with American music; say in Appalachia. The way the guys that play that old time mountain music, the way they heard the scale ... they heard those intervals, being influenced by African intervals. Another good analogy is with Middle Eastern music. Their lute players ... there is that funny note they play, in between a major and a minor second. *I* wouldn't know exactly what frequency or what pitch to play, because it is very precise.[43]

"This is the only underground song I know ... this is *really* underground," Dylan declares, introducing 'One More Cup Of Coffee.' It is taken markedly slower than on *Desire*, with Ronee Blakley singing the Emmylou Harris harmony part, and with a slightly more exotic, Middle Eastern flavor in both the violin and Dylan's Om Kalthoum-like vocal. Like this, it might have qualified as the world's first country & eastern song, with Dylan ending each line of the verse with a trill right out of a Tehran call to prayer. For those who claim Dylan's songs are weak on melody and that as an artist his music has not grown much, this version of 'One More Cup Of Coffee,' from Toronto on December 2 1975, represents a quantum leap from the relatively simple folk melodies with which the young Dylan first came to prominence.

The ensuing 'Sara' maintains the vaguely Eastern mood, with Rivera's violin playing almost continuously; something of which Dylan clearly approved. Again, there was no sense of Rivera leaving the lead vocal alone; her lines interleaved with, and yet framing, Dylan's melody. Even when he shifts to the harmonica, Rivera, who at rehearsals back in New York City would stop playing whenever Bob blew, carries on sawing as per Bob's instructions.

By now, the Toronto audience has been seated for over four hours, listening to largely new material or familiar material in startling new arrangements. Guam cut them some slack by collectively surging into a gypsy-like 'Just Like A Woman,' with Mansfield playing some gorgeous pedal steel beneath Rivera's swirling arabesques. The harmony singing with Ronee Blakley and a male voice (possibly Neuwirth) is less impressive, however. It's more reminiscent of last orders being barked at The Dog & Duck. Frustratingly, both Blakley and the unidentifiable male singer are off key at times; something which ought to have been worked out back at the SIR rehearsal studio, if not at soundcheck.

Was it bandleader Rob Stoner's idea to have the gang play a new, almost reggae rhythm on the bridge, and to make a subsequent drop in volume and dynamic immediately afterward? Whoever made the changes, it is a gorgeous reworking of the song – until, that is, the harsh chorus vocals return to ruin the mood. Blakely's singing, enunciation, and emphasis on the final word of the payoff line: "... breaks like a little girl" has to be heard to be believed, and not in a good way.

The evening draws toward its conclusion with Dylan's 1973 hit single, 'Knockin' On Heaven's Door.' Nowadays a folk warhorse up there in the firelight strumming canon alongside 'Kumbaya' and 'Michael, Row The Boat

Ashore' (both of which it melodically and structurally resembles), in 1975 it was arguably Dylan's best-known song after 'Blowin' In The Wind' and 'Like A Rolling Stone.' Roger McGuinn takes the second verse, singing gently in that unique, almost floating way of his. Beguiling as it is, it's soon obliterated by a "Knock, knock, knocking …" chorus which dispenses with subtlety in favor of a brutish chant, more readily associated with the crowd at a Premier League football match. The forceful chorus would prove to be something of a taster for the generally harsher approach the Rolling Thunder tourists would adopt on the following spring's second leg.

After the chorus, they return to the light, airy bridge, with McGuinn's 12-string guitar, Mansfield's pedal steel, and Rivera's violin weaving music of quite stunning beauty; it's as if they just remembered they were sensitive musicians again, and not a beery sports tribe. Thankfully, the final chorus is actually delivered with some grace and restraint, as befits a heartfelt plea for salvation.

From there, it is straight into a valedictory, if rather too rapid, swing through Woody Guthrie's 'This Land Is Your Land,' with the full Revue ensemble on stage and the audience clapping along merrily. It's an all-hands-on-deck finale, with even the otherwise under-used and overlooked Allen Ginsberg having his sing-along moment on stage. Amusingly, Dylan, Guam, and company are playing what is effectively an alternative American National Anthem, a rollicking folk hymn to the working masses of the United States – for a Canadian crowd. This incongruity doesn't seem to have occurred to anyone, on stage or off. 'Four Strong Winds,' written by Dylan's friend Ian Tyson (of Canadian due Ian & Sylvia) would have been a much more affecting choice in these environs.

Joan Baez takes the roll of MC, calling out the individual singers to take their verse. It is one surefire way of guaranteeing everybody knows when to come in. Levy slowly dims the stage lights to black as the song ends, holding the darkness for about ten seconds before bringing the lights back up to bright white to allow a final wave to the crowd from Dylan. Levy dims the lamps again to signal that the evening is over.

Playing venues such as Toronto's capacious Maple Leaf Gardens actually ran contrary to the original ethos of the Rolling Thunder Revue and there was some criticism of Dylan for abandoning smaller venues in favor of larger concert halls. However, the troupe-members knew Dylan had to pay for the shooting of *Renaldo & Clara* and, as much of the music they were collectively making was inventive, emotive, and, at times, unlike anything in rock's canon up to that point, it must have seemed counterintuitive not to present it to as large an audience as possible.

Besides all that, for the tourists, Rolling Thunder was a joy to be involved in, wherever they played. Larry Sloman wasn't alone in thinking that the spontaneous nature of the tour had propelled Dylan to new heights of performance. "Everybody was having a ball. I have never seen people on a tour with so much camaraderie. There were a couple of cat-fighting moments among the females, but other than that, everyone had such a great time. How could you not? I never saw Bob in the early days; I saw him in that period when he was first going out with The Band, and I have seen him ever since, but I have *never* seen him as inspired as on the Rolling Thunder tour. I mean, every night it was just *wow!* You could hear the two-volume *Bootleg* series of that (*The Bootleg Series Vol. 5: Bob Dylan Live 1975, The Rolling Thunder Revue*) and listen to the tracks on *Desire* and you can see how Dylan has grown into those songs and just blows the fucking place out with those songs!"[44]

After Toronto, there would be three further gigs on the fall Rolling Thunder Revue tour, including the Night Of The Hurricane benefit show at Madison Square Garden on December 8. Then, the leader of rock's best tour since, well, Tour '74 with The Band would make the rounds of various hip New York City parties before spending the holidays with his family.

He was already planning the next leg of Rolling Thunder, however, one that would commence in the spring of America's proud bicentennial year. In the interim, there would be six much-deserved weeks off for Dylan. If they'd left him relaxed and refreshed ahead of the next portion of the tour, then it wouldn't be obvious to anyone. Sometimes, although not often, the Hibbing Bard could be as easy to read as a dime-store novel; at most times he was as hard to decipher as the Rosetta stone, and his emotional state was as unpredictable as the weather. And the storm was coming.

CHAPTER 3
ROGER MCGUINN'S ROLLING THUNDER BUS TAPE

I n November 1975, Roger McGuinn made some *verité* sound recordings on the Rolling Thunder tour-bus. They provide a snapshot of the fall tour ensemble's camaraderie and capture the good feelings which abounded. In order to provide an insider's glimpse into the machinations of Phydeaux, the refurbished Greyhound bus rented to Dylan for the tour by Frank Zappa, McGuinn has kindly allowed a transcription of one of his Rolling Thunder tour tapes to appear in this book.

Here follows everything the microphone picked up one night in November 1975, as Phydeaux rolled through the New England darkness.

As the tape kicks to life, Jack Elliott is spinning an amusing anecdote. If you've ever wondered about the provenance of the Ramblin' nickname, wonder no more.

Elliott: "In Oxford, I was having some coffee and whatnot and June [Elliott's actress wife] suddenly pointed out, sitting over at the other table, 'Jack, that's Peter Ustinov, the guy in the picture!' 'Oh yeah, the guy in the Roman toga, that's him.' And I had seen him in a movie since then, too: a thing called *Desert Hotel* where he played the part of a hotelier in the desert, during the North African campaign. He is playing host to first the Germans, then the Italians, then the English, then the Americans, then the Italians [giggling is heard; it's a woman's voice] ... and he speaks all these languages! Turn here, you know [Elliott instructs the bus driver] ... he's the host ... funny man. He's the funniest man on earth.

"So there he is, right. I go over and say, 'Uh, Mr. Ustinov, I am Jack Elliott and I'm singing in concert here over at the college and, uh, I'd like to invite you over to the concert. My wife June met you on the set of *Quo Vadis* ... that was it; I think it was *Quo Vadis*. I never even saw the picture. He says, 'Oh, I'd be delighted!' and he walked with us along the street and came to this concert with us, and everyone had to sit around on the floor as there were not enough chairs. He had to sit on the floor. I didn't want to call attention to him and do all that star stuff. I was *thrilled* he was there, but I didn't want to let on that anyone special was there, or look at him for too long or anything. I didn't want him to feel ... you know? So ... but he, unbeknownst to me, would've liked to have had a little of that [star treatment]. When we were splitting, after the concert, I made him laugh a lot, too, and that really thrilled the hell outta me, 'cause he made me be funnier. I had only seen him in that one movie and I didn't know him. I didn't realize his full potential at the time; I just knew he was *great*. But, ah ...

so I was great and he loved it. As we were leaving, he stops in the doorway, as kids [Oxford students who'd been at the show] are filtering out, and he starts entertaining them with a little flamenco song he composed on the spot about me and June singing our way around the world [Elliott shifts into an absurd, Hispanic-accented nonsense song as he imitates Ustinov entertaining the students]; *Olé!* And he is standing there doing all this shit, man, in the doorway, and everybody's stopped, in a trance, listening to this stuff. Then, he gives us a ride back to London in his Aston Martin ... with the top down; it's freezing-ass cold. June's in the front seat with Peter and I'm in the back seat, lovin' every freezing-ass minute of it. And he's doing imitations of American singers, each one exactly right, not just a generalized thing. But like he does, like, Joe McCarthy [meaning Senator Joseph McCarthy, of Army-McCarthy hearings infamy, not a pop singer]; he does this guy, that guy. ...

"We get back to the house ... which used to belong to a famous old English actress, Ellen Terry [the celebrated Victorian thespian Dame and the great aunt of Sir John Gielgud]. It's got a bronze plaque on the building which says *Ellen Terry lived here*. We go inside and turn on the record player. We sit down and pull out a sketch pad and start drinking wine, drawing cartoons and telling jokes and stories, and listening to the records of Russian folk music and stuff, on into five o'clock [in the morning]."

Joan Baez: "This is called, 'This is how Ramblin' got his name.'"

Roger McGuinn: "I know! I've been a-sittin' here."

Baez: "Isn't this stupendous? I was waiting for the Peter Ustinov imitation and it never happened!" [There is laughter.]

McGuinn: "Never did. That's because he rambled from one subject to another."

Baez: "It never happened! My mind wandered."

Elliott: "A good time was had by all."

Baez: "Tell me you're not ... oh ... OK, do it now because you are losing me."

Elliott: "I'd do it now."

McGuinn: "We're running out of tape."

Unidentified voice [perhaps Mick Ronson]: "That's a very simple ..."

Elliott [interrupting]: "He went in the studio and [makes hurricane noises, talks more Hispanic gibberish, then suddenly shifts into television announcer voice, à la Ustinov]. Well, not since the dawn of motoring has this sound been heard near the fabled Rock of Gibraltar. And it was in the spring of 1906 that enlightened Governor Sir Original Blur-Cowley first inaugurated the *Grand*

Prix Du Rock. But perhaps his enthusiasm overrode his sense of the practical when, on the very first lap, Dan Brosio, driving the 900 cubic centimeter, 42-liter, 32-cylinder, six-and-a-half horsepower Bolsato, missed the turn and motored gently into the water. He was followed by some of the lighter cars: Walter Thurston, later Lord Gunnich, in the Doubleday Esquires, and Prince Hess Bless Hess riding in a chauffeur-driven vehicle with a masked lady by his side. Students of history will know British foreign policy inclined to be conciliatory during the period when the harbor was blocked by the hulks of racing cars. And it wasn't until the autumn of 1909 that the British got tough again with the raising of the Palmer Air, which was later converted into the sloop, HMS Incorrigible."

McGuinn: "Great."

Baez [laughing]: "Excellent, superb! I didn't know he did all that, but I'm sure he does, yeah."

Elliott: "Italian, German, French, Russian ..."

McGuinn: "He really did a lotta stuff."

Elliott: "Yeah, he did everything. A 40-minute record, that one ..."

Baez [interrupting]: "Good job!"

Elliott: "... I had memorized at one point."

Baez: "From Joni Mitchell, the primal scream, to rock, to Peter Ustinov, with a tad of rambling in between."

McGuinn: "A tad of rambling that got ... er ... not quite sniffed in the butt but ..."

Baez: "... snuffed in the boot?"

McGuinn [amusedly]: "Snuffed in the boot!"

Baez: "Who's passed out? I'm curious; just Ronee?"

McGuinn: "Just Ronee. She's down and out."

Baez: "She's tired. She did a good job tonight."

McGuinn: "She did a good job."

Baez: "You gotta tell her she did good ... because she does, you know?"

McGuinn: "Yeah, right. You gotta encourage her!"

Baez: "She was so happy when you just said it. Because you take if for granted everybody knows, and they don't know. We don't know ... we're insecure!"

McGuinn: "Somebody wrote in the news bulletin ... you are taken for granted if you are good, and fired if you're bad. That's true. There is no room for error, here. Some people are just barely cuttin' it, you know?"

Baez: "Yeah."

McGuinn: "Yeah, but it sure is fun. I mean, 'cause they keep it highly efficient as it is. It's a paramilitary kind of attitude they have about it ... but it is soft and gentle."

Baez: "Soft and gentle on us but not so good on [the tour] security [personnel]."

McGuinn: "It's highly efficient. Oh, yeah, security are goons."

Baez: "Yeah, they never eat."

McGuinn: "Nothing personal against them but ..."

Baez: "No. Not them. I mean they don't get treated too good."

McGuinn: "Oh, we don't treat them that well, huh?"

Baez: "No, we treat 'em OK."

McGuinn: "*We* treat 'em well but ... the management ..."

Baez: "The upper-ups [or, possibly, *the abrupts*] fuck 'em over."

McGuinn: "Well, we can't do anything about that."

Baez: "Yeah, you can; you can take them to your room. I take them my food at night."

McGuinn: "Aww ... you do? You are *so* considerate!"

Baez: "They swallow it in one lump, you know? I took my sandwich to Gene [Clark, a security man on the tour bus, not the Byrds man] ... *gulp* [she makes a hilarious swallowing sound] ... just like a dog or something!"

McGuinn: "That ten dollar bill you put under the ashtray for the waitress ... [a giggle is heard] ... who'd given ... such a hard time in that hotel room. And they'd opened especially, just for us!"

Baez: "We take too much for granted."

McGuinn: "We do."

Baez: "We are spoiled entertainers."

McGuinn [thoughtfully]: "I am glad you are such a conscientious person. You have a conscience working, there. Some of us may be a little too jaded."

Baez: "Oh, it's there you know."

McGuinn: "We have to be reminded, and I appreciate somebody who reminds me that my conscience is ... gone."

Baez: "Yeah, because you're a sweet guy; you're not a slob."

McGuinn: "I'm basically a sweet guy who can be a slob, easily, and I appreciate somebody wakin' me up to say, 'Hey, quit being a slob, jerk!' I appreciate that, thank you."

Elliott [in a crazy Hispanic accent, once again]: "No, no. No, *Ro-loo-hay-lee-yo*

... you are a gentleman, a prince, and a scholar.
[The unmistakable sound of Joni Mitchell is heard in the background at this point, even though many voices are speaking at once. "Besides all that, you are one of the best musicians I ever ... ever." An unidentifiable voice from a distant part of the bus says, "Fuckin'-a, *maaaannn*," in agreement.]
McGuinn: "I'm having a ball, man."
Mick Ronson: "I'm not a musician, I am a magician."
McGuinn: "You could do card tricks instead."
Elliott [amusedly]: "I like those sleight-of-hand tricks you do on them strings! [There is a sound of something being struck, followed by cries of surprise from several voices.]
Unidentified voice: "*Aieeeeeeee. ...*"
McGuinn: "I have to explain; Ramblin' Jack just kicked his spur up in the air and a whole bunch of tequila, about an ounce-and-a-half, went flying on Mick Ronson's shoulder."
Ronson [jokingly]: "Don't keep pressing up against me!"
McGuinn: "And on his back."
Elliott: "Here, take my sweater."
Ronson: "Ah, nuts!" [Various voices speak simultaneously about the tequila spill and how to clean it up.]
Joni Mitchell: "I'm passing the buck! It's running."
McGuinn: "Leave it recording!"
Steven Soles [almost certainly]: "David is looking for the microphone and the microphone is right there. It is a condenser microphone."
David Mansfield: *"All right!"*
Soles: "What do you have to say to the microphone today, David?"
Mansfield [very close to the mic, as if about to eat it]: *"Bbbbbllllllll-phew!"*
Soles: "Don't you know that many famous people have talked on this tape and you should say something extremely intelligent?"
Unidentified male voice: "Something extremely intelligent? And, of course, T Bone will have something to say [he doesn't]."
Soles: "Thanks, T Bone. I always did enjoy your spacey outlook. And then we move on to Rockin' Rob."
Rob Stoner [deliberately and professorially]: "Is it true this machine is picking up every word I say?"
Soles: "It's quite true, Rob."

Stoner: "Steven, could you please talk into that flower pot that is over on the table there? Just make sure you talk to that plant over there, that fruit bowl."
Soles [impersonating a television announcer]: "OK, we're going directly to the plant! [In the background, someone, probably female, sings a nonsensical song in a high-pitched voice.] The plant is very talkative today."
Stoner: "That's because it was planted here. It's a plant, you see. I used to work in a plant; a defense plant."
Mansfield: "Do you like plants?"
Stoner: "Yeah."
Mansfield: "What do you do with them?"
Stoner [proudly]: "I live on the planet Earth." [Soles, Mansfield, and Stoner enter a verbal riffing contest, repeatedly using the words 'plant' and 'planet,' as if in an Abbott and Costello routine.]
Stoner: "It's plane to see."
Soles: "It is?" [Gibberish erupts all around.]
Mansfield: "Is it blue? It's clear? Is it blue?"
Stoner: "Did you take Scientology? Did you make it to *clear*?"
Baez [obviously puzzled by Stoner's grammar]: "Did you *take* Scientology?"
Soles: "I am very clear. I am quite ..."
Stoner [interrupting, in the voice of a television announcer]: "Scientology Two [or possibly 'too']."
Soles: "*Scientology Two*, directed by Rob Stoner."
Stoner: "Maybe Miss Baez would like to say something into this machine – which picks up *every word you say* – about anything. Just give us your thoughts on life in general; or life. ..."
Unidentified voice [possibly Soles]: "Gee whiz, Rob; that's quite a question!"
Stoner [still in television announcer mode]: "Rather general, I understand. Ah ... life in general is a generality."
Soles: "How about a word from T Bone? [There is a pause.] Any word will do." [Laughter is heard from down the aisle, some of it coming from Joan Baez, who is obviously moving toward the microphone.]
Soles: "A laugh from Joan Baez!"
Stoner: "Yes, when the machine ... when the microphones are on I just come alive, have you noticed?"
Soles: "You have quite a sparkling personality, I understand ..."
Stoner [interrupting]: "I just come alive."

Soles: "I understand you got a write up in *Melody Maker*."

Stoner: "Would you like me to read it into this machine?" [There is a nervous pause. No one says a word.]

Stoner: "This is called 'Roger's Release,' it's called any day now, I shall be released."

Soles: "And of course, many other people have already talked on this tape and had far more interesting things to say."

Stoner: "Yes ... than this! We're just wasting tape; and electricity, and therefore ... *raping* the environment."

Soles: "*Melody Maker*, Rob, says in a review ..." [Soles is interrupted by Stoner. They then indulge in further comic banter about the *Melody Maker* article. It's reminiscent of the early Christmas fan club records by The Beatles. In the background, an unidentifiable woman talks of "writing good songs." Someone else is apparently "on the floor, passed out."]

Soles: "T Bone is always trying to be so artistic and he realizes that in all artistic endeavor when you become ... predictable ... then something manifests itself in a course of negative reactions."

Stoner: "Yes!"

Soles: "And this is precisely what happened to T Bone a moment ago, because he had to put in space for the third time and it became too predictable and he realized he must say something. So ... he did say ..."

Stoner [still using the television announcer voice, and obviously relishing entertaining the troops]: "So, he has got to come up with something, some statement of fact or thought and this is it. T Bone, for the blue Tourister luggage or the pink Chevelle!" [Baez is heard in the background talking about a picture of her son.]

Stoner [as if wildly drunk]: "Oh yeah, well ... we like fuzz tone in this band!"

T Bone Burnett [sounding tired]: "Turn it up to ten."

Stoner [admiringly]: "Pretty good for a starter, T Bone. What you got to follow it with?"

Burnett [thoughtfully]: "I realize that you have to put your ass on the line."

Stoner: "*What* line? The Mason-Dixon line?"

Burnett [amusedly]: "We gonna start fighting the Civil War again, kid?" [Relative silence descends as this thought is collectively contemplated.]

Stoner: "Are we gonna have to draw a line down the middle of this bus? [Burnett laughs.]

Stoner: I cannot believe this fuckin' tape is still going!"

Burnett: "I can't either."

Stoner: "God, why can't we think of anything interesting to say to put on it?"

Burnett: "Let's erase it! Let's erase it. Let's throw it out the window."

Stoner: "It's priceless!"

Burnett: "Let's throw the tape machine out the window."

Stoner: "It's priceless. It's Steven's machine."

Soles [as television announcer]: "It happens not to be my machine but Roger's machine; oh, Roger!"

Stoner: "Hey, Roger! How are you?"

Soles: "We're talking to Roger, now. When you listen to this tape, Roger, just remember … this is brought to you by Kemp Fisheries, Inc."

Stoner: "Thank you. Signing off. Over and out." [We hear the tape machine screeching off.]

[The tape is on again. An indistinguishable male voice says, with a laugh, "The tires are sagging, the fog is on the window, and the wipers aren't on, and there are frogs … *frogs.*"]

Burnett [now sounding completely exhausted]: "I didn't see it."

Soles: "You didn't see fog? Frogs?"

Burnett: "It was three to two the last time I saw it."

Soles: "Frogs are crawling underfoot."

Stoner: "There were frogs all over the windshield."

Burnett: "Luis Tiant [then a Boston Red Sox baseball pitcher, conceivably at large in the New England night] was standing up there."

Soles: "Yeah?"

Burnett: "Yeah, he was good. He was making his move there, he pitched a curve."

Soles: "Yeah, he was good. He was making his pitch there. He was a …" [Sound of the tape machine going off.]

[We resume with Allen Ginsberg singing a version of his song, 'Put Down Your Cigarette Rag (Don't Smoke).']

Allen Ginsberg: "250 million greens, what Madison Avenue gets, to advertise nicotine and hook your radical breath! Don't smoke, don't smoke, don't smoke; nope, nope, nope. Don't smoke weed, indeed, indeed; but don't smoke cigarettes, it's too obscene, indeed. Stay off your nicotine. Don't smoke!"

[The tape stops, and then starts abruptly. Ginsberg is still rapping.]

Ginsberg: "All you need, indeed, indeed, indeed. If you will get in bed, and give your boyfriend head, put something in your mouth like meat, not cigarette filth. [Laughter is heard.] Don't smoke, don't smoke, don't smoke, don't smoke, don't smoke!" [More laughter, then the tape is turned off and on again.]

Stoner: "Enema rising?" [Baez is heard in the background, singing a short phrase, beautifully.]

Unidentifiable male voice: "Since I was 17, love never bothered me."

Stoner: "Did someone say, 'Enema rising?'"

Unidentifiable female voice: "Animal rising?"

Second unidentifiable female voice: "No, 'Enema rising.'"

Baez: "All right then; now we're arguing? I wanna know what it means. It's like antidisestablishmentarianism, as far as I am concerned. It sounds very good *to the ear.*"

Second female voice, again: "Now what does it mean? Animal rising ... does it mean *anything*?"

Female voice [possibly Joni Mitchell]: "Yeah, it does."

Baez: "It better ... putting us on and we are all falling for it." [The tape is turned off, then on again.]

Ronson: "The full text?"

McGuinn: "Just do what you know of it."

Ginsberg [returning to his earlier song]: "Don't smoke, don't smoke, don't smoke, don't smoke, don't smoke, don't smoke, it's a nine-billion-dollar capitalist joke! Don't smoke, don't smoke, smoke, smoke, smoke, nope, nope, nope, nope. Smoking makes you cough, you can't sing straight, you gargle on saliva ... [speaking] I quit smoking again."

Ronson: "You serious?"

Ginsberg: "Yes sirree; I ain't had a cigarette in four days, man. And it ain't ... it is the 21st of November in 1975."

McGuinn: "On Phydeaux."

Ginsberg: "On Phydeaux, in the evening, after a full moon."

McGuinn: "Dynamite."

Ginsberg: "On the red curtain-windowed bus, rolling pleasantly up the highway from covered Harvard Square Theatre."

McGuinn: "Harvard Square, Cambridge, Mass."

Ginsberg: "Cambridge, Mass ... concert ... of Rolling Thunder."

McGuinn: "The concert was great tonight! Wasn't it fun?"

Ginsberg: "Yes."

McGuinn: "We all enjoyed it."

Ginsberg: "Ah ... to the ... where are we going?"

McGuinn: "We're going to a motel at ..."

Ginsberg [interrupting]: "A motel? What's the name of that?"

McGuinn: "... Foxboro, Massachusetts; the Sheridan Inn."

Ginsberg: "At Foxboro, Massachusetts; 20 miles away."

McGuinn: "The Sheridan Inn, Foxboro, Mass. 20 miles away. In Foxboro, Mass. Right." [The Rolling Thunder Revue did indeed play Harvard Square Theatre in Cambridge on November 20, 1975. It is now approximately 3am. The next destination would be Boston Music Hall for afternoon and evening concerts later that very day.]

McGuinn: "Mick Ronson has some interesting chord progressions. It is the interpretation of Joni Mitchell's song that she does."

Ginsberg: "Right."

McGuinn: "I'd like to ask him if he could ..."

Ginsberg [interrupting]: "... Right, we could get that down."

McGuinn [says something initially incomprehensible, as miscellaneous fellow travelers are chatting away merrily]: "Would you like to ask him yourself?" [There is more loud chatter.]

McGuinn [to Mick Ronson]: "We want to find out what those chords were that Joni plays in that open tuning. That is, you know, that strange open tuning, and you said that they were ... well, go ahead, tell us."

Ronson [his accent sounds very British, very Humberside, after so much McGuinn and Ginsberg]: "OK, well, I will just have to start from the top, right? And I will just have to sing it, OK? Like the beginning progression is *da, daa, daa*. The first three chords is C, B flat, F major seventh with an added sixth, and then the next bit is *da, dat, baa*, which is C, B flat, to E flat ... no, wait a minute. ..."

McGuinn: "Joni, do you know?"

Mitchell [softly]: "No, I don't."

McGuinn: "We were curious because we thought you might've written it on the piano and transposed it to the guitar."

Mitchell: "I don't know ... on the piano I know, you know, A, B, C, and I know all the names of all the individual keys, but I don't know, y'know, what chord I am playing, I mean, by its numerical or alphabetical title. I mean, I just know it by ear, right?"

McGuinn: "OK, well, Mick knows what the chords are and he was just telling me before."

Mitchell: "OK, I would like to hear what they are."

Ginsberg [amusedly]: "Note the funny little, heavenly smile on his face as he consults his consciousness and brain. His hands making gestures; as on the neck of the guitar."

Ronson [so serious that, curiously, he sounds like T Bone]: "What it is, is C, E flat, then, like, F9 with a major seventh, then it's C, B flat, then E flat with, like, a second. Then it's C, B flat, then, uh … it's a funny A flat chord with a B flat … it's a kinda combination of A flat and B flat; it's weird!" [The tape machine is turned off.]

[The tape starts again with Ronson sounding like a minor criminal in an Ealing Comedy. He is now warming to his explanatory task.]

Ronson: So, E flat, C, B flat, B flat again with an F in the root … F major seventh with an added sixth to C9 to G. And then the verse comes in and the verse is the major seventh with an added sixth to C9 to G. OK?"

McGuinn: "What key is it in again?"

Ronson: "It's in G."

McGuinn: "In the key of G, basically, based on a G, but it has all these jazz chords in it."

Ronson: "Yeah! And then, and then … the middle section is E flat, F, B flat to C, then it goes back to that sequence of F major seventh."

McGuinn: "That's great, man. It's really a …"

Ronson [impervious]: "With an added sixth, C9 to G."

McGuinn: "Wow!"

Ronson [intently]: "And then the end section, the last, the last … what finishes the song off is C, the *da daa daa*. Again, right?"

McGuinn: "Like the intro?"

Ronson: "Yeah. C, B flat, F major seventh with an added sixth; C, B flat, E flat major seventh, C, B flat, B flat."

McGuinn: "And that's the end?"

Ronson: "Yeah."

McGuinn: "Right. And it ends on that chord, just a-hanging?"

Ronson: "Yeah."

McGuinn: "Right. 'Cause this is really a great song!" [Everyone speaks at once.]

Ronson [his voice rising in emphasis]: "But no, there should be no [imitates a drum roll] at the end of it!"

McGuinn: "I would like to talk about the rhythm in the song and the way the vocal is ..."

Ginsberg [mishearing]: "When you say vision ..."

Ronson [still dismissing drum rolls]: "There should be no *boom de la da*."

McGuinn [undaunted]: "Between the beats. Would you [addressing Joni Mitchell] like to tell us, how did you get into spacing the actual words between ... sort of, you know ... it's almost a bossa nova or a ... no, it's a lilting sort of ... it is hard to describe. It's eclectic. It's a number of things."

Mitchell: "It's eclectic."

McGuinn: "It is highly eclectic and it is your own style."

Mitchell: "It is something that was developed by something similar to osmosis."

McGuinn: "Uh-huh."

Mitchell: "It is like a subconscious learning process. I can't articulate it consciously."

McGuinn: "I see."

Mitchell: "But it's a matter of ... a selection of energy ... it is like I couldn't ... it just goes in and it rings *true* and it is recorded in some manner, you know?"

McGuinn: "I know the feeling. I have a similar thing with my guitar picking."

Mitchell: "Right! OK."

McGuinn: "I understand from an artistic point of view."

Mitchell [softly]: "OK."

McGuinn [adopting a reporter's tone]: "OK, well, I think we've covered the subject, thank you." [Relieved giggling can be heard.]

Ginsberg: "Did you understand, Mr McGuinn, as those chords were named, did you understand how ..."

McGuinn: "... to form them on the guitar?"

Ginsberg: "How to form them on the guitar so as that you could play it?"

McGuinn: "No, some of them I would have to figure out."

Ginsberg: "Yeah ... yes."

McGuinn: "I'd have to get maybe a book and figure out ... I know a G9, I know the G6, I know the ... was there an F with a sixth? Wasn't it an F sharp? F with a sixth, I know that chord, I could make that. I know some of the ... I could mess around and figure it out."

Ginsberg: "How come he [Ronson] is so smart with it?"

McGuinn: "Well, I think ... let's ask him!"

Ronson [in best 'it wasn't me, guv' mode]: "Well, no, listen. When you play a chord, you can pick out the strings and you can tell what the strings are, OK? Like when I said, oh, an F sixth with an added seventh, you know [he pauses reflectively] ... the first note I am playing is an F, the second note I am playing is an open G, oh, it's got a ninth in it, too, whoa, that's *really* some going, isn't it? The second note is a G. OK, now, in the scale of F, right, the G is the second note, right? So, the second note would become a ninth, right, because there are eight notes in the scale. So, the second note would be the ninth which is the G. OK, now then, on the B string I play a D. Now then, the D in the scale of F is the sixth, like F, G, A, B, C, D ... that's six."

McGuinn: "Yeah, like one, two, three, four, but ..."

Ronson [interrupting]: "That's where you get the sixth from. Now, the top string is an open E string, I just hit the open E string. Now then, the E in the scale of F becomes the major seventh."

McGuinn: "The [unintelligible] note in the scale of F is the major seventh because it is the seventh note in the E scale and the ..."

Ronson [interrupting]: "If she was playing an E flat, it would become a seventh, right?"

McGuinn [thoughtfully]: "That's a very handy ... it is almost like a slide rule; a mathematical system that is memorized through experience."

Ginsberg: "Yeah!"

Ronson: "Well, it's down to ... I don't know how to play all these jazz chords, right? But I know what to call 'em if I play, because I think of the notes and then I think *that* is a sixth, *that* is a seventh, and then I name the chords that way."

McGuinn: "I just learned them as fabulous chords."

Ronson: "A seventh, a sixth. ..."

McGuinn: "What is this chord? And they said it was a G sixth."

Ronson: "Right."

McGuinn: "When you leave the E open on the G it is a sixth because on the scale of G the E is the sixth note up. I understand."

Ronson: "Right!"

Mitchell: "So, the letters and the numbers serve, really, as a language of communication between musicians; but there are musicians, now, who are experimenting with a system of music which is more related to the graphic arts. That's why you have a lot of these freaky, avant-garde guys who have distilled it to an essence; so it is sort of like a real inside ... it's a real *in* game, kind of, in a way, you know? It's sort of elitist but um ..."

Ginsberg: "Yes."

Unidentified male voice: "Bach wrote music like that but he had a whole pattern ... just wrote little road maps and his kids would write the charts. He would go [he makes a swishing sound] and that would be like a whole manuscript, you know?"

Mitchell [intently, although obviously becoming distracted]: "So, more and more I find that I can communicate to musicians in my own language. They've gotten over being amused by it and in my describing colors, pressure points, composition ... really ... with painterly terms. You know, like I've found guys who couldn't figure out what ... and I could show them a graph, but they are, like, from this other, this old form of music. They are obsessed with the bar, so they count by bars, but sometimes there are rhythmic figures which are hard to count within that system. But if they are memorized as a figure, as a long figure, they are really easy to communicate. But they try to dissect it into parts and it is like dissecting poetry and it loses its whole form, you know?"

[A few seats away, an unidentifiable male and his companions are talking commerce, just as Mitchell, McGuinn, Ronson, and Ginsberg are discussing art and music. It's quite a contrast in themes.]

McGuinn: "Well, I think it's *great*." [The male voice says something about "20 per cent" and another male uses the word "Rolf," as a verb. He may be referring to *golf*; it's hard to know.]

Joan Baez [walking up the aisle, becoming more audible as she does so]: "Yeah, I was gonna say, we are totally *rolfing*. Did you growl?"

Elliott: "I went and got rolfed one time ..."

Baez [sounding pleasantly tipsy]: Totally *grolfing*. Did you growl? I want a primal scream room next to the dressing room."

McGuinn [in soft tones, sounding like a television anthropologist sneaking up on some easily startled wildlife]: "We are talking now to Miss Joan Baez and Jack Elliott."

Baez: "Holding, rolfing, screaming, and all around is insane stuff. Hah!"

McGuinn: "Holding, rolfing, and screaming are all beneficial to your ...

something or other."

Baez: "Whatever ... psyche?"

McGuinn: "Psyche, yeah; your whole being."

Baez: "Psychoanalysis is about the same price, it takes a lot longer and I'm ... in my experience ... well, I shouldn't say that."

McGuinn: "Why not?"

Baez: "'Cause I've had it, you know? It's more ... beneficial."

Ginsberg: "Have you ever studied with anyone?" [A male, possibly Ronson, a few seats away, says, "I'm still not together."]

Baez: "'Cause you plow through it."

McGuinn: "Yeah."

Baez: "In the behavioral ... like pushing the armor of your body around so that you hit the soft spots and remember when your kid brother locked you in a closet or something."

McGuinn: "I remember when I was locked in a closet by a kid named Miller, in Tarrytown, New York, when I was about eight, and it horrified me. I got claustrophobia; ever since I've had that."

Baez [sympathetically]: "Yeaaaahhh. You bet your booties, yeah."

McGuinn: "It was awful."

Baez: "That's why we had to kick everybody off of Phydeaux, because we couldn't breathe anymore and everybody's getting claustrophobic."

McGuinn: "Here, now, today?"

Baez: "No, when it was too full up, you know?"

McGuinn: "Yeah, it was. Now there are six bunks open and everybody can crash."

Baez: "Yeah, right. Nobody wants to go to sleep because everybody is ..."

McGuinn [interrupting]: "Everybody is into staying up and rapping."

Baez: "... into each other, too."

McGuinn: "Yeah, we all like each other, too."

Baez: "Me, I'm getting to know Jack, here."

McGuinn: "Yeah, that's good. I didn't mean to interrupt it."

Baez: "No! You're not interrupting at all. Is he, Jack?"

Elliott [shyly]: "No, in fact we're gonna miss you if you go away." [Baez laughs contentedly.]

McGuinn: "Well, you didn't say anything, actually. Why don't you stick around ... I'll stick around."

Elliott [sounding pleased]: "All right!" [At this point, Elliott, several other males, Baez, and Mitchell are heard chatting away unintelligibly.]

McGuinn: "He had a musical question. It is because she uses that open tuning and he wanted to know what the chords were and I couldn't tell him."

Baez: "That is a beautiful tuning, yeah."

McGuinn: "I couldn't tell him because I didn't ... I hadn't played on it and I had to ask Mick. And he told me all the chords and they are like C9s, you know, and F6s and things like that."

Baez: "She marches right out there with her hair all scraggily and some dumb outfit on and ..."

McGuinn: "All scraggily. I was gonna say, Joni, you're ... comb your hair!"

Baez: "She does blonde on blonde and she goes off just fine."

McGuinn: "I was gonna say, you know, brush the back of your hair, and, you know ..."

Baez: "Oh, she's into leaving it ratty; what the hell."

McGuinn: "[unintelligible] ... to bother her, you know what I mean?"

Baez: "And then I said, 'Aren't you going to do a hit?' And she said, 'No,' and I respected her for it."

McGuinn: "She's doing that on purpose, she's pulling punches."

Baez: "She's pulling punches and she's gutsy, you know. I like that."

McGuinn: "She's real gutsy. She's OK."

Baez: "She's a tough old Canadian [she impersonates a Canuck vocal trait] *oot and aboot*."

McGuinn: "I like her a lot." [Baez sings a brief snatch of Mitchell's 'Don't Interrupt The Sorrow.']

Elliott [amusedly]: "She's the female Gordon Lightfoot." [Baez agrees, giggling. She then sings a bit more of Mitchell's song. Elliott laughs.]

Baez [struggling over the lyric]: "You gotta have a heart like Mary's to ... what?"

Elliott and McGuinn [together]: "I don't know."

Baez: "You gotta have a heart like Mary's to ... something or other."

McGuinn: "To bleed? I don't know ... I don't know the words. I can't make them out because there'd be ..."

Baez [interrupting]: "I can't either."

McGuinn: "I asked her how she got that and she said it was something that came from, you know, just the ether."

Baez: "I kinda get wafted out when she goes [she sings] 'ooooooohhhh, woooooooo oooooooohhhh.' [Elliott laughs.]

Baez: "I get lost! What, did she miss it? Or arranged it? Or trying to blow everybody away, or what?"

McGuinn: "It works with it." [Elliott is still laughing.]

Baez: "Yeah, it does work." [She sings another phrase, Mitchell-style.]

McGuinn: "It's like your 'Swing Low,' you know? [He is referring to Baez's nightly RTR rendering of the spiritual 'Swing Low, Sweet Chariot.' He continues, somewhat courageously.] Your 'Swing Low' would be corny if it didn't work so well."

Baez [unfazed]: "It is corny *anyway*."

McGuinn: "It works like a mother out there, it just *kills* them. They die!"

Baez: "You know why? Because nobody has sung ... Joni does now ... before Joni came, nobody had really sung that kind of song without all the noise ..."

McGuinn [thoughtfully]: "Uh-huh."

Baez: "... until then. And so I was sent up to ..."

McGuinn [interrupting]: "And you are also showing off your vocal craft which is extremely ..."

Baez [interrupting back]: "Bet your booties, I am. That's how I got on a rock'n'roll show. What the hell am I gonna do on a rock'n'roll show?"

McGuinn: "Yeah, right. It really is ... [unintelligible] a folk-rock show."

Baez: "Yeah, it is, but then, see, we slammed your rock right in there. That's neat."

McGuinn: "Well I'm a ... advanced folk-rock ... audience. It is advanced folk-rock; it is still folk music."

Baez [unsure]: "'Eight Miles High' is *folk* music?"

McGuinn: "Are you kidding? It isn't? I mean, how can you say that it isn't? Look, it is a native American music."

Baez: "Boogie!"

McGuinn: "It was created by John Coltrane, you know, who is a native American folk-jazz artist. I mean, to me, jazz is folk music."

Baez: "Right."

McGuinn: "OK, it is music of the folks, right? Folks made it and it is folk music. You know, just because we are using electric guitars and we are dancin' around like people in Africa, and we are doing beats that are foreign to the Anglo-Saxon, doesn't mean it isn't folk music. And I stand by that."

Baez: "*Thaaaaat's riiiight.* You're doing 'jigaboo' folk music."

McGuinn: "I am a folk singer … of a certain kind."

Baez: "And I am a dancer."

McGuinn: "You're a dancer."

Baez: "Having fun. That's great for dancing. That's why I got those little silver dancing booties. See?"

McGuinn: "That's folk dancing, you know?"

Baez: "You dance much better with them on."

McGuinn: "Yes, you do. They're dancing slippers."

Baez: "And you got knee-high things …" [Elliott speaks but his words are indistinguishable amid the hubbub. Joni Mitchell can be heard laughing.]

Baez: "… right behind a cloud … and I go 'Oh, shit' … [Further simultaneous conversations.] C'mon, Jack, what do you take me for? What is that story? I never get tired of … what?"

Elliott: "You wanna hear the one about the Grand Prix of Gibraltar?"

Baez: "The *what*?"

Elliott: "The Grand Prix du Gibraltar."

Baez [puzzled]: "… is that?"

Elliott: "Peter Ustinov?"

Baez: "Oh, let's hear it!"

Elliott: He did a thing … I met Peter Ustinov … well, first off, my wife, June, had a picture on the wall of herself, Peter Ustinov, and her mom and dad, on the set of some Roman toga movie – *The Ten Commandments* or something. It was Peter Ustinov. I had never heard of the dude, didn't know who he was. I said, 'Who's the guy up there in the toga?' She said, 'That's Peter Ustinov, he's great.' Then we went to England and I was singing in Oxford one day. I was doing a concert at the Oxford Heritage Society …"

[The tape ends: 33 minutes, 21 seconds completed.]

CHAPTER 4
MAIN TITLE THEME: THE BACKDROP TO RENALDO & CLARA

*"Stupid and misleading jerks sometimes these interpreters are ...
Fools, they limit you to their own unimaginative mentality ...
they never stop to think that somebody has been exposed to experiences
that they haven't been."*
(BOB DYLAN)[1]

The bitterness of the above quote is understandable, coming from a man who has not only experienced two generations of rock critics continually judging and second-guessing him, but who also felt the heat of a prying and intrusive media and a fanbase which clearly saw him as the 60s Elvis (which was OK with Dylan) and Spokesperson For A Generation (not so OK with Dylan), and which all but equated the Minnesotan with the Second Coming (not so OK with God). Trespassers had been so brazen they had been found in Dylan's grounds, on his roof, and even inside his house. One wildly enthusiastic nutcase (is there any other kind?) called A.J. Weberman spent a lengthy period of his young adulthood digging through Dylan's garbage for 'clues' – garbage that included his children's used diapers and the contents of the family cat's litter box. Try selling those on eBay.

Yet nothing, but *nothing*, with Dylan's name attached perplexes his public, even his most informed, dedicated fans, as much as *Renaldo & Clara*, his four-hour attempt at conquering the medium of film. Thirty-five years after it was shot, it still has Dylanphiles looking for 'clues.'

Renaldo & Clara is the single project in Dylan's creative life on which he spent the most time; from its 1975 conception to subsequent editing in 1976–77, and high-profile promotional interview rounds in late 1977 and early 1978. In fact, the editing of the 105 hours of raw *Renaldo & Clara* footage alone could take the prize as the single most time-consuming venture of Dylan's entire career.

Unavailable now for three decades, *Renaldo & Clara* was a project *extraordinarily* dear to Dylan's heart. As a youth, up in northern Minnesota, he'd had an uncle who owned several local movie theaters. Nephew Robert was allowed inside them, free of charge, whenever he chose. Combine that open invitation with lengthy, bone cold, Iron Range winters and you have the young Robert Zimmerman watching *a lot* of cinema.

At the present stage in his long career, many Dylan camp followers are discussing the influence on his later work of poets such as Robert Burns, Frank

97

Bidart, and Henry Timrod (the latter also a noted Civil War newspaper correspondent, that conflict being an ongoing Dylan fixation). Yet, while his songs' literary qualities are continually pored over, less has been made of a quarter century's worth of movie dialog which has appeared identifiably and uncomplicatedly in his lyrics – a facet of Dylan's writing which first manifested explicitly on 1985's *Empire Burlesque*. As a cinema enthusiast who writes songs which are frequently framed by the limits of romantic love and steeped in screenplay-like detail, it is surely logical that Dylan, having grown both wealthy and artistically restless, would try his hand at making his own movie.

The documentary *Dont Look Back*, filmed on Dylan's 1965 UK tour and released two years later, would certainly have whetted its star's filmic appetite, even though the movie was director D.A. Pennebaker's, from top to bottom. In it, neither the master of emotional disguise, Dylan, nor the master of provoking an emotional moment, his tour compadre Bob Neuwirth, could shake Pennebaker's focus in the slightest as he honed in on his subject, masterfully documenting Dylan's burgeoning superstardom and the task at hand for his inscrutable manager, Albert Grossman.

Dylan's first bona fide cinematic dabble came next, the rarely seen *Eat The Document*. Consisting of live performances filmed by Pennebaker during Dylan's 1966 world tour, along with subsequent footage shot by Dylan and Howard Alk in Woodstock, New York, the film finds Dylan and members of his redoubtable backing band The Hawks (for they were not yet The Band) acting, as best they could, in semi-improvised scenes. Although never formally released to the public either through its initial commissioners, ABC Television, or through nationwide movie theaters, *Eat The Document* leaked out via occasional, very special screenings and on bootleg videos and DVDs. Those who saw it were exposed to a confusing, almost cubist model of filmmaking; a cinematic experience as frustrating as it was periodically thrilling (for more on the film see my earlier book, *Million Dollar Bash: Bob Dylan, The Band, And The Basement Tapes*, published by Jawbone Press in 2007).

Eat The Document's combination of dynamic live footage, with Dylan fronting a rock group on stage, jarringly interrupted by cutaways to awkward (and not so awkward) action and dialog scenes, with musicians as actors, provides the template for *Renaldo & Clara*.

Both *Eat The Document* and *Renaldo & Clara* were edited by Dylan and his loyal friend Howard Alk, using a codified numbers system. That would mean, for example, footage of trains being ascribed the code *one*, imagery of rivers being logged as *two*, scenes of dogs *three*, concert footage *four*, and so on. To construct an edit, Dylan would describe to Alk a numerical pattern which was frequently based on musical notation within a given melodic scale. That systemized, arithmetic model would then dictate the order in which particular scenes were to be sequenced and also their duration.

It sounds like such a wonderful idea on paper. It also sounded like a wonderful idea when Allen Ginsberg described the editing of *Renaldo & Clara* to Pennsylvanian undergraduates in November 1978. "He [Dylan] shot about 110 hours of film or more and he looked at it all. Then he put it on index cards according to some preconceptions he had when he was directing and shooting. Namely, themes: God, rock'n'roll, art, poetry, marriage, women, sex, Bob Dylan, poets, death ... maybe 18 or 20 thematic preoccupations. Then he also put on index cards all the different characters, all the scenes. He also marked on the index cards the dominant color: blue or red ... and certain images that go through the movie like the rose and the hat and Indians, American Indians, so that he finally had an index of all that. And then he went through it all again and began composing it, thematically, weaving in and out of those specific compositional references. So it's compositional, and the idea was not to have a plot, but to have a composition of those themes."[2]

Indeed, while *Renaldo & Clara's* lack of logical narrative was immediately perceivable to its audience, it certainly did dwell on subjects close to its director's heart. It's noteworthy that the well-read Ginsberg didn't mention *The Woman In White*, Wilkie Collins's great Victorian mystery novel, as one of those recurring themes. Ginsberg was surely familiar with Dylan's favored literary references – and many more besides (although less so cinematic allusions: Ginsberg's biographer, Barry Miles, claims the poet rarely saw any kind of movie). While that literary leitmotiv was ignored by Ginsberg, he didn't fail to notice some of *Renaldo & Clara's* more superficial themes; not least Dylan's fetish for hats.

There is a potential connection between the way Dylan had Alk edit film footage and the way his friend Ginsberg wrote his poetry. Author Barry Miles, a friend and colleague of the poet's for over three decades, describes Ginsberg rewriting a later draft of his seminal 1956 poem 'Howl.' "Allen went through the manuscript of the first section, labeling all those lines that belonged together: A, B, C, and D. Those about Neal [Cassady] were A, those about Carl [Solomon] were C, and so on. He made a few vital tonal changes to the text ... then retyped the lines in their new order."[3]

This means that any student of Ginsberg, or any reader of Miles's Ginsberg biography, would recognize a similar rhythmic paradigm in the editing patterns of his poetry and that of Dylan and Alk's films. Dylan was, without question, a student of the Beats, and not just their biggest guns such as Ginsberg, Jack Kerouac, or Gregory Corso; he was known to admire the more obscure likes of Ray Bremser and Harry Smith, too. So, is it not possible that Dylan is emulating Ginsberg in his editing approach on *Renaldo & Clara*? Barry Miles thinks it unlikely. "I doubt Dylan even knew how Allen constructed the poem. Also, it [the grouping of scenes by theme] is a fairly usual way to organize footage of a documentary, if not the standard way. Even now, with Avid technology, the related scenes are grouped together."[4]

Dylan and Alk could have used today's Avid techniques. Linear editing software used to process and organize digitized film and video, Avid creates a newly edited version of existing visual source material not by cutting and rearranging the original footage with a razorblade or Moviola editing machine, as Howard Alk would have done, but by creating a detailed list of edit points based on a given list of subjects. The Avid editing software reads the constructed thematic list and creates a new edit by applying those given parameters to the raw footage. In other words, Dylan, who, as we've established, spent more time editing *Renaldo & Clara* than he did on just about anything, would have saved a great deal of time and stress had Avid been available in 1977. Alas, it was invented ten years later.

The potential for audience confusion in *Renaldo & Clara* is obvious even from a quick description of Dylan and Alk's rhythmic editing approach. Barry Miles is quite correct to suggest it had been used before in film. In fact, this particular technique had come to prominence with 60s French New Wave cinema directors such as Jean-Luc Godard and François Truffaut. *La Nouvelle Vague's* use of jump cuts (the opposite of classic 'continuity editing,' with scenes sequenced abruptly, randomly, or unrelated to any sense of linear narrative) helped define their genre. It is fair to say that Dylan and Alk were rather fond of jump cuts.

Dylan knew his French New Wave cinema and he made sure that those around him were equally well versed in European film. One such person was Pulitzer Prize winning playwright Sam Shepard, who had been hired to help write scenes for *Renaldo & Clara*. In the summer of 1975, Shepard arrived in New York City at Dylan's invitation. After arriving at Grand Central Station he was immediately summoned to an audience with the would-be film director. He found Dylan "lying horizontally across a metal folding chair like he's practicing a levitation trick." Dylan looked up at Shepard and said, without any other word of introduction: "We don't have to make any connections. None of this has to connect. In fact, it is better if it doesn't connect."[5] Bang! Ladies and gentlemen, the kid from Hibbing with the uncle who owned cinemas and who was generous enough to let young nephew Robert inside, gratis, had just articulated a perfect American layperson's description of one of the guiding tenets of French New Wave cinema (a continental European would surely know better and never say such a thing.)

There's more. In his published journal of the fall 1975 tour, *The Rolling Thunder Logbook*, Sam Shepard recalls that Dylan's very next utterance during that initial meeting was a question: "Did you ever see *Children Of Paradise*? How about *Shoot The Piano Player*?" When Shepard nodded affirmatively and inquired: "Is that the kind of movie you want to make?" Dylan replied, cryptically: "Something like that." More than "something like that," surely, Bob?

In his conversation with Shepard, Dylan had mentioned two of the five key artistic works that would influence *Renaldo & Clara*. To view Dylan's most personal film without knowledge of this quintet of resonating cultural signposts is, perhaps, to miss the point of the film entirely – just like so many of the paying customers and professional critics who moaned about the mystifying density of the four-hour *Renaldo & Clara* cut (the very kind of person Dylan complains about so bitterly in this chapter's opening quote).

Children Of Paradise is perhaps better known by its French title, *Les Enfants Du Paradis* – a heartbreaking tale of lost love directed by French auteur Marcel Carné. It was shot during World War II in Paris, during the Nazi occupation. Carné started production just as the city was falling to the oncoming German troops. Completing it was a staggering feat when one considers the film's outdoor sets, requiring vast crowds, and indoor location scenes staged in grand ballrooms and old theaters, not to mention Carné's miraculous ability to raise the funds to continue filming, piecemeal, over several years, despite the privations of wartime. *Children Of Paradise* was voted 'Best French Film Ever' in a 1995 poll of 600 French movie critics and professionals.

In common with *Renaldo & Clara*, Carné's film is dreamlike and many-faceted. Set in 1827, then deftly moving the narrative forward over seven years, the plot of *Children Of Paradise* revolves around a theater and the performers and performances therein. It also involves a rather complicated love quadrangle, with legendary French screen actress Arletty playing beautiful courtesan Garance, who, often dressed all in white, has everyone falling for her. Without any malice aforethought she proceeds to break the hearts of the sweet mime Baptiste Debureau (played by Jean-Louis Barrault), the ruthless Édouard, Count de Montray (Louis Salou), talented but pompous actor Frédérick Lemaître (Pierre Brasseur), and a murderous crook, Pierre François Lacenaire (Marcel Herrand). Baptiste is the only one of the four whose love for Garance is pure and without strings; naturally he is hurt the most when she leaves Paris at the end of the movie.

For many viewers, and, dare it be said, for Dylan, too, the film actually revolves around Baptiste rather Garance. His mime act requires him to perform in whiteface on stage, usually sporting a totally white costume. Dylan's adoption of whiteface on the fall 1975 Rolling Thunder tour is considered by many to be a reference to Baptiste. Scarlet Rivera remembers a heckling audience-member enquiring of Dylan at an early RTR show: "Why the makeup?" and Dylan replying: "I want you to hear my words, not see my face." [6]

At two hours and 43 minutes, *Children Of Paradise* is a long film for American audiences to digest, particularly in the 21st century, with the art-house circuit pushed to the far margins and DVD shops focusing heavily on Hollywood and stocking few foreign or leftfield releases. As a result, there is hardly any (young) American audience equipped to digest such a prolonged, cineastic experience, there being simply nowhere for them *to* digest it. In Europe, however, the film is almost always shown in a cut lasting over three hours; something Dylan would have appreciated. As he told *Rolling Stone's* Jonathan Cott, in 1978, "I know this film [*Renaldo & Clara*] is too long … I don't care … I'm not concerned how long something is. I want to see a set shot. I *feel* a set shot. I don't feel all this [contemporary Hollywood] motion and boom boom … ."[7]

Like the American movie to which it is most often compared, *Gone With The Wind*, *Children Of Paradise* has a necessary break in the middle, useful, not merely to break up the marathon duration but because there is simply so much to absorb. Carné's masterpiece is formally divided into two epochs: *Boulevard Of Crime* and *Man In White*. One could argue that this second epoch might equally have been titled *Woman In White*. Anyone with the slightest knowledge of *Renaldo & Clara* and a nodding acquaintance with classic French cinema must be breathtakingly aware of the similarities between it and *Children Of Paradise*. Both are long films with many layers and are, therefore, something of an endurance test for those weaned on formulaic Hollywood orthodoxy. Granted, Carné, an experienced filmmaker, guides his audience much more gracefully from narrative point to point than the novice Dylan. The latter creates a film that is, like his often primitively recorded musical output, a more rough and ready experience. It has often been said that those exposed to Dylan's art either get it right away or they never will – its creator seemingly unconcerned either way.

Of the two directors, Carné is certainly more overtly concerned with being understood by his audience; Dylan is seemingly ambivalent. Carné was known for his lengthy scene setups, carrying out his elaborate preparations even in the face of Nazi troops. Dylan shot on the fly and improvised scenes with many first-time actors. This suggests – to phrase it diplomatically – that Carné was the director more concerned with comprehensibility. While it also suggests that Dylan was artistically reckless, he might equally be seen as creatively bold and unafraid of pursuing his own, very particular celluloid vision.

In a 1978, Rochester, New York interview with music critic Mark Rowland, Dylan revealed his attitude to the audience when he suggested that he was: "... gonna go ahead and make another movie. I don't know whether that's gonna get accepted either, you know, but that's really not too much of my concern." If the director isn't concerned with the audience accepting his art then who, pray tell, would be? It's no wonder Bob was never inundated with offers from Hollywood.

For all that, there are resonant similarities between Carné's great, cinematic statement and Dylan's *attempt* at a great cinematic statement. Besides sharing the deep tragedy of failed romance and pure-hearted characters appearing dressed entirely in white, both films adopt a red flower as a metaphor for love's unpredictability. The floral metaphor is also used verbally. Before the end of Carné's film's first epoch, he shows poor Baptiste, wounded by his unrequited love for Garance, delivering his own eulogy. "Here lies Baptiste ... life gave him a red flower, a good thrashing, a wooden overcoat." It is the literal description of Carné's visual metaphor. This is comparable to *Renaldo & Clara's* red rose, which reappears several times in the hands of protagonists Sara Dylan and Joan Baez. "The rose," reports Allen Ginsberg in Clinton Heylin's *Bob Dylan: Behind The Shades*, "is like a 'traveling vagina'... those are his [Dylan's] words. The hat is masculine ... crowns. The rose travels from hand to hand ... it [*Renaldo & Clara*] is a painter's film and was composed like that."

Immediately after Baptiste delivers his own eulogy, Nathalie (María Casarès), the actress who loves him unrequitedly, boldly declares her devotion, completing a love triangle comparable to that played out by Dylan, Joan Baez, and Sara Dylan in *Renaldo & Clara*.

Jacques Levy's widow, Claudia, claims Dylan knew *Les Enfants Du Paradis* well and that his painting mentor, Norman Raeben, showed Dylan the film not long before embarking on the first Rolling Thunder Revue tour. "Norman, who was a very powerful influence, I think, on Bob ... had this film *Les Enfants Du Paradis*, and he showed Bob the film. There is a character in that film who's in whiteface ... played by Jean-Louis Barrault, a great French mime. It's a very romantic film ... about a traveling band of actors, real theater, street theater, mime ... and the children of paradise are the ones that sat way, way up [in the French theatre], just below the eaves."[8]

Mrs Levy was also eager to underline the direct visual connection between Dylan and the French film classic. "When Bob came out [on stage], in the second part of the [Rolling Thunder] show ... he would be in whiteface and Joan Baez came out also in whiteface. ... The light would be on the two of them, singing together ... they both wore the same clothing and the same hat and *then* you realized who was who."[9]

With all due respect to the tough, winter-hardened people of Hibbing and Duluth, Minnesota, it is hard to imagine *Children Of Paradise* being booked for a showing in one of the theaters owned by the adolescent Robert Zimmerman's uncle. It is easy to imagine it being shown periodically in New York City, the place to which the not quite so young Bob Dylan so willfully escaped in 1961. Knowing, as his audience now does, how open and receptive this young Dylan was to outside artistic stimuli, it is easy to see Suze Rotolo, John Cohen, Victor Maymudes, Bob Neuwirth, or any of the other struggling singer-activists-playwrights-actors who were his friends in Greenwich Village, dragging Dylan along to a screening (and gleefully reminding him, afterward, "I told 'ya it was great"). Whether or not Dylan was actually introduced to the film back in his scuffling days is not known, but he clearly saw it at some point and it left a deep mark on him, as those initial comments to Sam Shepard attest.

Shoot The Piano Player (or *Tirez Sur Le Pianiste* in French) is a 1960 movie by François Truffaut. It is considered a shining example of *La Nouvelle Vague*. It deploys such New Wave hallmarks as extended voice-overs (also called interior monologues), out-of-sequence shots, and our old friend the jump cut. Considered a breakthrough for cinema, then as now, the film's stylistic caprices initially alienated almost as many critics and viewers as they thrilled. (Seventeen years later, Dylan would witness a similar reaction to *Renaldo & Clara*, but in much harsher doses, particularly in the USA.) The abiding problem with such unorthodox filmmaking is the enormous potential for audience confusion. A befuddled viewer, alienated from the action on screen, soon feels their time is being wasted and is likely to dismiss a movie for being too chaotic, too arty, too pompous, and too difficult to digest.

About editing, Truffaut admitted, in a January 1980 interview with Hélène Laroche Davis: "It often happens that there are several versions of a film. One time, *Shoot The Piano Player* was on French television and for four minutes a scene was shown with the soundtrack from *another* scene. Nobody noticed, because they thought it was another pretentious experiment of the New Wave."[10] One cannot imagine this happening with *Gone With The Wind*, *Casablanca*, or *Four Weddings And A Funeral*. Someone would have spotted the incongruous soundtrack in no time. Yet, as with *Shoot The Piano Player*, there are several edits of *Renaldo & Clara* traveling today's information superhighway. Would anyone but the most fastidious Bobcat spot a misplaced soundtrack clip in Dylan's film? (An interesting sidebar: *Renaldo & Clara* has been denied a re-release even when requested by film festivals, and it has never appeared on DVD. Why, then, would Dylan and his management allow clips of the film to appear all over private websites and even portions of it on YouTube?)

The plot of *Shoot The Piano Player* is based around the fate of a has-been classical pianist, now playing in a crummy Paris bar, where a waitress falls in love with him. The musician, Charlie Kohler (played by Charles Aznavour), is not what he seems. Try as he might, he cannot escape his past, so he simply does what he knows best: he plays the piano. Later, he is dragged by his troubled brother into a messy scrap with local criminals, and is forced to return to the very dysfunctional family he has spent his recent years trying to evade by secreting himself in the lowlife saloon. Again, anyone with the slightest knowledge of *Renaldo & Clara* must be all too aware of the similarities between it and *Shoot The Piano Player*. Indeed, if you took a half-dozen bullet points out of *Children Of Paradise* and *Shoot The Piano Player* (a protagonist trying to escape his past, an intertwined and messy love life, a theatre troupe's troubles, intimations of criminality, an artist who feels trapped and who does the only thing he knows how to do to survive ...) and relocate them to New England in the fall of 1975 (with added dynamic live concert footage) you would pretty much have *Renaldo & Clara*.

In fact, in the same January 1980 interview with Hélène Laroche Davis, Truffaut inadvertently implies the correlation between *Shoot The Piano Player* and Dylan's film. "I was advancing instinctively, according to the actresses, too. I saw what was appropriate for these three different women. I consciously wanted to show three portraits of women who can pass through a man's life." Dylan could have made this same statement verbatim about *Renaldo & Clara's* Joan Baez, Sara Dylan, and Ruth Tyrangiel (who plays The Girlfriend) or possibly even Ronee Blakley, although she appears on screen as muse/lover with others such as Steve Soles and not solely Dylan. In fact, Dylan could have made it solely about Ms Baez's acting as she plays, variously, The Woman In White (although sometimes this role is played by Sara Dylan), a Mexican whore, and, occasionally, herself.

Truffaut's reference to "three portraits of women who can pass through a man's life" may lead any Dylan detective – for that is what his most ardent fans each become – to the poet Robert Graves. More specifically, it leads to Graves's 1948 critical work *The White Goddess*, in which he writes of poetic inspiration in a series of lengthy and quite complicated essays. In them he propounds the existence, in late prehistoric times, of a pan-European/Middle Eastern deity based on phases of the moon (Graves claims that this beautiful lunar goddess evolved into what we would now describe as an artistic muse). Although referred to in miscellaneous continental cultures by different mythological identities, this supreme divinity is actually based on the matriarchal cultures then prevalent in Mediterranean society. According to Graves, these cultures became overwhelmed by active proponents of patriarchy from late Minoan times (approximately 1450 BC). The patriarchies who deposed the goddess from her heavenly throne eventually pushed women out of earthly authority positions, too.

In *The White Goddess*, Graves maintains that purposefully reconstructed myths and religious rituals have been designed to conceal this shift from matriarchy to patriarchy, denying the existence of a culture which had elevated womankind, thanks to her life-giving quality (and, therefore, reducing men to a secondary function). He states that the reemergence of male-led societies signaled the end of a saner, happier mode of human existence. The alleged 'bad *guys*' were invaders, riding into Europe from Central Asia. It was they who replaced matrilineal institutions with patrilineal regulation and who subsequently remodeled myths and legends to support and justify these societal changes.

Graves refers to the White Goddess of Birth, Love, and Death – simultaneously a muse, an inspiration, and a reason for existence. With its references to Tarot cards, acceptance of mythology as fact, suspicion of the industrial machine, near dismissal of both science and urban life, and its elevation of poetry and love above all else, *The White Goddess* was a key text for young people knocking at the door of 60s liberation. When word reached those impressionable souls busy taking DuPont's advertising slogan *Better Living Through Chemistry* as a snappy justification for their own ingestion of hallucinogens, that Graves was no stranger to psilocybin-based stimulants (and had even lectured on the extraordinary visions he'd had while on mushrooms), *The White Goddess* and its author were quickly installed as benchmarks of the psychedelic revolution, right up there in the hippie pantheon alongside Aldous Huxley, Timothy Leary, and Hermann Hesse.

That scientists and archaeologists regularly attacked Graves in print, considering *The White Goddess* to be a collection of well-written fantasies and erudite but unfounded bunkum, was of no consequence to his young adherents. Robert Graves had found a new audience, or rather several new audiences: the restless young, followers of pagan religions, hallucinogenic hopheads, back-to-nature devotees, and refugees from the Beat Generation. They all marched towards Graves's proud standard as it flapped in the breeze, high on the hill of their own addled imaginations.

Graves's reaction to all this, and to *The White Goddess* specifically, is summed up in a letter to a colleague, Patricia Cunningham, dated August 22 1959: "… it's not a scientific book … some day a scholar will sort out *The White Goddess* wheat from the chaff. *It's a crazy book and I didn't mean to write it.*" [The italics are mine.]

That final sentence is an extraordinary one for an author to use, given the years of effort taken up by its writing. It sounds like something Dylan might say. Indeed, one can almost hear the person Joan Baez accurately called "the master of the evasive answer" telling an interviewer much the same thing about *Renaldo & Clara.*

Those who enjoy coincidence, and who also found *Renaldo & Clara* hard to follow, might like to know that in 1960 a movie version of *The White Goddess* was discussed. It would surely have been as unfilmable as Dylan's own unfathomable diversion into literature, *Tarantula*, although Graves and his friend Alistair Reid did get as far as writing a screenplay.

It is hard to believe that François Truffaut was not the owner of a well-thumbed copy of *The White Goddess*. Graves's Triple Goddess, taking the form of mother, bride, and hag, corresponding to birth, love, and death, resonates with *Shoot The Piano Player* (in which Charles Aznavour's character is re-born as a classical artist; his love for his wife, and her subsequent death, causing the demise of his own artistic soul).

Dylan has mentioned Robert Graves and *The White Goddess* in interviews on several occasions. He even met Graves, in 1962, in England. Michael Gray's *The Bob Dylan Encyclopedia* describes the young Bob meeting Hans Fried, son of Austrian poet Erich Fried, in Collet's bookshop in London and a conversation starting up between them after Dylan spied the copy of *The White Goddess* which Fried was carrying. It's a good bet that Fried had the updated, third British edition of the book which was published in 1961 and just available, for the first time, in paperback. Dylan even discusses the subject in *Chronicles: Volume One*: "I read The White Goddess by Robert Graves, too. Invoking the poetic muse was something I didn't know about yet. Didn't know enough to start trouble with it, anyway. In a few years' time I would meet Robert Graves himself. ... "[11]

First Truffaut and Carné, in films Dylan admired, then Graves, in a book Dylan admired, and, finally, Dylan in a film few admired; each artist had used the image of a woman in three states of being: birth/life, love/marriage, and divorce/death. Each time, the symbolic womanly muse is draped in white, whether Arletty as Garance, in *Children Of Paradise*, Nicole Berger playing Charles Aznavour's cold, almost Hitchcockian blonde wife in *Shoot The Piano Player,* or Joan Baez and Sara Dylan in their ambiguous *Renaldo & Clara* roles.

Both director Truffaut and director Dylan use women as something more than banal love interest, thematic distraction or, in the timeworn Hollywood tradition, mere eye candy. Truffaut (successfully) and Dylan (erratically) posit women as representations and reflections of freedom and the emotional condition of a given scene, or of the male protagonists' state of being. The two films are further entwined by Dylan's obvious passion for the European approach to filmmaking, particularly with regards to editing, while Truffaut was a frequent and vocal celebrant of American cinema, notably in the pages of influential film journal *Cahiers Du Cinéma*. As the French auteur admitted to Hélène Laroche Davis, *Shoot The Piano Player* – based on a hard-boiled detective novel entitled *Down There* by Philadelphia-born pulp fiction writer David Goodis – is "an homage to America cinema."

Editing is to movies what mixing is to recording. An artist can capture some fantastic music on tape, but if it is mixed poorly much of the art can be obscured (compare, for example, the vinyl murkiness of Dylan's 1978 album *Street Legal* with the clarity of the remixed, 1999 CD version). In motion pictures, excellent footage can be shot but if it's edited too clumsily, or if the wrong bits are left on the cutting room floor, the finished product can be less than the sum of its parts, its director's artistic vision left unrealized. *Renaldo & Clara's* editing team comprised the relatively experienced but experimentally inclined Howard Alk and the complete neophyte Dylan. By comparison, *Children Of Paradise* was edited by the estimable Henri Rust with help and advice from Madeleine Bonin, both extremely practiced hands. Similarly, *Shoot The Piano Player* was edited for Truffaut by the experienced Claudine Bouché and the director's trusted friend Cécile Decugis. These four European editors helped define styles of cinema storytelling which Dylan and Alk would effectively imitate, although Rust and Bonin cut in a relatively direct style, with Bouché and Decugis leaning more toward Alk's rhythmic paradigm.

It is perhaps interesting to note here that *Renaldo & Clara*, while critically slammed by US critics, received a much more sympathetic hearing in Europe where its unorthodox editing style was not so alien to audiences or critics. Had *Renaldo & Clara* been given to a safe pair of Hollywood editing hands, someone like Walter Murch, say; a hip guy, the same age as Dylan, who had edited the likes of *American Graffiti* and *The Godfather* on a Moviola machine, like the one Alk used (Murch would later edit Anthony Minghella's *The English Patient* using the new Avid system), then no doubt the film would have been easier for audiences to follow; particularly those American audiences who remain underexposed to European cinema.

One of the more infamous criticisms of *Renaldo & Clara* came from one of its stars, Joan Baez, in her entertaining autobiography *And A Voice To Sing With*: *A Memoir*. In it, she rails against the way all the female protagonists, not only herself and Sara Dylan, were used in *Renaldo & Clara*. "I had spent half an hour gluing on synthetic eyelashes and had been given a new wig ... naturally I was

to play a Mexican whore ... the Rolling Thunder women all played whores."[12]
It's a quote which has appeared frequently in Dylan books (and now it's in
another one). Perhaps Baez wasn't attuned to European cinema any more than
she was attuned to Dylan's artistic vision, or was privy to his dreams, but it is fair
to say that Dylan was typically unconcerned about how she, either as a cast-
member or, later, as an audience-member, would receive the film.

Steven Gaydos, executive editor of *Variety*, feels Baez may have a point but
is perhaps, rather like Allen Ginsberg, simply not enough of a cineaste to fully
appreciate Dylan's references. "I think Joan Baez is seeing it [*Renaldo & Clara*]
from the sense of her own relationship with Bob and her own ideology. You
want to talk about a huge influence on *Renaldo & Clara*? Maybe the single
biggest influence is [Federico Fellini's Academy Award-winning, 1963 Italian
cine masterpiece] *8½*. It's [about] the artist grappling with his art and his
relationship with women. There's a scene where Marcello Mastroianni has the
bullwhip and all the women are circling him. You could say, 'What a sicko,
Fellini; what a sexist pig, he's got women around him and he's using a whip to
control them.' OK, ideology aside, when we are talking about frailty, fear,
relationships, and power, and are exploring sexuality, love, and marriage ...
excuse me if it's a little bit messier than your ideology. I think that a guy [like
Dylan] should be applauded for showing, honestly, what's going on, rather than
sitting here and judging him on some scorecard of ideological purity. There's
always this romantic cinder burning in every damn song Dylan does, and to me
that is more profound and indicative of where Bob's at in terms of feelings
about women."[13]

Gaydos is right to point out the pertinence of Federico Fellini's classic film
about filmmaking, *8½*. Winner of the Best Foreign Film Oscar in 1963, its title
was arrived at by Fellini counting up his previous six solo directorial efforts plus
three collaborative movies (each being deemed 'half' his), making a total of *8½*.
In 1992, a poll by the British Film Institute's *Sight & Sound* magazine of 100
international filmmakers voted *8½* the second best movie ever. They also voted
Fellini the greatest director ever. Bob Dylan received no votes.

8½ will be confusing to the average American movie fan and DVD renter.
That is not the only thing it has in common with *Renaldo & Clara*. Hardcore
fans flocked to Dylan's film the moment it hit the theaters, yet it seems fair to
conclude that they, like the majority of US critics, found his movie considerably
short on plot. However, The Who's Peter Townshend wrote *Tommy*, another

grandly conceived, extracurricular rock star project, long on characterization and hardly overburdened with plot, and the public embraced it enthusiastically in both movie and Broadway musical formats. *Renaldo & Clara* obviously had other deficiencies.

Early on in *8½*, a film critic named Daumier (played by Jean Rougel) says to anxious, pressurized film director Guido Anselmi (Marcello Mastroianni), after perusing a treatment the director has given him: "What stands out at first reading is the lack of a central issue or a philosophical stance." Many would say the same, unfairly perhaps, of *Renaldo & Clara*. The Rougel character continues: "That makes the chain of gratuitous episodes which may even be amusing in their ambivalent realism … you wonder what the director is trying to do?" At this, director Anselmi looks frustrated, puzzled, almost angry, even though Rougel's writer isn't done yet: "The story doesn't even have avant-garde merits although it has all the shortcomings." Anselmi then takes Daumier's notes, crumples them up, and tosses them on the ground in frustration.

In 1978, Dylan would undergo similar torture, by real life critics, and would have to deal with essentially the exact same accusations as the fictional Anselmi. He would defend himself to *Rolling Stone's* Jonathan Cott. "To me, *Renaldo & Clara* is like my first real film. I don't know who will like it. I made it for a specific bunch of people and [for] myself, and that's all."[14]

Certainly, *8½* might be seen to have laid the groundwork for *Renaldo & Clara*. Both films depict the chaos surrounding the artist who finds himself a celebrity; creating his work and living a supposedly private life under the glare of the same bright spotlight. About halfway through *8?*, Anselmi's wife visits him on a film set where his mistress is already installed; predictable discomfiture ensues. This not only parallels various real life Dylan love triangles with Sara and a number of women in the 1975–76 period, it also echoes the relationship between Dylan, Sara, and Joan Baez (or whichever actress is playing The Woman In White) in *Renaldo & Clara*. Fellini's messy, fictional love entanglements are designed to illustrate Anselmi's hemmed-in creative soul, and Dylan, as director, does something similar, most overtly in his improvised scenes with his erstwhile real-life lover, Baez. In one notorious scene perhaps wisely cut from the final movie, Baez asks Dylan: "What would have happened if we'd been married, Bob?" Dylan replies, icily: "I married the woman I loved."

The similarities with *8½* continue. At one point, Anselmi moans: "I thought my ideas were so clear, I wanted to make an honest film, with no lies of any kind.

I thought I had something simple to say, a film that could be useful to everyone ... now I have a shambles in my head." It is easy to imagine Dylan thinking this aloud to Howard Alk, as they continued their marathon edit of the *Renaldo & Clara* footage deep into 1977. His critics would have no doubt found a more resonant comparison with Dylan in the moment midway through *8½*, when Anselmi declares: "I have absolutely nothing to say; but I want to say it anyway. ..." There are echoes, here, too, of Robert Graves's "it's a crazy book and I didn't mean to write it." Either statement could have easily served as dialog in *Renaldo & Clara.*

The stage cannot be fully set for Dylan's formal entry into the realm of movie-making without further discussion of the influential text mentioned earlier in the chapter; Wilkie Collins's *The Woman In White.* Published in London in 1860, after its successful serialization in Charles Dickens's magazine *All The Year Round* (and in *Harper's Magazine* in the USA), it would prove to be a bestselling novel. Collins was already a popular writer of Victorian 'sensation novels' – early precursors of modern crime and detective fiction. Although his name is not now as well known as that of Dickens, in his day, Collins was a favorite of British Prime Minister William Gladstone and Queen Victoria's consort, Prince Albert, and of T.S. Eliot in later years. During the serialization of *The Woman In White*, long lines of punters, eager for the next issue, would form outside the office of *All The Year Round.*

Collins, an opium addict prone to delusions and visions, had penned *The Woman In White* in 1859. It is a highly complex story revolving around the titular woman who is encountered in a distressed state on London's Hampstead Heath by drawing teacher Walter Hartright. He comes to the woman's aid even though she forewarns him about the threat of an untrustworthy aristocrat, Lord Percival. Hartright (examine that last name closely for a moment) lands a new teaching post at Limmeridge House, in Cumberland, falls in love with a pupil named Laura Fairlie, who bears a strange resembles to the mysterious 'Woman In White,' and eventually meets her half-sister, Anne Catherick (who actually *is* the book's eponymous heroine). Soon after that, an interchange of roles begins, with Laura eventually leaving Hartright to marry the caddish Sir Percival, who is after the family fortune.

In *The Woman In White*, romantic allegiances shift, as do identities and, indeed, the very meaning of romance. Having seen *Renaldo & Clara* and then read Wilkie Collins's most popular novel, it's difficult not to think of Dylan as a version of Walter Hartright, particularly the scenes in which Hartright confronts the near impossibility of creating meaningful art in times of emotional duress. It's a recurring theme shared with *Children Of Paradise* and *8½* (and one which manifests on the wet and windy *Hard Rain* NBC special, filmed in Colorado in 1976, with Dylan's own troubled personal life coming to the boil, causing him to appear on stage, and on camera, as if he'd rather be *anyplace* else).

Just as Hartright is faced with a muddled choice between Laura Fairlie and Anne Catherick, so Dylan's Renaldo is faced with the competing attentions of Sara Dylan and Joan Baez. Dylan's movie features a key scene filmed at the Lowell, Massachusetts graveside of Beat poet Jack Kerouac. There, Dylan and Kerouac's friend, and sometime lover, Allen Ginsburg discuss the meaning of Kerouac's life and work. In *The Woman In White*, there is also a crucial graveside scene in which Laura's death is faked and the unfortunate Anne Catherick is buried in her place, all of which causes Walter Hartright and Laura Fairlie to reassess their relationship and their life's true meaning.

Anne Catherick and Laura Fairlie are near mirror images, just as Dylan and Joan Baez were, dressed almost exactly alike, at several Rolling Thunder concerts in the fall of 1975. These included the Night Of The Hurricane benefit at Madison Square Garden, in which the duo's attire (identical broad-brimmed hats, with a flowers attached, white shirts and dark vests) was so similar that anyone further back than the second row had no idea if *either* figure was actually Dylan.

The 'theft' of Anne Catherick and Laura Fairlie's identities is the work of men, just as Joan Baez's and Sara Dylan's characters in *Renaldo & Clara* are blurred and then 'hijacked' by Dylan. What start out as strong companions and objects of respect are later reduced to the role of prostitutes (Baez wasn't alone in being upset by this twist, incidentally. Sara Dylan memorably said of the film: "After all that talk about Goddesses we wound up being whores."[15])

Like Collins's novel, Dylan's movie is unquestioningly an exercise in shifting allegiances and identities. While it is possible that Dylan never read *The Woman In White*, it is highly unlikely he had no knowledge of this great work of Victorian literature; the parallels with *Renaldo & Clara* are self-evident. Also, by the time the young Dylan left Hibbing, the novel had been made into a motion picture no less than five times. It's not hard to picture the young Bob Zimmerman in his uncle's nice, warm movie house, the Minnesotan winter raging outside, glued to the 1948 Hollywood version starring Gig Young as

Walter Hartright and Sydney Greenstreet as Sir Percival's accomplice, Count Fosco. It is equally easy to imagine a weekday afternoon, c1963, on which Dylan and his songwriting shadow, Phil Ochs, a man also deeply smitten by cinema, trot off to see *The Woman In White* in a double feature at some Manhattan movie palace.

Back in its immediate post-war heyday, Warner Brothers chose Peter Godfrey to direct *The Woman In White* and the director helped select a heavyweight cast (including Eleanor Parker in the dual role of Anne Catherick/Laura Fairlie). However, the movie did the novel few favors, as the final cut featured a ghastly, tacked-on happy ending, reminiscent of the equally contrived denouement to Orson Welles's second directorial effort, *The Magnificent Ambersons* (the result of RKO's corporate suits demanding a feel-good conclusion and wresting control from the much-harassed Welles. Curiously, both films feature Agnes Moorhead in a similar supporting role). It is difficult to believe that the director who made *Renaldo & Clara* could possibly be unfamiliar with either the stark, gothic night-crawl of Collins's groundbreaking novel or the truncated 1948 movie version.

The Dylan novice who raises a quizzical eyebrow at this point, wary of the mounting similarities between Dylan's immediate influences and his finished work, should bear in mind that His Bobness is as much a congenital borrower as he is a consummate craftsman; always has been, always will be.

Minnesota winters; a kindly uncle; a love of certain kinds of foreign cinema; a tendency to place women on a pedestal and bestow on them attributes they may not actually possess and a darkness they may not deserve; an artistically restless soul; some finances and free time; all these factors contributed to Bob Dylan seeking to make as ambitious a movie as *Renaldo & Clara*. Why start with something simple like a backstage documentary or a concert film? That had been done before. Why not start with something revolutionary? Dylan had already changed popular music dramatically, and for the better. Why not do the same thing to American cinema? Bob was certainly not short of artistic courage and in his friend Howard Alk he had an experienced filmmaker who knew a thing or two about revolution.

Certainly, embarking on so grand and radical an artistic adventure involved a degree of courage. Might it have been Dutch courage, or worse? Drugs definitely played their part on Rolling Thunder. Allen Ginsberg had been shocked by the level of cocaine use on the tour (which is quite something for a

Beat writer) and had even penned a poem called 'Snow Blues' mocking the rock-star lifestyle, which he printed in the traveling troupe's newsletter. ("When it snows in yr nose you catch cold in yr brain," it concluded.[16])

Howard Alk was, alas, no stranger to drug abuse and his narcotic intake went hand-in-hand with the depression and low-self esteem which would ultimately cause his premature death. However, Dylan's principal motivations were almost certainly those of a true, visionary artist, coupled with an ego reinforced by success and a decade's worth of 'yes men' sycophancy. Bolstered by the above and, no doubt, Dylan's intake of legendarily high-octane coffee, and seemingly undaunted by any possible negative consequences, the pair would set to work on *Renaldo & Clara*.

Dylan and Alk are to be admired for setting their sights so high and it is understandable how they would be inspired by the likes of Messrs Carné, Truffaut, Fellini, et al. But they were remarkably naïve, to say nothing of their vanity, in thinking that their film would prove anywhere near as powerful or influential as the work of such experienced and celebrated directors. Remember, too, that *Renaldo & Clara* was effectively Dylan's cinematic debut as an auteur, as hardly anyone had seen *Eat The Document*. This did not stop Alk from mentioning to friends that he and Dylan were of a mind to rewrite the filmmaking rule book.

That they attempted to deploy European art cinema editing techniques proved how unconcerned Dylan was about where the chips might fall and how little interest he had in his audience's taste or sensibilities. Was this audacity or hubris? Either way, ten years after these very same artful editing techniques caused *Eat The Document* to be rejected by an understandably confused and concerned ABC Television network, an undaunted Alk and Dylan used them all over again to edit *Renaldo & Clara*.

Howard Alk had some history as both a musician and filmmaker. Born in Chicago, he ran a folk club in the city called The Bear which had booked Dylan in April 1963. From those gigs, a friendship grew and sustained until Alk was found dead at Dylan's Rundown Studios in Santa Monica, California, on New Year's Day 1982. (Dylan collectors will have seen Alk, leaning against a limousine, behind Bob, on the poster and DVD cover of Martin Scorsese's *No Direction Home: Bob Dylan*.)

Alk was also a filmmaker with a valid and deserved reputation. He had edited Edward Bland's short film *Cry Of Jazz* in the late 50s, worked with D.A.

Pennebaker on *Dont Look Back*, was Dylan's co-conspirator on *Eat The Document*, and edited (quite probably using the numeric system he and Dylan so loved) the disjointed footage photographer Barry Feinstein shot for his beyond avant-garde counterculture celebration, *You Are What You Eat*, in 1967.

In addition, Alk had made two political documentaries which best show his cinematic talents. *American Revolution 2* was a film essay about the violent protests that disrupted the 1968 Democratic Convention in Chicago, while *The Murder Of Fred Hampton* was a terrific cine portrait of the eponymous Black Panther activist who was shot dead, while sleeping, on December 4 1969, during an organized raid by the Illinois Special Prosecutions Unit, Chicago police, and the FBI. Alk was also the editor of *Snapshots*, a 1972 film by *Renaldo & Clara* cameraman and associate producer Mel Howard. Dylan had seen *Snapshots*, according to Howard, who described it as: "A rambling film about the lifestyles of a variety of people in the late '60s ... full of Chinese boxes within boxes." It was definite influence on Dylan, he maintained. "Dylan had similar notions ... to make a film that reflected the American tradition of the troubadour, the poet who goes on the road, recording and creating history as he goes along."[17]

Alk could certainly make dramatic, meaningful cinema. And he was also capable of jarring, cubist, almost non-sensible edits; the kind that might try the patience of anyone used to the predictably orthodox fare on show at the suburban shopping mall movie houses of Middle America. A politically left-wing folk-music enthusiast, a true friend and faithful companion, and a movie-maker unafraid of risk or failure; Howard Alk was certainly Dylan's kind of guy.

Renaldo & Clara was, of course, disparaged by film critics in the USA upon release and its initial four-hour version received only a limited release before a frustrated Dylan pulled it out of stateside cinemas. Europe was more amenable (it played in one Paris movie house for a solid month) but not so much so that it encouraged Dylan to continue directing films. *Renaldo & Clara* remains, for many, the work of the talented rock star floundering out of his artistic depth in a foreign medium. As such, it joins the roll-call of misbegotten musician-turned-actor-director vehicles alongside The Beatles' *Magical Mystery Tour*, the television special *James Paul McCartney*, *Abba: The Movie*, *The Great Rock'n'Roll Swindle*, any Madonna film, *Slade In Flame*, Prince's *Under The Cherry Moon*, *Pink Floyd The Wall*, and *Head* by The Monkees (and, yes, I'm aware that several of these films are now considered classics ... *of a sort*).

The rocker-turned-auteur film which *Renaldo & Clara* most closely resembles is by Bernard Shakey, alias Neil Young, a jumbled yet fascinating first cinematic effort called *Journey Through The Past*. Like the *Renaldo & Clara* sequences which are inspired by Dylan's dreams, parts of *Journey Through The Past* came direct from Young's nocturnal imagination. Both films faired better with Joe Average when concert footage appeared on screen. The director of photography on *Journey Through The Past* was David Myers and the sound production credit went to L.A. Johnson, both of whom would be heavily involved with *Renaldo & Clara*. Suffice to say, the majority of the audiences exposed to both *Journey Through The Past* and *Renaldo & Clara*, whether Young fans, Dylanphiles or not, found both these movies taxing and impenetrable (both may yet be deemed classics … *of a sort*).

In a very open and insightful interview with Shelly Livson in *The Telegraph*, the classy fanzine dedicated to archiving and discussing Dylan's work, no less a filmmaker and Dylan associate than D.A. Pennebaker discussed the inherent problems faced by an accomplished rock singer trying to make work in another creative medium. "This is always a question you get into with people like Dylan … can that fantastic kind of sovereignty that surrounds a name that gets emblazoned on the public mind … can you do *anything* off it? And always the answer is no, you can't. Whoever's the greatest movie actor of all time can't just walk out and make a hit record. It took Barbara Streisand a long time to be able to conquer two worlds and she had to work her way up. And I think Dylan found that out with … *Renaldo & Clara*. No matter how interested people were in Dylan and the myth of Dylan you can't just deal off that."[18]

Dylan's cinematic ambitions began to be reignited in October 1972 when scriptwriter Rudy Wurlitzer, one of the few Hollywood veterans who could pass as a stunt double for The Band's Garth Hudson, sent Dylan his script for *Pat Garrett & Billy The Kid*. James Coburn, who was signed up to play Sheriff Pat Garrett, would later refer to this as: "A beautiful script. I thought it was one of the best scripts I have ever read." Wurlitzer's first feature film was the previous year's *Two-Lane Blacktop*, a road movie starring singer-songwriter James Taylor and Beach Boy Dennis Wilson. Although it was greeted with mixed reviews and went largely ignored at the box office, *Two-Lane Blacktop* has, over the years, become the archetypal 'classic … *of a sort*' movie.

Rudy Wurlitzer was aware that Dylan loved cinema and that he had originally penned the song 'Lay, Lady, Lay' for John Schlesinger's movie

Midnight Cowboy, but had delivered it too late to make the movie's final cut. Wurlitzer had also heard the story of Dylan writing some lyrics down on a cocktail napkin for actor Peter Fonda to pass on to The Byrds' Roger McGuinn, who would go on to use them in the soundtrack song 'The Ballad Of Easy Rider.' Rudy Wurlitzer correctly surmised that the artist who had recorded an album called *John Wesley Harding* could write a song about another outlaw of the Old West. He was hoping Dylan might contribute something as strong as 'Lay, Lady, Lay' to the soundtrack of *Pat Garrett & Billy The Kid*. He would duly oblige.

While he read and re-read the script, Dylan began to wonder if there was a part for him in Wurlitzer's screenplay. Sam Peckinpah was going to direct and was soon rewriting the script – Wurlitzer pulling out his hair at some of the combative director's alterations. On location in Durango, Mexico, Peckinpah admitted to James Coburn that he had never heard of Bob Dylan. Coburn was a Dylan fan, however, and Bob was duly flown down to Mexico to meet the great director. After a welcoming dinner, Peckinpah asked Dylan to play guitar and sing him some songs. Coburn later recalled that Peckinpah stopped the private concert after four songs saying: "Who the hell *is* he? Who is that kid? Sign him up!"

Soon, a role was written for Dylan, although as Vince Farinaccio points out in his book *Nothing To Turn Off: The Films And Video Of Bob Dylan*, Dylan's character, Alias, was no blithe contrivance and was actually based on a known sidekick of Billy The Kid's. Dylan was commissioned by Peckinpah to create the movie's soundtrack and, on November 23, he arrived in Durango with Sara, ready to start work. This would continue until Christmas when the Dylan family flew to London to spend time with George and Patti Harrison.

While Wurlitzer and Peckinpah didn't always see eye to eye, they basically liked and respected each other. The studio backing the movie, MGM, didn't seem to like, respect, or trust Peckinpah, however, and things soon began to fall apart. Bad luck blighted proceedings. At one point, a camera was dropped and footage captured on it, when later printed, appeared blurred along the bottom of the frame. Then a bout of influenza floored a number of cast-members. One of Dylan's children was also taken ill with an undiagnosed ailment. Cast-member, and Dylan's chum, Harry Dean Stanton found himself at odds with Peckinpah, making Dylan doubtful about his putative role in the still-morphing script. At the same time, Peckinpah began to wonder about the musically untutored Dylan's ability to formally score a major motion picture and so, partly at MGM's behest, Jerry Fielding, a veteran Hollywood arranger, was brought in to help with the soundtrack.

Fielding and Dylan did not get along, nor did they respect each other. They should have. Dylan was not the uber-primitive naïf Fielding assumed he was, just as Fielding was anything but the stiff, establishment figure Dylan construed him to be. Indeed, Fielding had quite a history. He was a past member of several political organizations which had been considered 'fronts' for socialist and communist cells and had been called to testify before the House Un-American Activities Committee in December 1953, whereupon he took the Fifth Amendment and was promptly blacklisted for the next eight years. Fielding's 'crimes' included being friends with left-leaning screenwriter/novelist Dalton Trumbo and hiring African-American musicians for television orchestras (meaning Middle America being exposed to the novel images of white and black folks making music *together*). When his career finally recovered, Fielding's résumé included the soundtrack to Otto Preminger's 1961 movie *Advise And Consent* and Oscar nominations for his work on *The Wild Bunch*, *Straw Dogs*, and *The Outlaw Josey Wales* (the former pair directed by Sam Peckinpah). MGM and Peckinpah decreed that Fielding would be the man to keep Dylan on the musical straight and narrow. As if.

In mid January, filming began afresh, as did work on the soundtrack. Things did not go any more smoothly. Fielding was unimpressed by a Dylan recording session overseen in Mexico City by Gordon Carroll, MGM's on-set unit manager and nominal producer. The January 20 1973 session would generate a solitary song for the soundtrack: 'Billy 4.'

Peckinpah soon realized that the final edit of his film would be taken out of his hands by MGM's bigwigs. He was not pleased. In early February, Dylan was asked by Fielding for another song for the soundtrack. Dylan gave him 'Knockin' On Heaven's Door.' The song's simplistic chord progression and repeated, "Knock, knock, knockin' …" refrain offended the sophisticated Fielding, who compared it, unfavorably, to a nursery rhyme. Fielding may have known his children's ditties, but he apparently didn't, or couldn't, recognize a pop song's most obvious hook. To be fair, Jerry Fielding's tastes never ran to country or gospel music, much less rock, acoustic folk, gospel, or any of the other elements that were heard in Dylan's song. Jerry Fielding discusses the song in C.P. Lee's book *Like A Bullet Of Light: The Films Of Bob Dylan*. "He finally brought to the dubbing session another piece of music, Knock, Knock, Knockin' On Heaven's Door ... everybody loved it ... it was shit ... and it was infantile, it was sophomoric. It was the stuff you learn not to do the second year you score a piece of film."[19]

It is only fair to say that many veteran film critics agreed with Fielding, thinking the song's lyrics too literal to accompany a scene where a man, wounded from a gunshot, is shown slowly dying.

Nonetheless, in February, at Burbank Studios, northeast of Hollywood, 'Knockin' On Heaven's Door' was committed to tape (with Roger McGuinn playing his trusty 12-string Rickenbacker), along with the remainder of the soundtrack and other, miscellaneous material which would eventually leak out via re-releases of the movie, the director's cut, Betamax, VHS, and DVD versions, and also among the currency of Dylan's bootleg tape traders, some of the most dedicated of their breed to be found anywhere.

Discussing 'Knockin' On Heaven's Door' for the liner notes of the 1985 boxed set, *Biograph*, Dylan told Cameron Crowe: "I wrote it for Slim Pickens and Katy Jurado. I just had to do it." In the movie, Katy Jurado plays the Mexican wife of Pickens's Sheriff Colin Baker. In real life, Jurado was the ex-wife of actor Ernest Borgnine and had a fine cinematic career of her own, earning a Best Supporting Actress Golden Globe for her work in *High Noon* and an Academy Award nomination for her work in *Broken Lance*. It's more likely that Dylan actually wrote the song for Sam Peckinpah. 'Knockin' On Heaven's Door' plays as Sheriff Colin Baker is shot; he dies as wife Jurado hurries over to comfort him. To the veteran US shopping-mall movie house habitué, it is arguably the most effective scene in a film which shows a lawless American West on the cusp of domestication; the wilderness about to be tamed into a garden.

As well as providing its distinctive soundtrack, Dylan is a not insignificant visual presence in *Pat Garret & Billy The Kid*. Frequently on screen as the enigmatic Alias, he gives a mixed bag of a performance. Depending on the viewer's prior opinion of Dylan (and, indeed, their predisposition to the 'horse opera' genre, Sam Peckinpah, and movie history in general), his acting could be described as anything from awkward to effective. The critics were certainly torn. *Variety* judged Dylan's performance "embarrassing," while the *Times*, in London, thought his Alias "captivating." This difference in critical opinion is indicative of the chasm between American and European attitudes to cinema – the same polarized stances that would see *Renaldo & Clara* derided in the USA while achieving a modest level of recognition across the pond. Perhaps US critics were unprepared for the kind of spontaneous turmoil which Dylan brought to the movie (literally, if inadvertently, so when he and Harry Dean Stanton started a stampede of horses one morning, thus providing inveterate tippler Sam Peckinpah with a fine reason to start drinking early that day). Whether Alias was awkwardly throwing a knife at a man in one scene (Peckinpah's idea; it was not in Wurlitzer's original script), reading aloud the contents of various food cans (a humiliation ordered by James Coburn's Pat Garrett), or making a socially awkward and completely non-Western-hero introduction to Kris Kristofferson's tough-guy Billy The Kid, Dylan certainly knew how to upset an applecart. He later confessed to a level of confusion during the film's shooting, a feeling compounded by his problems with the soundtrack. He told Cameron Crowe how this insecurity was worsened by witnessing the difficulties Peckinpah was having with MGM during production and later tribulations over the film's editing.

There is a school of thought which suggests that Dylan and Howard Alk's insistence on complete, autonomous control of *Renaldo & Clara* was a reaction to everything Dylan had witnessed during the making of *Pat Garrett & Billy The Kid*. C.P. Lee and Vince Farinaccio certainly subscribe to this view, as does Dylan biographer Clinton Heylin, who quotes Bob thus: "I learned by working in *Pat Garrett* that there is no way you can make a really creative movie in Hollywood ... you have to have your own crew and your own people to make a movie your way."[20]

Variety's Steven Gaydos, a man who regularly watches five movies in a single day, maintains a different angle. "A studio feature costs millions and millions of dollars; *Renaldo & Clara* did not. I think Dylan knew he was making his home movies and he didn't want anyone else to own this stuff. I think, also, just like Paul Simon and a couple of other smart guys early in the 60s, Dylan was concerned about owning copyright; it's similar to owning song publishing. I don't think his experience with Sam [Peckinpah] had that much influence on his decision to own it [*Renaldo & Clara*]. If he had never met Sam and had never worked with him on *Pat Garrett*, he [Dylan] would have done exactly the same thing."[21]

In the end, *Pat Garrett & Billy The Kid* was released to an indifferent world, much to the frustration of Peckinpah (who sued MGM's chief Jim Aubrey for two million dollars in damages over Aubrey's re-editing of *Pat Garrett*) – a feeling shared by Messrs Wurlitzer, Kristofferson, Coburn, and Dylan, not to mention

Dylan's long-suffering family, who had hated being on location for so much of the shoot. Ironically, the MGM big shots that had so harassed Peckinpah during the filming were all out of a job a little over six months after the movie's release – victims of a stockholders' revolt after the studio released a string of box office disasters. Retribution would be Peckinpah's, as the new MGM regime was much more sympathetic to his original conception of the movie and allowed him into their Culver City studios to re-edit his flawed diamond of a film.

Peckinpah died on December 28 1984, aged 59. His drinking and carousing had finally caught up with him. Four years later, his cut of *Pat Garrett & Billy The Kid* (with an additional 17 minutes of footage) was completed, using the director's notes. It was shown on cable television in the US. The following year, this restored version played in cinemas – shopping-mall multiplex, art house, and otherwise. During the Slim Pickens/Katy Jurado death scene, an instrumental version of 'Knockin' On Heaven's Door' was now heard, having been deemed less distracting than the full song. It is not known if this was the idea of Peckinpah or an MGM executive. Jerry Fielding died in 1980, so, while he would have been pleased with the change, he wasn't the one who made the call.

If Peckinpah was the most disappointed in the fate of *Pat Garrett & Billy The Kid*, he was not alone in his misery. Coburn and Wurlitzer were right there with him in their dismay over the studio's mishandling of the movie, as was Bob Dylan. If a respected director like Sam Peckinpah could get messed around, surely any auteur could. Dylan and Howard Alk would have much to discuss the next time they met.

In fact, Dylan and Alk were seldom out of touch for any length of time. Dylan was drawn to those who knew the visual world, or, more specifically, the art of interpreting the world visually. That meant filmmakers, painters, photographers, urban graffiti artists, sculptors, and even those who drew their self-portraits in chalk on the cement of city sidewalks. Alk belonged to this crowd. In a way, he was Dylan's own D.A. Pennebaker, or his private Nick Broomfield (the British documentary filmmaker); available for whatever cinematic scheme Bob might be brewing up. Alk was a fellow artist and provocateur, no less afraid to rock the boat than Dylan.

Being a friend of Dylan's was one thing, but, having inspired him with his own cinematic oeuvre, Alk would be deemed crucial to whatever success *Renaldo & Clara* might achieve and equally liable should the film meet with failure.

Without question, Alk's documentary work showed Dylan how to achieve a lot of his own cinematic goals; it also proved to him something more fundamental: that such goals were attainable in the first place. If you're gonna shoot for the moon you have to have someone supply the rocket fuel.

Almost as important as Howard Alk to the development of Dylan's visual sense was painter Norman Raeben. A talented but brusque mentor to painting students for over 40 years, Manhattan-based Raeben had come to Dylan's attention after being recommended by some friends of his wife, Sara, who had studied under him. Bob had attended similar classes for at least two months, starting in late April 1974.

Raeben taught at a cluttered studio within Carnegie Hall, in Midtown Manhattan, with 22 students per class. The days were structured like a regular school timetable: 8:30am to 4pm with an hour for lunch at 11:30. These classes would prove invaluable to Dylan as both songwriter and moviemaker. Raeben was himself a student of the warts-and-all, Ashcan school of urban realist artists. His basic premise was to teach students how to re-think their visual and mental perspectives of the painted subject and to co-ordinate the mind, eye, and hand so as to realize a realist (as opposed to *realistic*) version of this subject. In other words, to achieve graphic art that faithfully represents what the mind retains (with no need for exaggeration) without necessarily resorting to literal replication of what the eye sees. Another of Raeben's tenets was a disregarding of temporal normality; a belief that art can, in effect, stop or redefine time. He was teaching painting as an expression of interpretation, feeling, and intuition. His passionate, five-day-a-week lessons had a major influence on Dylan and inspired him to begin writing songs again after a considerable hiatus; hence his oft quoted avowal that Raeben "put my mind and my hand and my eye together in a way that allowed me to do consciously what I unconsciously felt."[22] It was a technique Dylan would call upon in the songwriting for *Blood On The Tracks* and a number of other subsequent projects.

In many ways, the build-up to *Renaldo & Clara* and the entire fall 1975 Rolling Thunder Revue tour is reminiscent of the arc of Dylan's early career. Beginning around 1962, the momentum of Dylan's artistic life moved ever faster, the sense of constant evolution and the need to create something new becoming increasingly paramount as the decade rolled on. Many have written that Dylan peaked with the album *Blonde On Blonde* and the phase of his career that concluded soon after its release; a closing signaled by his motorcycle accident of July 29 1966. Apogee or not, it was certainly a bookend moment, Dylan's subsequent 60s work being more reflective and no longer governed by the former kinetic urgency.

There is a direct parallel with the process of renewal which took place almost exactly ten years later. From the moment he set foot in Norman Raeben's studio and began "to do consciously what I unconsciously felt," it is clear that it wasn't just Dylan's creative restlessness reemerging but, rather, evidence of suppressed *need* to be creatively restless, which is not quite the same thing. Arguably, the ultimate fruit of this was not *Blood On The Tracks* or *Desire* (terrific as they are) or the two *Rolling Thunder Revue* tours (memorable as they were) but *Renaldo & Clara*, a film which was Dylan's greatest creative gamble, and, perhaps, greatest misstep, and which sucked up more of his time than any other project he had ever devoted himself to.

For a film that was barely shown on release and rarely seen in his native country, it's worth pointing out that *a hell of a lot* has been subsequently written about *Renaldo & Clara*. Every single respected Dylan biographer has had a turn dissecting this easily misunderstood film. The consensus remains that the movie is pretty much indefinable; the genie has left that particular lamp. Putting it back in is no easy task.

Renaldo & Clara is notoriously tough to analyze and describe. As has been made clear, Dylan most probably constructed the film this way deliberately. The director of *Renaldo & Clara* is the same Bob Dylan whose responses in interviews generally avoid the inquisitor's question, allowing him to later deny any interpretations of what he actually *did* say. Perhaps Winston Churchill should be invoked here. On October 1 1939, in his first radio address to the British nation as First Lord of the Admiralty in Chamberlain's wartime cabinet, Churchill famously said of the Soviet Union: "It is a riddle, wrapped in a mystery, inside an enigma; but perhaps there is a key."

If nothing else, *Renaldo & Clara* is certainly "a riddle, wrapped in a mystery, inside an enigma." However, there are a number of keys: Wilkie Collins's enigmatic *The Woman In White*, the traveling performance troupe and red rose imagery of *Children Of Paradise,* the jump-cut editing of *Shoot The Piano Player* and *8½*, the influence of the Beats ("I came out of the wilderness and just naturally fell in with the Beat scene, the Bohemian, BeBop crowd ... ," Dylan told Cameron Crowe in 1985), and Robert Graves's idea of womanhood, as expressed in *The White Goddess*. Perhaps there are just *too many* keys to the kingdom that is *Renaldo & Clara*, resulting, for the viewer, in both superficial mystification and also a kind of emotional confusion in trying to digest the film's multi-layered meaning.

How did Dylan interpret his own film, emotionally speaking? In 1978 he gave an unprecedented torrent of interviews to the likes of Robert Hilburn, in the *Los Angeles Times*, Jonathan Cott, in *Rolling Stone* (twice), Ron Rosenbaum, in *Playboy*, Pete Oppel, in the *Dallas Morning News*, and John Rockwell, in the *New York Times*, in which he discussed *Renaldo & Clara* as he had never discussed a single work before. Yet, despite this volume of verbiage, all that was revealed was Dylan's ability to remain elusive. Certainly, he was rigorous in never making explicit what the movie-goer should expect to see should they sit down in front of his film. Witness this exchange from an interview with Jonathan Cott, published in *Rolling Stone*, January 26 1978:

Dylan: "There's Renaldo, there's a guy in whiteface singing on the stage, and then there's Ronnie Hawkins playing Bob Dylan. Bob Dylan is listed in the credits as playing Renaldo, yet Ronnie Hawkins is listed as playing Bob Dylan."
Cott: "So Bob Dylan may or may not be in the film."
Dylan: "Exactly."
Cott: "But Bob Dylan made the film."
Dylan: "But Bob Dylan didn't make it. *I* made it."

Dylan was a little more forthcoming in his interview with Ron Rosenbaum published in *Playboy*, March 1978:

Rosenbaum: "Let's talk about the message of *Renaldo & Clara*. It appears to be a personal yet fictional film in which you, Joan Baez, and your former wife, Sara, play leading roles. You play Renaldo, Baez plays a "woman in white," and Sara plays Clara. There is also a character in the film called Bob Dylan played by someone else. It is composed of footage from your Rolling Thunder Revue tour and fictional scenes performed by all of you as actors. Would you tell us basically what the movie is about?"
Dylan: "It's about the essence of man being alienated from himself and how, in order to free himself, to be reborn, he has to go outside himself. You can almost say that he dies in order to look at time and by strength of will, can return to the same body."

A partial examination of Dylan's answer confirms, to anyone who knows his literary influences, he is an artist in thrall to French symbolist poet Arthur Rimbaud and his infamous philosophical dictum, "I is another" (*Je est un autre*). It also reveals an artist in tune with his sense of self ("He not busy being born is busy dying," as he had once sung); someone familiar with The New Testament (with Lazarus arising from the grave, and with Christ being 'reborn'); and an artist familiar with Norman Raeben's quest to create an art which stopped or redefined time.

A partial examination of the same Dylan answer by the *Renaldo & Clara* audience would reveal even more confusion than they expressed on leaving the theater; that and a failure to recognize references to French symbolist poets, European cinema, or, most probably, The New Testament.

Is *Renaldo & Clara* to be as easily dismissed as so many Dylan fans and critics would like it to be? Certainly, Dylan's biographers, and key members of his most faithful flock, find some merit in it. Michael Gray refers to it as "a grand failure," which seems neither unfair nor inaccurate. Vince Farinaccio feels the film helped Dylan answer questions about his own myth and the machinations of the music business. C.P. Lee found that *Renaldo & Clara*, while flawed, proffered "mesmerizing achievements." Paul Williams said, bravely, that it "reinvents film" and calls it a "masterwork," while confessing to having seen it "perhaps a dozen times."

For those who have seen *Renaldo & Clara* fewer times than Paul Williams, Howard Alk, or Bob Dylan, and still find it impenetrable, it is perhaps pertinent to remember Joan Baez's frequent observation about never getting a straight answer out of Dylan. Indeed, she appears early on in *Renaldo & Clara* snapping at Dylan: "Why did you always lie?" Dylan's answer is perfect for a guy who never gives a straight answer in real life and who isn't about to give one in a film about mutable identities. "I never lied. That was that other guy."

CHAPTER 5

RENALDO & CLARA:
THE FOUR-HOUR
DREAM

Here is an incomplete list of the cast and characters in *Renaldo & Clara*:

Bob Dylan: Renaldo
Sara Dylan: Clara
Joan Baez: The Woman in White
Ronnie Hawkins [misspelled "Ronny Hawkins" in opening credits]: Bob Dylan
Ronee Blakley: Mrs Dylan
Ramblin' Jack Elliott: Longheno De Castro
Harry Dean Stanton: Lafkezio
Bob Neuwirth: The Masked Tortilla
Allen Ginsberg: The Father
Mel Howard: Ungatz
David Mansfield: The Son
Jack Baran: The Truck Driver
Ruth Tyrangiel: The Girlfriend
Helena Kallianiotes: Helena
Rubin 'Hurricane' Carter: Himself
Anne Waldman, Denise Mercedes, and Linda Thomases: The Sisters Of Mercy
T Bone Burnett: The Inner Voice
David Blue: Himself
Roberta Flack: Herself
Arlo Guthrie: Mandolin Player
Joni Mitchell: Herself
Scarlet Rivera: Herself
Luther Rix: The Drummer
Mick Ronson: Security Guard
Sam Shepard: Rodeo
Steven Soles: Ramon
André Bernard Tremblay: Maurice

And that's not to mention Roger McGuinn, Rob Stoner, Howie Wyeth, and Peter Orlovsky (Allen Ginsberg's longtime companion and Rolling Thunder's chief baggage-handler), all of whom are spared absurd character names of the Longheno De Castro and Masked Tortilla variety. Unlike camera shy singer-guitarist T Bone Burnett (who hardly appears in the film narrative, despite his prominence in the credits), bassist Rob Stoner was apparently keen to get in front of the camera on as many occasions as he could. The credits are arranged in two camps: one features, broadly, those performers who have some acting role, and hence have character names in the film, while the other is made up of musicians who generally appear when they are providing music, on stage. Roger McGuinn says he didn't appear in any of the film's dramatic scenes simply because: "I wasn't invited to. It was Bob's movie and he did what he saw fit."[1]

The final edit of *Renaldo & Clara* reflects the credits' division of labor: roughly half the film has Dylan, Mrs Dylan (and *Mrs Dylan*), Hawkins, Baez, Elliott, et al, acting in dramatic scenes, while the other half features some of the most pulsating concert footage ever shown on the big screen.

Anyone who has seen *Renaldo & Clara* will understand the dilemma with which Dylan and Alk must have wrestled: should they put out the greatest concert film ever, or should they stick to Dylan's artistic guns and facilitate all the improvised acting scenes? It was a quandary which became even more pronounced when they later attempted to trim the edit from four to two hours in order to release a more accessible version.

The temptation for anyone who has seen this film, and who loves both cinema and Dylan, is to imagine themselves in the editing room. How best to make a palatable *Renaldo & Clara* while remaining true to Dylan's vision? It's something I'd like to attempt. So, find your seats, the lights are dimming, and the curtain is parting. Here is the four-hour-plus *Renaldo & Clara*, scene by scene, with edit instructions, showing how it might be slimmed down to achieve this apparently implausible compromise. At the time of writing, it is available on YouTube, but in piecemeal fashion, meaning some scenes are missing.

The film opens with Dylan and Bob Neuwirth on stage, singing 'When I Paint My Masterpiece' as the credits roll. Dylan has on a clear mask, the first but by no means the last sign that this flick is no date movie. Neuwirth's 'harmony' is mainly a shouted unison vocal which drowns out his partner at some points. Nonetheless, Dylan is patently happy to be singing with his old friend again. *KEEP THIS SCENE*

The next scene is a poorly lit shot of *Rolling Stone* reporter (and documenter of the tour) Larry 'Ratso' Sloman in a hotel lobby, complaining that he wants a room, while McGuinn, Dylan, and others stand by. Sloman asks for a per diem payment and discusses renting a car. In his book, *A Life In Stolen Moments*,

Clinton Heylin suggests that this scene was shot November 19 1975, at the Worcester, Massachusetts hotel in which the Rolling Thunder Revue party were staying. If this scene is designed to introduce us to the tedium of life on the road then it is doing its job rather too well. Larry Sloman remembers how it felt. "I had been getting hassled by Louis Kemp. He really didn't know anything about the music business, but Louis was asked to come along and be Dylan's road manager. ... So, we'd get on tour and all of a sudden the access that I had to Bob via *Rolling Stone* magazine, you know, 24 hours, was now, 'Oh you are just another reporter, you can't get close to these people, you know, there are rules. ...' A lot of my book (*On The Road With Bob Dylan*, published in 1978) is me butting heads with these guys. So [one of] the ground rules they set up was that I couldn't stay at the same hotel with the troupe, but I could come and arrange interviews. So I had my rented car, which *Rolling Stone* was paying for, and I stayed in a little seedy motel about a mile down the road from where they were staying."[2] *LEAVE ON CUTTING ROOM FLOOR*

Cut to singer-songwriter David Blue, playing pinball beside an indoor swimming pool. There follows a famous monologue scene in which Blue (born David Cohen) talks about growing up in Providence, Rhode Island, and about his early days in Greenwich Village.

Renaldo & Clara soundman L.A. Johnson, a veteran cinematographer who died in January 2010, recalled capturing the scene. "That was [cinematographer David] Myers and me who shot that interview, which I think is a really good example of the *cinéma vérité* style. David's sensibility, his sense of humor when shooting ... he had very good interaction with people. I think that is what Bob Dylan saw, that combination of self-reliance, of finding stories and shooting them, and enjoying the humor in all of it."[3] *KEEP THIS SCENE*

After that, Dylan is shown playing blues guitar riffs in a dirty garage in Fenway, Maine, while sporting the hat that he wears on the jacket of *Desire*. The dark-haired Helena Kallianiotes is next to him. Dylan is in his Renaldo guise (he looks like Dylan, but he is Renaldo), so it is fitting that the identity of the woman Helena plays in this scene is uncertain. A mechanic asks him, "Are you running from the law?" Whether this comment is prompted by Dylan, or by nominal scriptwriters Sam Shepard or Allen Ginsberg, is unknown. Renaldo's reply is unequivocal: "I am the law." Wow, man! *KEEP THIS SCENE*

Next, Bob Neuwirth is shown on stage at the Other End. He is wearing a black Zorro mask and stands at a microphone in the role of MC. An obviously challenged African-American named Tony Curtis (but of course) reads a poem and attracts some heckling before being finally applauded. A puffy-looking Phil Ochs (at this point, still hoping to be invited on the tour) then jumps up on stage; he is wearing Dylan's *Desire* hat. Ochs hits a chord on an out-of-tune acoustic guitar. According to Larry Sloman, this footage was captured at Mike Porco's 61st birthday party, which would make the date October 23 1975.

"They decided to throw a huge birthday party for Porco," says Sloman. "Bob and Joan Baez were just going to show up and everybody else from the tour, and it was amazing. … Phil [Ochs] was so far gone at that point that you really didn't know what you were going to get out of him. One time, he came to Folk City and slammed a hatchet into the bar and started ranting and raving. He was in really bad shape. At one point, I think Neuwirth invited Phil up to the stage and on the way up Phil took Bob's hat, that kind of gray hat that he wore the whole tour, and Phil got up on stage and started singing these incredibly beautiful old folk songs. It was just so moving, and of course Bob, the whole time [was saying], 'I gotta get that hat back, gotta get that hat back.' It was an amazing night."[4] *LEAVE ON CUTTING ROOM FLOOR*

Cut to the same *Desire* chapeau resting on a coffee table at a business meeting where Dylan is discussing how to get the song 'Hurricane' out to the public. *LEAVE ON CUTTING ROOM FLOOR*

Next, Hank Williams's song 'Kaw-Liga' is performed by Dylan in a rhythm & blues style. A girl scrambles up a fire escape and into a building. *LEAVE ON CUTTING ROOM FLOOR*

Dylan and Scarlet Rivera are then seen tuning their instruments, backstage. *LEAVE ON CUTTING ROOM FLOOR*

Now, a truck is seen rolling down the highway with a Native American head logo on its side. This is probably evidence of Dylan and Alk's numerical/thematic editing system (different numbers representing trains, rivers, Native Americans and so on). In context, it is distracting and makes little sense. *LEAVE ON CUTTING ROOM FLOOR*

After that, we're with a DJ is shown in his booth at the station making an on-air announcement about the Rolling Thunder Revue coming to Providence, Rhode Island. The DJ wears headphones so large they look comical. *KEEP THIS SCENE*

Sara Dylan and Helena Kallianiotes are now seen; they are seated in a diner and are discussing travel. *LEAVE ON CUTTING ROOM FLOOR*

Concert footage follows. Dylan and the band perform 'Isis.' An intense Dylan, in whiteface, introduces it as "a song about marriage," while appropriately flashing his wedding ring. He sings it like he means it; he's wailing from the soul and testifying mightily. This is like an updated scene from *Children Of Paradise* – with Dylan as a rock'n'roll Baptiste. He is not playing guitar, just singing and periodically playing bursts of harmonica. Dylan knew he was on camera and may have raised his game accordingly. It is riveting footage. Michael Lindsay-Hogg and Martin Scorsese, eat your hearts out. *KEEP THIS SCENE; IN FACT, FIND MORE OF IT*

We then see Sara Dylan/Clara picking up a rose. *KEEP THIS SCENE*

Cut to entertainment reporter Sheila Shotton, from the Canadian Broadcasting Corporation. She is in a Toronto hotel lobby waiting for Bob Dylan. She obviously has no idea who Bob Dylan is, or what he looks like. Told that "Bob Dylan is wearing a hat," she spies Ronnie Hawkins in a white Stetson and proceeds to interview him. She can hardly be blamed, since Hawkins has announced that he is, in fact, Bob Dylan. Looking, sounding, and acting nothing at all like Dylan (he's not a Yankee but an Arkansas boy; is much bigger and far more gregarious than Dylan; and is the hail and hearty life of the party, not an inscrutable introvert), this is one of the most flagrant examples of inappropriate casting in the history of cinema, and a fine example of both God's and Dylan's sense of humor.

Ronnie Hawkins: "Let me tell you how that got started. The old gal that was going to do the interview [Sheila Shotton] ... she didn't know what Bob Dylan looked like! I mean they staged it and I didn't know anything about it, but she wasn't staged ... she couldn't act that good! We just got going and she said, 'Is Bob Dylan here?' and I said, 'Yeah, here I am!' and I walked up there and did a whole interview as Bob Dylan."[5] *KEEP THIS SCENE*

Next, we're in a hotel room where Ronnie Hawkins (as Bob Dylan) attempts to get Ruth Tyrangiel, playing an innocent farm girl, to go on the road with him "for 30 or 40 days." An actor Hawkins is not; he cannot improvise and repeats himself on camera like a nervous schoolboy. To be fair, some direction from a formal film director would have helped greatly here. Hawkins/Dylan wins the fair maiden's hand, nonetheless, saying: "I don't mind playing second fiddle as long as it's on the front row," while Beethoven's *Moonlight Sonata* plays in the background. Hawkins is a huge presence, but he is not playing to his strengths. When Tyrangiel says she needs to ask her father's permission before she goes on the road, Hawkins replies: "Girl, I was turned down by the Ku Klux Klan, so he's certainly not gonna approve me!"

Despite questionable thespian skills, Hawkins relished being in the film, even if the circumstances could be demanding. "It was the first time I had anybody that'd actually want to take my picture! They woke me up at three in the morning, the film crew, and Bob Dylan says, 'We are going to start filming now' and I said, 'Well, I haven't gotten my script yet,' and Dylan says, 'We are going to wing it.' They stayed up all night."[6] *LEAVE ON CUTTING ROOM FLOOR*

We then jump cut to a slice of pure Alkian documentary realism. A preacher is telling the Good News to a not entirely friendly group of passersby on Wall Street, with the New York Stock Exchange framed rather poetically right behind him. It is God and Mammon juxtaposed. It's possible, in fact, that Alk may not actually have shot the scene. There was more than one crew involved in the making of *Renaldo & Clara*, as L.A. Johnson recalls. "David [Myers] and I had been a crew going back to before [we filmed at the] Woodstock [Festival]. We had a rep as a *cinéma vérité* documentary crew, and we could go onto any sort of situation and capture it. I think Bob had a sense of our skills and had a real good idea of what that was about stylistically, setting up situations and then letting the crew sort of extract something from that. Howard Alk was a great man, and Howard had known David [Myers] previously. Howard was the 'A crew,' as it was called, and we were the 'B crew.' Basically, David and I were hired guns and we were brought in to scope out the situation and contribute what we could."

Alk was certainly the main cameraman when it came to capturing Dylan on stage, Johnson recalls. "During the concerts, he did those big close-ups of Dylan. That was all Howard. David would shoot the hand-held, onstage stuff, and then we would hire other cameramen. But we [Myers and Johnson] were the core group who did all the stuff away from the concerts." Johnson is quite clear that it was Dylan who was pulling the film's strings. "Louis [Kemp] would call us up to say that Bob had an idea and wanted to shoot something down in the ballroom. He was really the one coming up with the situations and we would hear about them usually from Louis; he was our conduit to Dylan. We would have these short conversations with Bob about what the scene was, what the situation was, and then he would sort of motivate the environment and we would go with it."

Some members of the entourage would be manipulated simply to create cinematic situations, Johnson remembers. "We discovered, as we went along, that people like Larry 'Ratso' Sloman, even though he was a great sport, was being treated like the bastard dog. One day he would be able to get a meal and then the next he would get kicked out of the venue without a pass. Myers just loved messing with Ratso. I remember we were in some snowy place in Massachusetts and he [Sloman] was out in the snow waiting, trying to get in the backdoor. Myers said, 'If you go round the back, we will let you in,' and we opened the door ajar and got this shot of Ratso under a tree, shivering. Those were the kind of things that we loved shooting."[7] *KEEP THIS SCENE*

The next scene finds the same Larry Sloman, and several others, discussing theology in a New England diner. This ensemble appears several times in *Renaldo & Clara* as a kind of Greek chorus. *LEAVE ON CUTTING ROOM FLOOR*

Next, Dylan is filmed leaving a theater's rear exit in the cold early morning; his song 'Ballad In Plain D' is heard on the soundtrack, sung by Canadian Gordon Lightfoot; and a fine version it is, too. Dylan then enters a café where diners are chowing down short-order grub. He discusses the subjects of hope, romance, and commitment (the very subjects of the film, perhaps) with award winning French-Canadian filmmaker André Bernard Tremblay, who is playing the part of Maurice. Here, Dylan has real screen presence. He wears a winter coat, scarf, and Cossack hat, despite being inside the warm diner. Somehow, he never looks foolish, which is a neat trick to pull off. *KEEP THIS SCENE*

Cut to Sam Shepard and Sara Dylan walking down a street discussing Jack Daniels sour mash whiskey. Shepard: "There are particular Irish gods who like

Jack Daniels." It's a patent lie, as no true Irish person would touch Jack Daniels given that they have distilled world class malts on the Emerald Isle for a few hundred years. Shepard goes on: "There is a god who is thin but cruel and addicted to this particular sour mash, and if you don't take it, I'm gonna give it to him." *LEAVE ON CUTTING ROOM FLOOR*

A chaotic scene then occurs in yet another diner in which several brunette women are talking about God with Dylan. Although the tone of one of the women is the very definition of pretentiousness, to her credit, she avoids mention of the drinking habits of either the Irish or the divine. *LEAVE ON CUTTING ROOM FLOOR*

Cut to an eye-catching montage of bare trees and statues in a graveyard. Leadbelly's 'Black Girl' (a song more identified with Kurt Cobain by younger music fans) is sung by several people off-screen, accompanied by Scarlet Rivera's out-of-pitch fiddle. This is the Lowell, Massachusetts graveyard where Jack Kerouac is buried. *KEEP THIS SCENE*

Now we're back with David Blue who is playing pinball again. He's talking about the old Greenwich Village days, a club called the Fat Black Pussycat, and about Dylan's writing 'Blowin' In The Wind' one afternoon. He recalls going to the Monday night hootenanny at Gerde's Folk City and how Gil Turner learned the song and sang it for the first time there, while the young Dylan watched him from the bar. *KEEP THIS SCENE*

A belly dancer is then seen writhing rhythmically across the floor of one of the eateries shown earlier in the movie. She has her back to the camera, but it appears to be dancer and choreographer Claudia Carr, who was known to be on the tour. It could be seen as a precursor to Dylan's 2004 Victoria's Secret lingerie television commercial, but then again, it's probably just a scantily clad woman, gyrating. *LEAVE ON CUTTING ROOM FLOOR*

Ronnie Hawkins, still playing Bob Dylan, tries to get into this same eatery, but a make-up-wearing Mick Ronson bars his way. The guitarist is surely the world's first glitter-rock bouncer. The slender Ronson telling the beefy Hawkins, "You're not getting past my face, sonny boy," is, frankly, laughable as theater and as improbable as snow in July. One of the true low points of *Renaldo & Clara*, the scene is reminiscent of the 'acting' in Prince's ghastly *Under The Cherry Moon*. It's easily the most awkward dramatic scene involving a talented English guitarist since Mick Jones appeared in *Rude Boy*. *LEAVE ON CUTTING ROOM FLOOR*

Now we see several elderly ladies sitting in a restaurant watching the belly dancer do her thing to 'Hava Nagila.' Then a lounge singer, identified by Dylan biographer Clinton Heylin as one Merlin Wild, performs the song 'Willkommen' from the film *Cabaret*. How Dylan and Neuwirth must have loved the name Merlin Wild. This is another hastily lit sequence, and it shows. Larry Sloman reports that they filmed in two different diners and three different restaurants. Perhaps it was the only time they could get some people to sit still? This footage is from the Sea Crest Motel in North Falmouth, Massachusetts, where the troupe was rehearsing and where, on October 29 1975, they performed an intimate show for the other guests. *LEAVE ON CUTTING ROOM FLOOR*

Next, we're back on what looks like Wall Street, where Christian evangelists are seen speaking from the top of a Volkswagen bus. The crowd on the street is hostile; cries of "what a waste" and "comb ya hair, ya stupid idiot" are heard. Then a chant of "We want Jesus, we want Jesus" goes up. Two evangelists on the top of the VW bus chant back "We have Jesus, we have Jesus." It is an early and admittedly accidental example of the hostility that would greet Dylan's imminent Christian phase. A man in the crowd shouts angrily, "You're a scumbag hypocrite, you know that?" One of the evangelists cannot take the abuse and leaps off the VW and assaults a young heckler. The preacher reminds the crowd, in a quote worthy of Dylan's *Slow Train Coming/Saved* era interviews, "I'll tell you this ... whatever you say to a man of God, you say directly *to* God!" *KEEP THIS SCENE*

Dylan then appears in whiteface, performing a fine, up-tempo electric version of 'A Hard Rain's A-Gonna Fall' which is completely unlike either the familiar acoustic classic or the version from the *Hard Rain* television special that would be captured in Fort Collins, Colorado, the following year. The camera pans round to Ramblin' Jack Elliott and Sam Shepard as they look on in wonder at this performance from the side of the stage. *KEEP THIS SCENE*

The next scene returns us to a familiar diner, where Dylan is being interviewed by Larry Sloman. The interview is intercut with footage of an anonymous fan trying to speak like Dylan in 1965, using put-ons bordering on non sequiturs. "I interviewed fans of Dylan and then talked about the songs," recalls Sloman. "These were people that I found outside the tour, on the edge; people I didn't know and that I came across and wrangled up as the crew filmed me. There is tons of that stuff which never made the final cut ... you can't imagine how many hours were shot."[8] *LEAVE ON CUTTING ROOM FLOOR*

Next, Sara Dylan is seen buying coffee in a bus station. She is carrying a copy of *Playgirl* magazine. Yes, *Playgirl*. *LEAVE ON CUTTING ROOM FLOOR*

Allen Ginsberg, introduced by the delightfully named Merlin Wild, is now seen taking the stage at the Sea Crest Motel to read 'Kaddish,' his Beat ode to his mother. It's a poem which does not flinch from graphic references to her insanity. It is October 29 1975; the warm-up show for the tour. Ginsberg's audience is primarily aging Jewish ladies brought together by a love of mahjong. The effect upon them of such a tender, aching, and yet brutal poem about the loss of a beloved Jewish mother cannot be readily calculated.

Rehearsals would reveal the Jacques Levy-directed Rolling Thunder Revue concert to be well over four hours in length; and yet no provision was made for Ginsberg to get up and read his poetry or perform his mantras. Dylanologist Clinton Heylin confirms this. "As far as I know, Allen only ever appeared [on stage] for [the nightly Rolling Thunder ensemble finale] 'This Land Is Your Land.'"[9] T Bone Burnett concurs. "I never saw him [Ginsberg] perform musically on stage, other than the encore, and he would come up and wail some background parts on 'This Land Is Your Land.' [The Band's] Rick Danko and Allen Ginsberg did [a version of] Rick's 'What A Town,' in New England someplace, I think; but Ginsberg just kind of wails on that. He'd get up and sing to his shoes. He was a courageous guy, Allen, in his own way; a beautiful dude."[10]

Burnett is right; Ginsberg did perform on stage once, during the first RTR tour, other than during the encores. It was in Hartford, Connecticut, on November 24 1975, and the song was indeed 'What A Town,' the opening cut from Danko's soon-to-be-recorded debut solo album. Given that he was there each night, and was America's most famous poet at the time, to not have Ginsberg read (while allowing some of the other tour performers under the spotlight to play what was sometimes, by comparison, modest fare) has to be seen as a major oversight if not something of an insult. Did Dylan or Levy think the RTR audience would not embrace the honest pain of 'Kaddish,' the protracted scream of 'Howl,' the subconscious unburdening of 'Dream Record,' or the sweet tenderness of 'Elegy For Neal Cassady'?

"I think everyone was underused on the shows: Joni Mitchell, for instance," suggests Ginsberg biographer Barry Miles. "Allen was hired largely to write scripts for 'spontaneous' playlets and performance pieces for the film, rather than as an onstage performer. He did do the 'Kaddish' reading, but that was for the film, not to a paying audience. I don't think he read any poems at all on the tour." Despite this, Miles also suggests that Ginsberg and his immediate associates were of no little significance to Dylan on the tour. "[Poet] Ann Waldman was on the tour, at Allen's suggestion, to add more 'poetic sensibility' to the proceedings and help with the film scripts. Allen traveled with his boyfriend, Peter Orlovsky, who was the baggage handler, and Peter's girlfriend, Denise Felieu (alias Denise Mercedes), who painted Dylan's face white for the show, made sure his hat had fresh flowers on it, and was also, I'm told, one of Dylan's girlfriends. She also ran errands, like buying him six pairs of blue jeans. They were pretty good friends, or as much as you can be in those circumstances. Later, when Denise had her guitar stolen, Dylan happened to call up and she told him she had a gig and no guitar. Dylan told her, 'Choose any guitar, any guitar you like. It would give me a lot of pleasure to know you were playing a guitar I gave you.'"[11]

Roger McGuinn remembers Ginsberg being a significant presence on the tour but thinks that the very length of the show dictated certain restrictions on performance. "People like Allen gave their art to us and to others ... on this tour. It was Felliniesque and more fun than you can imagine. The only possible downside I would see, looking back, was that you could not possibly give all the performers the amount of airtime they deserved."[12]

Ginsberg was asked by writer and professor Alan Ziegler of Columbia University if he had ever read any poetry during Dylan's Rolling Thunder gigs. Ginsberg answered: "He [Dylan] was dubious about my singing but he kept pushing me to recite poetry, until finally in Fort Collins [the May 1976 RTR show captured in the *Hard Rain* television special) I did, and then again in Salt Lake City ... I sort of had this fatuous idea of myself as a singer. They had enough singers and musicians and rock'n'roll stars. He [Dylan] was interested in the poetry part. I was shy about that; partly scared. I couldn't figure what you could say to 27,000 people; what could engage the minds of that many people in the hysteria of a giant rock'n'roll thing?" [13] What Ginsberg fails to mention is that the Fort Collins and Salt Lake City shows were the very last Rolling Thunder concerts.

The absurdity of having Ginsberg along but not allowing him to read his powerful poetry on stage, particularly at the relatively intimate early Rolling Thunder gigs in the fall of 1975, is underscored when one reads the notes Bob Dylan wrote for the jacket of Ginsberg's *Collected Poems 1947–1980*. "Ginsberg is both tragic and dynamic, a lyrical genius, conman extraordinaire and probably the greatest single influence on the American poetical voice since Whitman."[14] True enough. So why keep Walt Whitman's heir backstage? *KEEP THIS SCENE. IN FACT, FIND MORE OF IT*

We now cut to David Blue, who is still playing pinball. He is perhaps no less a Greek chorus than the punters in the diner which Dylan keeps cutting to. Blue talks about Ginsberg, who we've just seen reciting (thus making this a *Renaldo & Clara* rarity, an almost logically placed scene), and how impressed he had been, back in the day, to know that Dylan was friends with a major Beat poet. He eulogizes about a time when art was for art's sake, and not, as Bob Neuwirth phrases it in Martin Scorsese's movie *No Direction Home,* "dollar driven." Blue also mentions Luke Faust, a fine banjo player on the early-60s Greenwich Village scene who chose not to seek fame. *KEEP THIS SCENE*

Dylan's entourage is then seen being served food by Native Americans at Tuscarora Reservation in Niagara County, New York. The date is November 16 1975. Dylan and Alk have slotted this in here, presumably, using the numerical/thematic editing system. While there may be some hypothetical point to the scene, it clearly does not hold the viewer's attention. It arrives out of nowhere and fails to move the film along *LEAVE ON CUTTING ROOM FLOOR*

Ginsberg is next seen singing and playing harmonium at what looks like Gerde's Folk City. A girl accompanies him on a strummed electric guitar. The song has a rising, repeated chorus: "All the hills echo it / All the hills echo it," and is quite captivating. It is a piece Ginsberg often played live, an interpolation of poems from William Blake's *Songs Of Innocence And Of Experience*, which he called 'Nurse's Song.' *KEEP THIS SCENE; IN FACT, FIND MORE OF IT*

Next, we see Bob Neuwirth on a train, roaring past snow-covered countryside, in a scene shot December 3 1975. He asks the conductor what the direction of the train is. He says he has been on it for six days. The conductor smiles and says, "This train has only been on the road four hours; I think you got lost in Toronto." The conductor is as verbally adept and poised as can be; he is everything Dylan's fans and friends in the diner scenes are not. *LEAVE ON CUTTING ROOM FLOOR*

In the ensuing scene, we're backstage at what looks like a performance at the Tuscarora Reservation. Neuwirth appears in the guise of The Masked Tortilla. With a mask now painted on his face. A sprightly fiddle tune plays in the background. Indian activist Wallace 'Mad Bear' Anderson welcomes the Revue. People dance wearing 18th-century costume. Ramblin' Jack Elliott sits in with the local fiddle band. Native Americans are seen drinking spirits from the bottle (never a good sign). Neuwirth is so verbally provocative to the Native Americans and the locals in their period costume, it's a miracle he isn't dead. Doug Boyd is introduced. He is an American Indian medicine man and guardian of many secrets passed down from countless generations (as well as being the author of an excellent book, called *Rolling Thunder*, no less, about the eponymous tribal leader and spiritual healer).

On the soundtrack, Dylan is heard singing 'People Get Ready,' the classic 1965 rhythm & blues song by The Impressions, and is then shown arriving at the show and slowly moving through the crowd like a politician on the campaign trail. *KEEP THIS SCENE*

We remain at the reservation for the next scene. Dylan's piano-based 'People Get Ready' is still on the soundtrack and we are treated to a rare offstage cameo by the lanky T Bone Burnett. He looks like a cross between Ichabod Crane and John Lennon. Joan Baez is also shown; she is greeting several Native Americans warmly. Dylan enters the room and the crowd parts like the Red Sea as he passes. He is greeted cautiously and like the celebrity he is. In contrast, Baez is greeted like an old friend. *KEEP THIS SCENE*

Rather annoyingly, the scene then cuts to a truck which is driving across the snow-covered countryside, and then back to Neuwirth, asleep on a train, wearing a T-shirt that bears the slogan "Bob who?" *LEAVE ON CUTTING ROOM FLOOR*

The Woman In White stares out of the window for a few seconds. But is it Sara Dylan, Joan Baez, or someone else? *KEEP THIS SCENE*

Next, we're backstage at an unidentified concert hall. Equipment is being unloaded from a truck. This is a sizeable arena, not one of the small venues to which Dylan had initially aimed to restrict the tour's activities. The footage of roadies with cases of Studio Instrument Rentals' equipment could be of 100 different bands in 100 different places. Perhaps that is Dylan's point. More distinctively, a blond, male roadie plays Chopin on a piano as the Rolling Thunder Revue backdrop banner is unfurled. *KEEP THIS SCENE*

The scene cuts to the Guam musicians backstage, preparing for the concert. No one says or does anything of consequence. *LEAVE ON CUTTING ROOM FLOOR*

Dylan is next seen driving a motorhome. Jack Elliott is in the front passenger seat next to him. A Rolling Thunder version of 'I Want You' plays in the background. It sounds like a rehearsal tape recorded at SIR in New York City, in October. There is too much instrumentation on it to be from any smaller room, yet it doesn't have the ambient sound that would accompany a concert hall recording. Dylan says: "We're off to see the gypsy who runs a sporting house." *KEEP THIS SCENE*

Singer-guitarist Steven Soles is departing the tour-bus and entering a hotel. *LEAVE ON CUTTING ROOM FLOOR*

Steven Soles plays Ramon, the boyfriend of singer/actress Ronee Blakley. In the next scene, he tells her to hurry up with preparations for the evening's show. Suddenly this erupts into a nasty "I know who you've been fucking" fight, Ramon using those very words. The scene, acted for all it is worth by an amateur (Soles) and a movie veteran (Blakley), is probably the very kind of thing Dylan had in mind for the film all along. It's the sort of drama he would often refer to during interviews promoting the film. It is also a scene which is completely out of context in the longer, four-hour edit of the movie, and its improvisational nature shows how little input the likes of Sam Shepard, despite being recruited for the job, had in writing any kind of screenplay.

Anyone who has been through a divorce will find this scene painful to watch, as will those who have had acting classes. Blakley actually improvises a line, "You have not fucked me for three years," dialog which comes rather out of the blue, with no dramatic buildup. Dylan is less a director than a puppeteer, here, making his pals 'act' when he wants them to (be it 3am or whenever). This scene is less crucial to *Renaldo & Clara* than it is to an understanding of the ego drama of being Bob Dylan, with those around him all too eager to jump through whatever hoops he ordains. *LEAVE ON CUTTING ROOM FLOOR*

Another (almost) logical scene follows, as Blakley sings 'Need A New Sun Rising Every Day,' her own fine ballad, first recorded for her 1975 album, *Welcome*. This is a wonderfully filmed sequence. It begs the question: why must the almost universally thrilling concert footage in *Renaldo & Clara* (and that of *Eat The Document*, for that matter) always play second fiddle to the bizarre, frequently nonsensical, 'action' scenes? Granted, if someone were to see *Renaldo & Clara*, having previously watched *Children Of Paradise, Shoot The Piano Player*, and *8½* (and having recently read *The White Goddess* and *The Woman In White*), then they might 'get' exactly what Dylan is trying to do in these non-musical scenes. It is the safest of bets, however, that the average *Renaldo & Clara* viewer knew little of the above, and went to see the film based on their love of Dylan's music, period. No wonder they would be left puzzled for the duration of the film, and, no doubt, for most of the next week, too. Is Dylan, popular music's ultimate wordsmith and one of his lifetime's major cultural figures, showing his audience how artistically limited he feels by being 'merely' a rock superstar? *KEEP THIS SCENE*

We then get a totally fabricated scene, gleaned from several locales. It should be pointed out that this is what 'real' movies frequently do: manufacture a coherent single narrative moment from shots actually taken in several different locations at different times. In the scene, Ramblin' Jack Elliott and others from the tour ensemble are in a bar; the reality is they are in Mama Frasca's Dream-Away Lodge, dreamin' away. Ramblin' Jack announces that last time the barmaid Leonora saw him he'd recently been married. Dylan would have us believe they are in a bar, in a gypsy-run house of ill-repute. Theresa, Leonora, and Regina, Mama's three daughters, work at the bar in the scene. Leonora greets Ramblin' Jack warmly; they've obviously met before. She makes a remark about the way Jack looked last time they saw each other. *LEAVE ON CUTTING ROOM FLOOR*

Next, we're introduced to redoubtable matriarch 'Mama' (Maria) Frasca, proprietor of the Dream-Away Lodge, in Becket, Massachusetts. She sings a poignant Italian song to Joan Baez. Its lyrics concern a brunette in love on a moonlit night (in the credits the song is called 'Mama's Lament'). Mama Frasca plays a small green guitar in open tuning while, off camera, Rob Stoner accompanies her on bouzouki. Baez is wearing the white wedding dress which Mama Frasca has just handed her, insisting that she don it.

Mama Frasca was functionally illiterate, and while she was unaware of exactly who Dylan was, she was nonetheless excited to have the famous Joan Baez in her establishment. According to Clinton Heylin, the Dream-Away Lodge scene was filmed November 7; one of several shot that day. Most of the footage ended up on Howard Alk's cutting room floor.

Books on the tour by Clinton Heylin, C.P. Lee, Sam Shepard, and Larry Sloman all refer to Mama's Dreamaway *Lounge*, but a phone call to the establishment confirmed that it was a lodge first and forever and the only lounge is the bar. It had been operated by Maria Frasca since 1942 and it was local boy Arlo Guthrie (son of Dylan's musical hero, Woody Guthrie) who told tour photographer Ken Regan about the place. Regan then informed Dylan and Alk of the Lodge's possibilities as a location for some *Renaldo & Clara* scenes.

Thirty-four years later, Arlo Guthrie remembers Mama Frasca's hostelry warmly. "It was the kind of place where there was no menu; you had whatever she was cooking, and she usually cooked the same things: chicken and potatoes. Mama would sit around after dinner playing her guitar and singing the songs she had written. Sometimes, one or two of her daughters would sing and play along with her. We knew the songs she loved, and had even made a professional recording of her with some of the guys in our band. Mama kept a single of herself on the jukebox until the day she died."

Dylan had been looking for a place to hang out after Rolling Thunder had played Springfield, Massachusetts, and local lad Guthrie knew just the spot. "I thought it'd be a great, out-of-the-way place where we could have some fun and be away from the gathering hordes of people. I don't think Mama knew who Bob Dylan was, or who any of these people were, but she was very quick to see that this was something special. She hit it off extremely well with Joan Baez and presented her with a beautiful white dress. All the while we were there, the cameras rolled, and we were just enjoying the chaos."[15]

Nestled at the edge of October Mountain State Forest, in the Berkshires, the

Dream-Away had started life as a hunting lodge for local businessmen interested in shooting a mammal or two before bagging a few single malt whiskeys. Rumors of the lodge once being a home to women of easy virtue are apparently quite true, thereby making it a perfect setting for *Renaldo & Clara's* white-clad women/brothel scenes. *KEEP THIS SCENE*

Which is where we go next, as Joan Baez and Sara Dylan appear on screen, briefly, dressed as ladies of the night. Baez speaks in a ridiculous French accent about where her life is going and Sara suggests a happy marriage will be the answer to her problems. This improvised dialog seems a tad cruel, as Baez was by then divorced. Although she famously protested about having to repeatedly play the role of a whore in *Renaldo & Clara*, Baez does so here with no little aplomb. No doubt the likes of Bob Guccione or Russ Meyer would point out how hot Sara Dylan and Baez look in this scene and, fair enough, they do. Can you imagine the argument required to convince your wife to dress up as a prostitute and appear next to one of your well-known old flames for a movie which will be seen internationally? *LEAVE ON CUTTING ROOM FLOOR*

We cut to Mama singing, again. Baez chimes in with a wordless but sweet high harmony line. *KEEP THIS SCENE*

Jack Elliott is then seen petting a Scottish terrier. *LEAVE ON CUTTING ROOM FLOOR*

According to tour accounts from participants such as Sloman and Shepard, Dylan and company gathered around the Dream-Away Lodge piano to sing a version of Gene Vincent's 'Be-Bop-A-Lula,' but this was not filmed. Nor was Ginsberg's dramatic reading at the Lodge of passages from Herman Melville's *Moby Dick* (Ginsberg was obviously aware that Melville had at one time resided in nearby Pittsfield). Instead, Ronee Blakley at the bar confesses to Dylan that she likes "tough, nice men ... strong men who are also very sweet." The camera then cuts to Dylan for a reaction shot; he gives a quizzical "Yeah?" It might have reminded cinema fans of Marlon Brando's famous nostrum: "Just because the director yells 'action' [it] doesn't mean you have to do anything." Blakley looks quite pretty perched on a barstool, wearing a sky blue beret. "I'll take you," she says to Dylan with enough meaning in her tone to get any man interested. This is the Renaldo/Clara, man/woman dynamic in full swing. It's like a snippet of a 1975 update of *Casablanca*. Just as things heat up, Alk and Dylan cut away. For shame, gentlemen, for shame! *KEEP THIS SCENE*

We return to Mama Frasca singing, this time in English: "It wasn't you and it wasn't me," goes her refrain. A startlingly fresh-faced Arlo Guthrie is now her bouzouki accompanist. Then we see Mama's bedroom and the moment Baez is shown the white wedding dress. Baez remembered her time at Mama's Dream-Away Lodge in her autobiography. "[We] went to see Arlo Guthrie at a gypsy's place [sic] in upstate New York. It was a restaurant with a bar, and while everyone sat around drinking hot toddies, Bob was wildly trying to get a scene to happen, and the old gypsy lady spotted me and said I must go up to her room … On the bed lay a faded, beaded white satin wedding dress. It was ankle length and had lace straps over the satin bodice. Next to it were a little antique embroidered opera purse and a choke necklace of fake pearls and rhinestones.
  "'Put the dress on,' she said cheerfully, and I did. It fit perfectly. She brushed a tear from her grubby cheek and shook her head sagely, saying that she had known I would be coming that day, though she had no idea who I was [in fact, Mama Frasca did know who Baez was, although she was unfamiliar with the other musicians], and that the dress and purse and necklace were mine. Then she kissed me and said to go down and join the crowd. I felt positively magical gliding down the stairs, and everybody spotted me at once and said 'ooh' and 'aah,' and Bob decided to do a 'scene' with me."[16] *KEEP THIS SCENE*

Next, we are back in the Lowell, Massachusetts cemetery where Jack Kerouac is buried. This footage, shot November 3, is a brief montage of Madonnas and a Christ on the cross, each of whom is looking up toward the sky in the post-Reformation fashion. *LEAVE ON CUTTING ROOM FLOOR*

Cut to David Mansfield playing the violin angelically while dressed like, well, an angel, with wings and a dime store halo on his noggin. Cameraman David Myers, of the 'B crew,' is seen shooting the scene from a different angle. Mansfield, not yet in his twenties, actually looks about 12 as Baez and other painted ladies tempt him with their charms. Baez cannot help but smile at the absurdity of all this and, frankly, in such heavenly garb, young David is more likely to attract the attention of Allen Ginsberg than any hot-blooded woman.

Clinton Heylin places this scene in a Quebec City hotel room on November 28. It was all in day's work for David Mansfield. "Things were coming at you fast and furious and so having a film crew around was no easier or difficult than any of that other stuff. It was one camera, one sound guy ... maybe three people. Nothing was lit, they weren't laying track, and they weren't doing any of the stuff you would think of when you think of filming a musical production. It was filmed much more like D.A. Pennabaker might shoot a documentary. They [the film crew] were just part of the theme, and some of them hung out with us, too, so they were, socially, part of the whole thing, the whole tour. Where the musicians were, they were, too."

Mansfield was a musical wunderkind who had no ambition to act in a film. "When I knew the crew was going to be around, I wasn't lobbying to get into the scenes. I was just trying to sort of pretend that this is what happened to me everyday – taking it all in my stride. The Bobs [Dylan and Neuwirth] would be drinking after the show and say, 'Hey man, next week we are going to be in Massachusetts, let's go to Kerouac's grave.' But nobody said we are going to do this, this is the situation. The thing would just sort of invent itself. There was no discussion or dialog, and there was no second take."[17] *KEEP THIS SCENE*

We now cut to Ramblin' Jack Elliott leading Guam and a Dickensian looking, banjo-playing Roger McGuinn on a fine version of Louis Jordan's 'Salt Pork, West Virginia.' *KEEP THIS SCENE*

In the next scene, an unidentified man in a diner philosophizes, as Larry 'Ratso' Sloman looks on. *LEAVE ON CUTTING ROOM FLOOR*

Now, Ramblin' Jack Elliott is seen yodeling on what sounds like a song by Jimmie Rodgers. The scene is so brief it is unclear which one. *LEAVE ON CUTTING ROOM FLOOR*

We are then transported back to the Sea Crest Motel in North Falmouth, Massachusetts, where Allen Ginsberg is getting a chant going while Burnett, McGuinn, and Ronson add counterpoint; it's all very 50s, "Yeah, yeah, baby ... go-go baby ... bop-shoo-wop ... do wah diddy ..." Stoner let's rip with an "aaaahhh ... aahhhhh ... aaaaHAAA ... ahhh," which sounds frighteningly close to the opening of Led Zeppelin's 'Immigrant Song.' Outside, Dylan and

Neuwirth are wandering away with a wine bottle apiece, staring at the sun setting over the bay. They then walk slowly toward the shore, Dylan clasping a bugle, for no good reason. *LEAVE ON CUTTING ROOM FLOOR*

Cut to David Blue, who is still playing pinball. This time he does not speak. This 14-second shot exemplifies the randomized pointlessness that is the corollary of the Dylan/Alk film-editing system. *LEAVE ON CUTTING ROOM FLOOR*

Next, we're with Dylan, on a public bus. He spots something on a New York City street. He disembarks in a mad rush while, on the soundtrack, he and Guam perform 'What Will You Do When Jesus Comes?' This song was rehearsed relatively extensively at SIR in Manhattan, before the RTR set out. It shines a bright light in the direction of Dylan's future musical adventures. *LEAVE ON CUTTING ROOM FLOOR*

We then hear the sound of Anne Waldman reading her poem 'Fast Speaking Woman,' although she is not seen on screen. A devotee of William Blake and Jack Kerouac, and a lecturer, along with Allen Ginsberg, at the newly opened Jack Kerouac School of Disembodied Poetics at the Buddhist-oriented Naropa University in Boulder, Colorado, she was a perfect addition to this bohemian, multi-artist road-show. She's a great poet too; there ought to have been more of her. Dylan reappears at the corner of Bay Street in Manhattan and wonders aloud which train takes him uptown. *KEEP THIS SCENE*

The next scene begins with a a tired-looking Sara Dylan in close-up wearing a white scarf and white hat. It is apparently cold. She really does have sad eyes, Dylan was right about that. This six-second scene is another example of the potential of the Dylan-Alk editing technique to confuse. *LEAVE ON CUTTING ROOM FLOOR*

Next, some of the main film crew, Larry Sloman, and a few hangers-on are show back in the diner. This is a 22-second scene that is, again, entirely superfluous. *LEAVE ON CUTTING ROOM FLOOR*

Of much more value is the next scene, in which Dylan and Guam play an arresting reinvention of 'It Ain't Me, Babe' – a performance captured on November 20 at the Harvard Square Theatre concert. Howard Alk is the cameraman here; the lens's gaze rests firmly on Dylan's face and doesn't cut away, even when Bob's bopping causes his head to leave the frame entirely. This creates a great sense of dramatic tension. Alk may have had his flaws as an editor, but he was an undeniably great cinematographer. After a little over two minutes, the camera cuts to a shot of the band playing away for all their worth; the tension is released. As Dylan delivers the line "A lover for your life and nothing more," the camera cuts to Ronee Blakley at the side of the stage, wearing her sky-blue beret. This is the type of semi-abstracted scene which nonetheless strengthens the underlying theme of Dylan/Renaldo's romantic travails. *KEEP THIS SCENE*

Next, we see The Woman In White leaving a mansion in a horse-drawn buggy. Is it Sara Dylan, Joan Baez, Ronee Blakley, or Ruth Tyrangiel? This is a 17-second scene. It is worth saying, here, that when Dylan was editing this footage, in 1977, he had recently broken up with wife Sara; he may not have been in the best state emotionally (or in terms of sobriety) to be left in a darkened room with scissors and endless cans of film. *LEAVE ON CUTTING ROOM FLOOR*

The scene cuts to a neatly-shaven Allen Ginsberg joining the troupe on the choruses of 'Knockin' On Heaven's Door,' which is being performed for the inmates of the Clinton Correctional Facility For Women (now known as the Edna Mahan Correctional Institution For Women), in Clinton, New Jersey. It is Pearl Harbor Day, 1975. The jail, for that is what it is, held over 1,000 women prisoners and a handful of males, including Rubin 'Hurricane' Carter. In a role reversal, McGuinn is singing lead and Dylan joining in at the chorus. A lithe Joan Baez dances gracefully with a handsome African-American male who is wearing a loud pink outfit, of all things. Various reports state that during this benefit concert, Joni Mitchell apparently lost faith in Rubin Carter's cause, mainly because the boxer preferred to talk to reporters and supporters during the show rather than listen to the music. Mitchell does not go over well with the incarcerated women and by the close of her first number she is attracting hisses and catcalls. Off camera, someone says to her, "When I get out, I'll come see ya." Mitchell replies, unconvincingly, "Yeah."

Roger McGuinn had noticed that Joni Mitchell was performing new material with which the audience was unfamiliar. "She wasn't doing any of her hits and I was thinking, 'Gee, Joni, it would be nice to see you go out there and turn them into hamburger.' She could have done that but she didn't," McGuinn recalls. "She had this attitude that I was copping out, sort of, by doing old material, but I had the attitude that *she* was kind of copping out. I told her that and she said, 'Well, I know I'm good,' and I said, 'Well, I know you know you are good, but I want to see it happen.'"[18] *KEEP THIS SCENE*

The diversion from *Renaldo & Clara's* core themes continues as Rubin Carter is interviewed by reporters. A rehearsal version of 'Hurricane' plays on the soundtrack. This is very confusing. It feels like another film has been edited into the middle of *Renaldo & Clara*. A good documentary filmmaker, like Howard Alk, should have been allowed to make a separate film about Rubin Carter. As it is, scenes of the imprisoned boxer feel awkward and out of place. *LEAVE ON CUTTING ROOM FLOOR*

On the same theme, we then cut to Howard Alk's footage of street interviews, shot outside the Apollo, in Harlem. The disaster movie *Earthquake* is playing there. One erudite young male interviewee expounds on the Carter case; a woman behind him conspicuously covers her face with a newspaper. Again, this seems like footage for another movie entirely; it feels as if two or three tracks from *The Freewheelin' Bob Dylan* have suddenly appeared in the middle of *Oh Mercy*. *LEAVE ON CUTTING ROOM FLOOR*

Rubin Carter is then seen in full press conference mode. One reporter asks: "Have you benefited at all from prison? Has it done anything positive for you?" We don't learn the answer. *LEAVE ON CUTTING ROOM FLOOR*

Then it's back to the Harlem streets, once again. Another man gives his views. "As long as blacks realize they are not part of the system ... they live in the system but are not part of it ... and will never be part of it ... then they'll never expect these things." Sadly, the man is talking about justice; perhaps he lived long enough to see Obama elected. Anyway, he is in the wrong movie; he should be in a documentary about Rubin 'Hurricane' Carter, the prison system, or social injustice. *LEAVE ON CUTTING ROOM FLOOR*

Now we are whisked back to the press conference for a quick Carter quote about meeting Dylan. Carter repeats the story of his sending his book *The Sixteenth*

Round to Dylan and how, when Dylan came to visit him in prison, the two men realized their race had nothing at all to do with their ability to communicate. *LEAVE ON CUTTING ROOM FLOOR*

Cut to the street outside the Apollo, again, where first a retired cop and then one Sister Roberta Smith air their views. The latter is an African-American Woman In White. She speaks of the prophecies of Daniel in The Old Testament. It's another hint, intentional or otherwise, of Dylan's incipient born again status. *LEAVE ON CUTTING ROOM FLOOR*

We're not done with Rubin Carter yet; the scene cuts back to the press conference. "I love America," the boxer states, categorically. He answers further questions as 'Hurricane' plays on the soundtrack. This should be a separate film, Bob! *LEAVE ON CUTTING ROOM FLOOR*

We're back in Harlem, now. An interviewer demands to know why Carter isn't a free man. The cameraman wouldn't be able to tell them. *LEAVE ON CUTTING ROOM FLOOR*

Next, we see Mama Frasca and Joan Baez, back at the Dream-Away. Baez is wearing the white wedding dress. She harmonizes on a song called 'God And Mama.' Mama then announces that she has her records available and that they are "… only one dollar and I got 'em for sale." Perhaps Rubin Carter will buy one. *LEAVE ON CUTTING ROOM FLOOR*

Cut to Dylan, Neuwirth, and entourage entering CBS Records' Manhattan lobby. They have come to see label chief Walter Yetnikoff. Security men demand that they turn off the camera. *LEAVE ON CUTTING ROOM FLOOR*

Dylan and friends take the elevator for what must be cinema's longest lift ride. They walk down the corridor to Yetnikoff's office and pressure him to hurry the release of the 'Hurricane' single. *LEAVE ON CUTTING ROOM FLOOR*

Then it's back to David Blue who is, inevitably, still playing pinball. This man cut some excellent records but he will probably be better remembered for his appearances in this film and for his presence on the jacket of the 1975 CBS issue of Dylan and The Band's *The Basement Tapes*. In this scene, Blue talks about Dylan's first album, discusses commercial folk music, The Kingston Trio, and how the ethnic folk music crowd "played old-time traditional music the way it was, and that was the line they stuck to." He recalls Dylan playing "harmonica for Fred Neil for a buck a night ... at the Café Wha? That was *the* gig." This scene signals a move away from the Rubin Carter saga. *KEEP THIS SCENE*

Next, we see Sara Dylan, as Clara, looking very tired and, again, sad-eyed, wearing a wig. She leaves a church and walks down an urban street in what looks like Montreal. Someone, possibly Sam Shepard, is heard reading a poem about a woman's eyes, and then Dylan is heard on the soundtrack doing a rough piano version of 'She Belongs To Me.' In his book, *Tangled*, author Glen Dundas suggests that Dylan's piano songs on the *Renaldo & Clara* soundtrack were captured in a Niagara Falls hotel room on November 14. The bluesy guitar fills heard against Dylan's piano assist in making this a fine version of the song. It is also a coherent, evocative piece of filmmaking. There should be more of it. It brings to mind an axiom of Truffaut's, about which Alk and Dylan would have been all too aware, which states that a person involved in any action whatsoever, no matter how mundane, is given extra resonance and gravitas simply by doing it on screen. Add to that Dylan and Bob Neuwirth's belief in the moment, in serendipity, and in letting the cards fall where they may, and you begin to understand both the intensity and the chaos of *Renaldo & Clara*. *KEEP THIS SCENE*

Cut to Sara Dylan/Clara speaking to Bob Neuwirth, who is in a car, which he then exits. He takes a rope and throws it over a stone wall. An initially unidentifiable man climbs down the wall wearing a baseball cap and prisoner's garb; he is obviously escaping jail. Neuwirth runs one way, the criminal the other. The latter then strolls along an urban street in his prison clothing and, lo and behold, he is revealed to be Harry Dean Stanton. One of the diner customers from an earlier scene is heard on the soundtrack talking about *his* time in prison. Is this a 'Hurricane' Carter reference? *LEAVE ON CUTTING ROOM FLOOR*

Now, we are with Dylan and Neuwirth on a train. Ohio Bob tells Minnesota Bob that he is being followed wherever he goes. A rather corpulent man with an earring and dark glasses is seen looking suspicious (and suspiciously *like* Howard Alk). *KEEP THIS SCENE*

Cut to a brief shot of snow-covered countryside. *LEAVE ON CUTTING ROOM FLOOR*

Harry Dean Stanton is now seen on the train, smoking nervously. Joan Baez is seen sleeping peacefully and the train pulls into a station. Is this what writers call contextualization? *KEEP THIS SCENE*

Cut to The Woman In White, in the horse-drawn carriage. Again it is impossible to tell if it is Joan Baez, Sara Dylan, Ronee Blakley, or none of the above. *KEEP THIS SCENE*

Next, we see Dylan and Guam performing 'It Takes A Lot To Laugh, It Takes A Train To Cry,' the ensemble swinging in a brilliant re-positioning of a classic Dylan composition. Mick Ronson's lead guitar is exemplary; he could have written a tutor book for advanced guitar which would have dazzled the world of music. Scarlet Rivera is shown searching for the stage. *KEEP THIS SCENE*

Now, Dylan and a dark-haired woman are seen standing in a train yard. Yawn. *LEAVE ON CUTTING ROOM FLOOR*

Cut to Ramblin' Jack Elliott, singing at the Other End. Folk singer Eric Anderson enters the shot. This is confusing, that's about all. Larry Sloman thinks this footage is from Mike Porco's birthday party/concert. Ramblin' Jack registered the confusion at the heart of the film, yet relished his role in it. "I enjoyed it even though I wouldn't expect anyone to understand anything about it, because it's inexplicable. I mean, there is no way to describe what was in anybody's mind as far as the construction or the editing of the film [is concerned]. It has very little to do with what we were doing on the Rolling Thunder Revue. It's not a documentary about our trip at all. It was just a whimsical kind of modern hippie operetta, on film. It was five hours long and they cut it down to two. I enjoy watching it 'cause I was in it, although I can't understand how anybody would get any enjoyment out of the thing; it just mystifies people."[19] *LEAVE ON CUTTING ROOM FLOOR*

Next, Harry Dean Stanton is seen in a small cabin, smooching with Joan Baez. Ramblin' Jack, as if to prove his above cinematic observations, enters and asks: "You just traded your horse for this woman?" Stanton replies: "He took the horse. He's got the horse and he's left the country." Stanton and Baez smile and laugh; Ramblin' Jack looks frustrated. Stanton and Baez return to their kissing. Jack is holding a rifle and looking like he could shoot the pair of them (or the cameraman). He repeats his original message. Stanton and Baez begin to sing in some faux gypsy accent; they clearly know it is all absurd. Ramblin' Jack repeats his question a third time: "You just traded your horse for this woman?" His character apparently does not rate Ms Baez very highly, but obviously values the horse.

In the 70s, more than 200 *Rock Around The World* radio shows were syndicated in over 160 major radio markets via the American RATW Radio Network. They were also broadcast via Armed Forces Radio to US servicemen around the globe. Two such broadcasts were devoted to the Rolling Thunder Revue. In the May 2 1976 broadcast (long before *Renaldo & Clara* had been seen by anyone other than Dylan and Alk), Joan Baez was already expressing her frustrations about the film. "The movie was Bob's baby. He wanted to be making a film, so while we were on the road, he was doing double-time. He was doing ... the concerts, and, in between, directing, producing, or whatever, for this insane movie.

"Nobody really had an inkling of what it was about ... and I got involved because I was there and because I wanted to. And it seemed to be, if you'd think up a scene and everybody liked it, you could go ahead and do it. I think I ended up in something like six or seven versions; [in] different parts, [as] different people, rather than playing myself. I was in a brothel scene with Sara, Bob's wife, and myself. Sara was laughing, she said we looked rather like mystical, powerful, life-force things ... but what were we doing? We were playing a bunch of whores!"[20] *LEAVE ON CUTTING ROOM FLOOR*

Cut to Ramblin' Jack, back on stage at the Other End, finishing his song. *LEAVE ON CUTTING ROOM FLOOR*

Next, Joan Baez comes out of the shower and wraps her hair in a white towel. She muses aloud about how she misses having somebody to talk to on the tour. She then handles a hair-dryer suggestively while commenting: "A guy ...

wouldn't follow anything. ... With a guy ... they're all screwed up." On the soundtrack, her voice is heard singing a wordless harmony at a rehearsal while the onscreen Baez reclines on the bed. *KEEP THIS SCENE*

Cut to Baez on stage, singing her song 'Diamonds And Rust' while bathed in a blue spotlight. *KEEP THIS SCENE*

Baez is in the next scene, too. She is in the lounge of the Dream-Away Lodge, once again wearing Mama's white wedding dress and looking radiant. She's talking to Dylan, who is sitting on the barstool next to her, smoking. They converse. Baez says: "What do you think it would have been like if we'd gotten married?" Dylan replies: "I don't know. I haven't changed that much. Have you?" Baez: "Maybe. ..." Mama Frasca enters and says: "Look at that beautiful girl there [Baez] ... she looks like a bride; she's gonna get married today." Dylan: "Yeah? To who?" *KEEP THIS SCENE*

Now, Dylan and Baez are walking through snow. Beside a barn, there is a white horse with a black mane (like Traveller, Robert E. Lee's horse, something Civil War buff Dylan would have known). This is clearly a reference to Ramblin' Jack's "You just traded your horse for this woman" statements in the earlier scene and is so out of sequence here that the effect is jarring. On the soundtrack, Dylan sings 'If You See Her, Say Hello' at the piano (another song apparently captured in his Niagara Falls hotel room), as a stable boy points out a cabin which, it transpires, belongs to Harry Dean Stanton. Dylan and Baez walk up some stairs toward this cabin. Dylan mounts and rides away on the horse. He looks surprisingly at home in the saddle. There is real potential in this footage but, again, it seems to have been edited by an addled resident of Phoenix House. *LEAVE ON CUTTING ROOM FLOOR*

Next up is a shot from the driver's seat of a Manhattan (or perhaps Montreal) horse carriage. An unidentifiable Woman In White is again the passenger. *LEAVE ON CUTTING ROOM FLOOR*

Baez is then seen talking to Harry Dean Stanton, in a Mexican accent, about the impossibility of making Renaldo happy. Is she now Clara? Discuss. *LEAVE ON CUTTING ROOM FLOOR*

Dylan and Guam now perform 'Romance In Durango.' Alk and Dylan many not have wanted a concert movie but moments like these are where the film truly comes alive.

L.A. Johnson, who supervised the music recording for *Renaldo & Clara* (and would go on to shoot many fine concert movies, including Martin Scorsese's *The Last Waltz*) recalls capturing the performance footage. "I remember those gigs which most of the music [scenes] came out of, at that theatre in Boston [The Boston Music Hall]. I remember, I was standing there, I had a video monitor and I could see the stage from a road truck. We were looking at those shows with wide-eyed amazement. When that band got together and snapped into it, they were fantastic. I think they left their egos somewhere else because it was just amazing. And then, off the stage, everybody was like a family, a traveling circus, which is what it really was."[21]

With Bob Neuwirth and Steven Soles strumming acoustics, and T Bone Burnett on electric, there were no fewer than three rhythm guitarists in the band, in addition to Dylan, with Mick Ronson on lead and David Mansfield on pedal steel (amongst other things). Having multiple onstage guitarists may be visually exciting but it's often a recipe for musical messiness and a perplexity of volume. However, the RTR came armed with a proficient road crew and the musicians were generally savvy enough not to outgun one another on stage. "We weren't playing at the kind of ear-splitting onstage volume that even Dylan did later on," says David Mansfield. "We had good monitors, good stage crew and mixers, and a lot of the show was acoustic. When it wasn't, when we did the big ensemble pieces, like 'Romance In Durango,' and there were 10,000 guitar players, with everybody playing at once, that was a very strange, almost Grateful Dead-like cacophony at times. But people were *listening* to each other. They were playing with small amps, and we could hear one another. It wasn't nearly as crazy as it would be if you tried to pick the same kind of music and put it into a big arena show today."[22] *KEEP THIS SCENE*

Sam Shepard is in the next scene. He is no longer a scriptwriter for *Renaldo & Clara* but has become one of its actors. He and Sara Dylan sit around a cheap-looking room in what appears to be the Dream-Away Lodge. They talk about their relationship. This feels like voyeur territory; their improvisations are not unlike those of a million other couples discussing their life together. Sara says she is lonely and would like to be asked to stay. Shepard replies: "I don't want to be responsible for you." Sara says: "I think I've heard this before." On the soundtrack, Sara's real life partner (probably, and not for long) is heard at the piano performing 'One Too Many Mornings,' a perfect accompaniment to a scene in which a couple seems to be splitting up. "I think you want me like some kind of amulet," says Sara." Shepard replies: "You got everything you need." Sara: "Yeah? But I don't got you." It is a tender moment and for someone who is not a professional actor, Sara Dylan is heartbreakingly convincing here. A dog then jumps up between Shepard and Dylan, one of several 'canine shots' which Alk and Dylan slot into the film for no sensible reason. Shepard was recommended to Dylan as a scriptwriter by Jacques Levy. He could also act, however, and his thespian experience kept him around even after it was decided to improvise all the action. *KEEP THIS SCENE*

Sara Dylan is then seen entering a phone booth and placing a call. We see the phone being picked up at CBS Records in New York City. It's Walter Yetnikoff, again. He says: "Yes, I'm with Bob." This is New Wave-style jump cutting. Dylan is indeed in Yetnikoff's office; he is seen staring at a poster for Dr Hook's LP, *Freakin' At The Freakers Ball*. Milton Glaser's iconic poster of a stylized Dylan, sporting psychedelic rainbow hair (as found in the packaging of *Bob Dylan's Greatest Hits*, released in 1967) is also seen on the office wall. Yetnikoff is speaking on the phone and turns down the volume on Willie Nelson's then new *Red Headed Stranger* album to better hear the conversation. After Yetnikoff finishes speaking, the scene cuts to a distant shot of Sara Dylan hanging up the phone in the booth. *LEAVE ON CUTTING ROOM FLOOR*

Sara Dylan, Joan Baez, and several others are then seen dressed as hookers (again). David Mansfield talks to the ladies who are sitting on a sofa. Allen Ginsberg attempts to come on to a woman – this is acting, after all. Mansfield nervously fingers his glass of red wine and bites a cookie, or cracker, as if taking Communion on a Sunday morning. Sara Dylan's bustier is straight from the pages of the Victoria Secrets catalog. Ginsberg appears shirtless, his arm around the waist of a beautiful but unidentifiable woman. He discusses a hooker's "ego protection bracelet" before the shot moves to Rob Stoner, kissing a brunette. Stoner: "Please come and fuck me, please come and fuck me" – possibly not the soft, poetic words a girl wants to hear. Stoner is then seen in an alley, smashing something. She obviously said no. *LEAVE ON CUTTING ROOM FLOOR*

Next, Stoner and Dylan sing/shout 'House Of The Rising Sun' in a hotel room (in Quebec City, on November 28, according to L.A. Johnson and Glen Dundas). The scene ends abruptly and Dylan shifts, on a dime, into pensive/enigmatic mood. *LEAVE ON CUTTING ROOM FLOOR*

Then we see Stoner, dressed as his hero, Gene Vincent, walking alone backstage while T Bone Burnett is heard telling a woman that he is not an insurance salesman, and that "I gotta go; I play music; I play it for people. ..." Stoner, replete with lit cigarette in mouth, makes a good rocker. T Bone says: "Don't get between me and my music because I'm telling you ... you'll have to go."

Burnett remembers the improvised scenes clearly. "Bob would say, 'You get on the bus and you go there with this person and do this' and then we would all go off and do that, not having any idea what we were supposed to be doing [laughs]." He doesn't remember a lot of formal direction from Dylan, Neuwirth, or anyone else. "Sam Shepard was directing as much as anybody; although there was no real direction. It was all improvised, all just sketched out. We would get a sketch: an angry clown meets a golfer at the seaside – or something like that. I played a scene where I was 'Buddy Holly'; I was with 'Maria Holly' on the bus, the day before I took off on my last tour, in February 1959. There were lots of things like that." Burnett was a reticent actor. "I asked them [Alk and Dylan] not to put me in it at all; I've never liked to be filmed. I'm probably in a couple of shots. I really did ask them to leave me out of it. Even when they were editing it, I would go by and say, 'Bob, please leave me out of this.'" [23] *LEAVE ON CUTTING ROOM FLOOR*

Next, Dylan's motorhome is seen cruising past Madison Square Garden, and then through a snow-covered, moonlit town. *LEAVE ON CUTTING ROOM FLOOR*

Cut to Dylan, in whiteface, singing 'One More Cup Of Coffee.' "I remember being backstage, talking with Ramblin' Jack," recalls Arlo Guthrie, who guested on a number of Rolling Thunder fall shows, "and Bob comes around the corner with some white make-up on his face. I asked him, 'What's that stuff doing on your face?' and he said, 'What face?'" [24]

On this version of 'One More Cup Of Coffee,' Scarlet Rivera is playing an electric violin (an acoustic violin with a pickup, to be exact) on Dylan's right, while Stoner is singing a high harmony. Rivera is then seen walking down a backstage corridor, holding a red rose; by now we're well aware that the rose and a brunette woman are two major metaphors in Dylan's cinematic world. The shot ends with Rivera taking the rose to Dylan in his dressing room (a symbolism that's not too tricky to interpret). *KEEP THIS SCENE*

Now, we're back at the Sea Crest Motel in North Falmouth, Massachusetts. It's October 29. Allen Ginsberg is reading 'Kaddish' to the elderly, Jewish, mahjong enthusiasts. At the line "A long black beard around the vagina" the screen is filled with the image of Mama, at The Dream-Away Lodge, massaging Ginsberg's head. This is the kind of jump-cut editing which really works and has an emotional, cinematic logic. Mama accurately reads Ginsberg's palm, reporting that: "You're a healthy man ... you have a good brain and a good heart, except that you let money go out from you."

In the first of the of the two-part *Rock Around The World* Rolling Thunder radio broadcast, Rob Stoner recalled the mahjong ladies. "They were having their tournament by day and having their banquets by night. One night, we decided that we would provide a little entertainment, and get it on film. So, this audience of about 200, middle-aged mahjong enthusiasts got to see Allen Ginsberg reading a poem and Bob Dylan doing a song on the piano, accompanied by Luther Rix on drums. Ramblin' Jack also did a song. It was quite a variety show for the old ladies. They were rather taken aback. They had no idea that Bob Dylan was going to appear."

It really was "quite a variety show." Ginsberg's 'Kaddish' is an extremely powerful poem, easily the equal of his more famous 'Howl.' By all reports, the Sea Crest Motel audience of Jewish matriarchs was deeply moved. Sam Shepard remembered the scene in his tour diary, *The Rolling Thunder Logbook*: "Allen approaches the podium, brown suit, papers in hand, looking for all the world like a latter-day Whitman with black trimmings instead of gray. He mounts a small stool and hunches into the microphone. The ladies smile charitably and Allen begins his piece. His long, terrifying, painful prayer to his mother. These are mothers too, but the needle's too close to the vein. The mothers go from patient acquiescence to giggled embarrassment to downright disgust as Allen keeps rolling away at them. His low rumbling sustained vowel sounds becoming more and more dirgelike and persistent. Dylan sits in the background, back against the wall, hat down over his eyes, listening stilly. Since I was raised a Protestant, there's something in the air here that I can't quite touch, but it feels close to being volcanic. Something of generations, of mothers, of being Jewish, of being raised Jewish, of *Kaddish*, of prayer, of America even, of poets and language, and least of all Dylan, who created in himself a character somehow outside the religion he was born into."[25]

Ginsberg's father, Louis, was also a poet and he wrote to his son to say how much he admired the courage of 'Kaddish,' although he specifically objected to the "bad taste" of the beard/vagina line quoted above. Back in the early 60s, renowned English poet and essayist Stephen Spender had heard a Berkeley, California recital of 'Kaddish' given by Ginsberg. Afterward, he criticized the poet for putting such intrusive personal intimacies into his poem. Spender, who had not written a poem for some years, would recant completely a few days later, stating that, after reflecting on 'Kaddish,' he was once again inspired to write poetry and that his new verses would be full of highly personal material.

The Sea Crest Motel 'Kaddish' footage *is* very moving. Once again it raises the question: why was Ginsberg not allowed on stage to read during the Rolling Thunder Revue tour? On the second leg, the following year, actor Dennis Hopper would be permitted on stage to read, of all things, Rudyard Kipling's 'If.'

Without question Ginsberg's cultural import dwarfed that of anyone on this gypsy roadshow, other than Dylan. His poetry reading might have been brilliant punctuation for the song-by-song revue format which Jacques Levy had to so carefully design. If Ginsberg had been allowed to deliver just one song, just one of his mournful, modal, elegies, it would have been unlike any of the more orthodox musical fare on offer and would have, by reflection, underscored Dylan's credentials as rock's premier poet. If 'Kaddish,' had been read, particularly in the smaller venues that characterized the tour's initial leg, it might easily have provided a time-stopping epiphany. A theatrical mind such as Jacques Levy would surely have been aware of this potential; so why was Ginsberg only seen on a crowded stage for the massed choral encore of 'This Land Is Your Land'?

Ginsberg had even written poems of real worth about Bob Dylan: 'Postcard To D____' (1972), 'Blue Gossip' (1973), and 'On Reading Dylan's Writing' (1973). He could have read one of those to a partisan audience and surely have been warmly embraced for it. "I remember sitting in the stands on numerous occasions with Allen Ginsberg [and thinking] what's he doing on the tour?" recalls Larry Sloman, who remembers Ginsberg finding another outlet for his literary talents. "He was going to be in *Renaldo & Clara* and he decided, in his own way, 'since I am going to be on the tour, I am going to create a newsletter,' and he put together a Rolling Thunder newsletter."[26]

Dylan's own opinion of Ginsberg, a man he called "holy" couldn't have been much higher. As he told biographer Robert Shelton: "What I mean by 'holy' is crossing all the boundaries of time and usefulness ... if we are talking now in terms of writers I think can be called poets, then Allen must be the best. I mean Allen's 'Kaddish,' not 'Howl.' Allen doesn't have to sing 'Kaddish,' man ... he just has to lay it down. He's the only poet that I know of. He's the only person I respect who writes, that just totally writes. He don't have to do nothing, man. Allen Ginsberg, he's just holy."[27]

So there we have it. A distinguished poet, a scholarly professor, a winner of the National Book Award, a member in good standing of the literary establishment, and a champion for the right of free expression and for social justice, reduced to churning out a semi-private newsletter for rock stars and their backing musicians. Missed opportunities don't come much more heartbreaking. *KEEP THIS SCENE; IN FACT, FIND MORE OF IT*

Ginsberg *is* a memorable presence in the movie, however. In the next scene, he and Dylan visit Jack Kerouac's grave at the Edson Cemetery, in Lowell, Massachusetts. This footage was shot on November 3. They have a guitar and a harmonium with them; soon a typically Ginsbergian song arises. The picaresque Kerouac, author of the Beat Generation's signature novel, *On The Road,* and a notable influence on Dylan's writing, had died in 1969, of cirrhosis bought on by years of sustained alcohol consumption. He was just 47. His grave bears his dates of birth and death and the epitaph *HE HONORED LIFE.* In fact, the man ended up a recluse in his mother's house. The redoubtable Gabrielle Kerouac prevented any visits from old literary chums such as Ginsberg or William Burroughs, in a vain attempt to help her son control his drinking. Incredibly, in his last years, the free-spirited, libertarian Kerouac's politics had shifted to the reactionary right. Ginsberg reads a portion of Kerouac's 'Mexico City Blues' in honor of his old companion. It's a moving scene and one which sustains the emotional piquancy of the earlier shots of Ginsberg's poetry reading.

At the graveside, Ginsberg talks about the last resting places of other poets. He says to Dylan: "You know what's written on Keats's grave? 'Here lies one whose name was writ in water.'" Dylan asks Ginsberg where Keats is interred: "He's buried in a beautiful cemetery in Rome; the American Cemetery, in a pyramid, next to Shelley," he replies. (In fact, Keats and Shelley both lie in Rome's beautiful Cimitero Acattolico, or non-Catholic Cemetery, often referred to as the Englishmen's Cemetery. The American Cemetery, while certainly noteworthy, is in Nettuno, south of the city, and is the final resting place for US World War II combat casualties, not English Romantic poets.)

Ginsberg and Dylan then discuss Kerouac's work and are soon engrossed in a conversation about what they they've both been reading of late. They sound like two university professors comparing how they teach English Literature to graduate students. The well-versed Ginsberg is interesting to listen to. He says of Kerouac: "He quit football because he wanted to study Shakespeare," and begins another monologue about the graves of great writer's he has seen. Dylan confesses to having visited the graves of Chekhov and Victor Hugo. They are silent for a bit, looking down at Kerouac's last resting place. Ginsberg inquires of Dylan: "This is what is going to happen to you?" Dylan is thoughtful and then replies: "No ... I wanna be buried in an unmarked grave." *KEEP THIS SCENE; IN FACT, FIND MORE OF IT*

A man, looking suspiciously like Howard Alk, is then seen walking down a hotel corridor with a pretty girl at his side. He is holding what appears to be a small Klieg light; Ginsberg is heard chanting "The skull is ugly." (The possessor of this unsightly cranium is never made clear.) Ronee Blakley is shown helping to shave off Ginsberg's beard. None of it makes any sense. Dylan's creative obsession with having "no sense of time," something taught him by Norman Raeben in those New York City painting classes 18 months earlier, had paid great artistic dividends on *Blood On The Tracks* but could create chaos and confusion in *Renaldo & Clara*. As Dylan told *Rolling Stone's* Jonathan Cott: "When I started doing it [the painting lessons], the first album I made was *Blood On The Tracks*. Everybody agrees that that was pretty different, and what's different about it is that there's a code in the lyrics and also there's no sense of time. There's no respect for it: you've got yesterday, today and tomorrow all in the same room, and there's very little that you can't imagine not happening."[28]

A little later in the same interview, Dylan states: "From that point I went on to *Desire*, which I wrote with Jacques Levy. And I don't remember who wrote what. And then I disappeared for a while. Went on the Rolling Thunder tour, made *Renaldo & Clara* in which I also used that quality of no-time. And I believe that concept of creation is more real and more true than that which does have time."

While it may have worked in lyrics and on vinyl, Dylan's penchant for temporal disordering simply didn't work on celluloid. The likes of François Truffaut, Jean-Luc Godard, and Jacques Rivette certainly changed cinema and are understandably admired for their hand-held camerawork, improvised location shooting, and, most importantly for Dylan, time-manipulating editing techniques; but theirs was a language learned after years of filmmaking and one they articulated with authority. Dylan, well read and au fait with European cinema as he may have been, was a greenhorn filmmaker. Howard Alk's oft-repeated comment that *Renaldo & Clara* "broke the grammar of film" is absurd. There's a parallel, here, with Dylan's musical career. His songwriting and singing style in the mid 60s were so influential that he launched legion imitators, from P.F. Sloan and Donovan to David Blue. While they each got the façade right and used elements of Dylan's technique and style, none of their recordings succeeded in making a similar artistic impact. *LEAVE ON CUTTING ROOM FLOOR*

We then cut to the band on stage, led by Roger McGuinn playing the unmistakable, chiming introduction to The Byrds' classic 'Eight Miles High.' When McGuinn starts to sing, Alk and Dylan cut, for no good reason, straight to the instrumental passage. The band is really cooking, here; you would have felt it in your cinema seat. Joan Baez takes to the stage to dance during this instrumental section. She busts some moves that aren't too far from Madonna in her 80s pomp (although the equally limber Baez remains contrastingly clothed). *KEEP THIS SCENE*

Cut to McGuinn singing a rapid-paced 'Chestnut Mare.' Although he co-wrote other Byrds songs with Levy, including 'All The Things,' 'Just A Season,' 'Kathleen's Song,' and 'I Wanna Grow Up To Be A Politician,' 'Chestnut Mare' was the primary motivation for Dylan writing with Levy and was, therefore, an apposite choice for the Levy-directed, Dylan-starring Rolling Thunder Revue. Howard Alk is obviously the main cameraman here, as McGuinn's face is held in characteristic, close-up focus as he sings into the mic. *KEEP THIS SCENE*

Next, Sara Dylan (again in a wig) is seen backstage talking with husband Bob as he absent-mindedly picks a guitar. This scene arrives a good three hours into the long edit of the movie and yet is the first time we clearly see Renaldo and this particular and most intriguing Clara together. *KEEP THIS SCENE*

Then we're back in the bordello. We hear women's dialog: first a question, "What was the problem?" then a reply, "I was in love with him." Baez and Sara are again dressed as whores (according to Joan), or mystical, powerful, life-force things (according to Sara). Baez is positively glowing and smiles to someone off screen; it's a huge, happy grin, as if she just cannot help enjoying herself or, perhaps, the absurdity of her situation. A close-up of four roses follows. It's a recurring motif, for sure, but also a possible early example of product placement (Four Roses whiskey). Baez, in the role of The Woman In White, says: "Did you ever have another name?" Sara Dylan's reply is drowned out by piano playing on the soundtrack. Baez: "That's very interesting ... because there was one time ... I was involved with somebody ... I think perhaps it was possible he was involved with you." Baez remains The Woman In White for the remainder of the film; identities are finally starting to come into focus. What a great film this could have been if Dylan had kept the non-concert footage just to scenes depicting this intriguing love triangle. *KEEP THIS SCENE*

We then get another shot of Baez, as The Woman In White, in a horse-drawn carriage. She is holding the inevitable rose. The carriage stops; she gets down from it and enters a building. She walks upstairs and knocks on a door. Clara answers. The Woman In White asks: "Is Renaldo in there?" She is let in. Renaldo stops playing guitar and looks speechless. "Who is she?" Clara demands as she puts her arms possessively around Renaldo. *KEEP THIS SCENE*

Cut to Dylan on stage, singing 'Sara.' It's another of Alk's typical extended close-ups. The song has different lyrics form the *Desire* version: "You fought for my soul against the odds / I too young to know you were doing it right / And you did it with strength that belonged to the gods." A beaming Ronee Blakley is shown putting her arms around bassist Rob Stoner at the end of the song. *KEEP THIS SCENE*

Suddenly we're back to the Toronto hotel lobby, where television announcer Sheila Shotton is trying to identify 'the real' Bob Dylan. She is interviewing Ronnie Hawkins, who is, of course, *playing* Bob Dylan. Ronee Blakley enters the lobby and is interviewed as Mrs. Dylan *KEEP THIS SCENE*

Next, we're back to David Blue and his interminable pinball. (He must be a

Grand Master at it by now. He should have been in *Tommy*.) He's still musing about Dylan (or, perhaps, Renaldo): "He lives like a human being. He has a wife, a family … you know what I mean? It's ridiculous." *LEAVE ON CUTTING ROOM FLOOR*

We then return to Dylan, as Renaldo, and Sara, as Clara, in their hotel room; Baez is outside the door. The intimacy is building for the camera and the audience. In his interviews, Dylan is always rigorous in his denial of personal interpretations of his work, always fighting to cover up his past and his private life; yet, sometimes in his art, whether it be *Blood On The Tracks*, the song 'Ballad In Plain D,' much of *Desire*, or the best footage of the Dylan/Sara/Baez triangle in *Renaldo & Clara*, he will readily express some of the rawest, most personal intimacies any postwar popular artist has placed before the public.

With undeniable tension mounting, The Woman In White enters the room where Renaldo has Clara wrapped in his arms. How odd, and how difficult, this scene must have been for at least two of its protagonists. Baez watches the lovers and then turns her back. On the soundtrack, Baez and Dylan are heard singing a duet, 'The Water Is Wide,' a tender British folk ballad, thought to date back to at least the 1600s, about lost and impossible love. Clara asks: "Who *is* this lady?" Renaldo turns to Baez and says: "Sit right here, I was getting up anyway." Clara asks why The Woman In White is taking notes like a cub reporter. Renaldo/Dylan is wearing dark trousers and a waistcoat with no shirt. He is pale and without hair on his chest. He clearly does not work out at a gym and seems, in this poorly-focused shot, like he could be David Mansfield's older brother. Baez sits on the mattress where Renaldo has just stopped romancing with Clara. This is obviously a key scene to filmmaker Dylan. The Woman In White reads aloud a note in her hand: "I love you. Meet me in the appointed place at twilight, my darling." Renaldo, in the quick-thinking mode of unfaithful husbands the world over, turns to Sara/Clara as the seemingly damning note is being read and shrugs. The Woman In White continues to read the note as Clara throws her arms around Renaldo, pulling him close to her breast. As The Woman In White leaves, Clara delivers a stinging line to her onscreen romantic rival: "Are you sure you have the right room?" Bette Davis would've killed to have said that in a film, and Dalton Trumbo would've been proud to have penned such a line. Clara asks Renaldo if he has been lying to her. "I hate liars," she says. Proving Dalton Trumbo didn't actually write this screenplay, Renaldo looks blank and answers: "Me, too." 'The Water Is Wide' (recorded November 11, at the Palace Theatre in Waterbury, Connecticut) continues on the soundtrack, its lyrics seeming to comment on the action: "But love grows old and waxes cold / And fades away like morning dew."

It is entirely possible the Dylan/Sara/Baez circle of romance is Dylan's onscreen attempt at the brutal, autobiographical honesty heard on *Blood On The Tracks*, or in individual compositions such as 'Sara' and 'Wedding Song.' *Renaldo & Clara* offers the public spectacle of a surprisingly shy, habitually guarded artist, suddenly exposing his previously fortified private life in raw cinematic depictions of love and romance. The shy Mr R. A. Zimmerman of Minnesota *must* realize his onscreen depiction of lovesick Renaldo, and his wife's portrayal of Clara (and her periodic appearance as The Woman In White) – while a real life old flame (Baez) plays, well, an old flame – will undoubtedly cause his faithful audience to regard the movie as a *roman à clef*; a page right out of Dylan's life story suddenly read aloud. Dylan seems to have been fine with this as the backbone of his grand cinematic statement, although it must have been awkward for his wife and genuinely painful for Baez. Can this be the same Dylan who so frequently grows angry at reviews or critiques that claim his work reveals elements of his personal life? Why point your faithful followers to a particular pool of water if you are not going to allow them to drink? *KEEP THIS SCENE*

Again trying to manipulate time, Dylan the filmmaker then cuts back to footage of Dylan the singer, and Ginsberg the poet, in the Edson Cemetery in Lowell, beside Kerouac's grave. A professorial Ginsberg discourses about Christ carrying his own cross, as well as translating certain Latin and French phrases inscribed on various graves close to Kerouac's. It has to be said, the grimy old mill town of Lowell has one hell of a graveyard. *KEEP THIS SCENE*

Now, we're back in the hotel room with Renaldo, Clara, and The Woman In White. The two women are bonding; they begin to question Renaldo. Clara, quite understandably, demands of him: "Do you love her?" Renaldo replies: "Do I love you like I love her? No." He turns to The Woman In White and says: "Do I love you like I love her? No." The master of the evasive yet seemingly honest answer has all the coals burning in his furnace and is running on full power. *KEEP THIS SCENE*

While we're still digesting this intrigue, Guam are shown performing 'Catfish,' Dylan's ode to the late New York Yankee pitcher Jim 'Catfish' Hunter, then in the prime of his career. Rob Stoner takes the lead vocal and Mick Ronson plays guitar like he has four hands – the word virtuoso doesn't begin to describe his playing. Nonetheless, if Dylan had really rated this song he would not have given it away. A song about a baseball star adds nothing to any of the film's themes, least of all the love triangle it has just interrupted. *LEAVE ON CUTTING ROOM FLOOR*

Fortunately, we then return to the hotel room where an exasperated Woman In White asks Dylan/Renaldo: "What on earth are you up to?" He replies: "Well … it's hard to … I couldn't explain it to you in a minute." She responds: "You never did. Nobody ever asks." Then Clara pitches in: "They ask but he never explains. He never gives straight answers." Renaldo: "What is a straight answer? No one's ever given me a straight answer." At this, The Woman In White appears to give up. Renaldo: "Evasiveness is all in the mind. Truth is on many levels." At this, perhaps the quintessential Dylan aphorism, the women really begin to join forces, talking back and forth and nodding affirmatively toward one another. Dylan is heard in the background singing his own composition 'Patty's Gone To Laredo.' Not copyrighted by Dylan until December 1977, it sounds a fine song; it's a shame it's hidden away like this on a soundtrack, partly obscured by dialog. Some Dylanologists source its recording to a Quebec hotel piano session in mid-November, but it sounds like someone is tapping along on a drum kit, which makes that seem unlikely. If those are drums, then surely it originates from the New York City SIR rehearsals, back in October. *KEEP THIS SCENE*

Cut to shots of a train transporting Rolling Thunder band-members through snow-covered New England countryside. Roger McGuinn is seen talking into an astonishingly large mobile telephone. The head Byrd and gadget freak obtained his first mobile phone in 1969, it came housed in a capacious briefcase containing a transmitting and receiving system. That same year, the technophile McGuinn also had a CB radio installed on his motorcycle. *LEAVE ON CUTTING ROOM FLOOR*

The scene then cuts back in the bordello. Allen Ginsberg's character confesses that he originally wanted to be: "A labor leader, saving the suffering masses."

This is quite true, in fact. The young Allen Ginsberg did indeed seek to become a lawyer representing labor unions. For all that, this scene does nothing but dilute the burgeoning Renaldo/Clara/Woman In White dynamic. *LEAVE ON CUTTING ROOM FLOOR*

Cut to Rob Stoner in the role of 50s rocker Gene Vincent. He complains to the camera. "They took everything from cats like me. I've made a million and I can spend a million, and I can do it again." Joan Baez is seen on stage singing Leonard Cohen's 'Suzanne.' *LEAVE ON CUTTING ROOM FLOOR*

We're back in the tense hotel room, yet again. The Woman In White makes to leave. What is deadly serious to filmmaker/actor Bob Dylan seems less so to Joan Baez; she starts to laugh as she exits the room. She turns her face to the floor; it's a wry, human moment. Then she drops her rose; Renaldo picks it up and hands it to her as she departs. Again, the symbolism is not difficult to interpret. He has made his choice. *KEEP THIS SCENE*

The theme is carried over elegantly and (for once) logically into the next scene, with Dylan and Baez on stage, duetting on Johnny Ace's 'Never Let Me Go,' the Memphis rhythm & blues singer's final Duke Records single, from 1954, released just before he'd accidentally shot himself dead while playing with a handgun, backstage at a Christmas night concert in Houston. Alk's super-tight close-up at one point shows only the microphone and the eyes, noses, and mouths of the two singers. It's a powerful, intimate shot which seems to comment on the hotel scene witnessed beforehand. *KEEP THIS SCENE*

Now, we see The Woman In White leaving the hotel room. Renaldo is seen reading a newspaper review of the last Rolling Thunder show which includes a photo of Dylan and Baez. Clara says: "Look at her, she's cold, she's frigid, just look at her, for Christ's sake … she's probably barren." A defensive Renaldo replies: "You don't even know her." Clara responds: "I know her; we're like sisters." In the hallway outside, two other lovers start to embrace and kiss. In the hotel room, Renaldo puts on theatrical whiteface make-up. A piano version of 'Sad-Eyed Lady Of The Lowlands,' Dylan's hymn to his wife, is heard on the soundtrack. It would be tough for any artist but Dylan to deny this is autobiographical; Dylan has the ability to deny anything and make it plausible. *KEEP THIS SCENE*

Cut to Larry Sloman and others chatting away in a diner. They are discussing 'the movement' (meaning the leftwing political agenda as galvanized by civil rights and anti-Vietnam War protest). Nothing substantial is actually vouchsafed, however, and, as Dylan once had it, nothing is revealed. *LEAVE ON CUTTING ROOM FLOOR*

Next, we see Dylan performing 'Tangled Up In Blue.' Alk's camera is again static as it frames Dylan at the microphone. If the singer's face leaves this close-up field then it leaves the screen entirely; there is no effort to track Dylan's movements. The lyrics of the song have been changed from the familiar *Blood On The Tracks* cut (and are not the same as those found on the 1984 version captured for the *Real Live* album). With whiteface make-up slapped on and the by now familiar wide-brimmed hat in place, Dylan projects undiluted intensity. The performance was recorded at the Boston Music Hall on November 21, during the evening show. The Rolling Thunder Revue would occasionally play additional matinee shows. The ability to sustain a pair of four-hour performances in one day is a reflection of the musicians' relative youth (Dylan, for example, was then 34, halfway to his 35th birthday) not to mention, perhaps, their daily stimulant intake. *KEEP THIS SCENE*

We then cut to Ginsberg and Dylan, back in Lowell. They have left the Edson Cemetery, and Dylan stroll through a nearby playground. The body language and the tone of the conversation signify that the poet is the teacher here; almost a father figure, and the singer is his curious, precocious student. Ginsberg biographer Barry Miles confirms that, while Dylan definitely viewed Ginsberg as a wise counselor, he was also capable of treating the poet's learning and enthusiasm too casually. "Sometimes Allen would make good suggestions that were ignored or not credited. He sometimes complained to me about it. I know there were endless complications over the sleeve notes [which Ginsberg wrote] for *Desire*, for example. But yes, Dylan often said that Allen was a mentor, a teacher, and that all of the Beats were."[29] Ginsberg asks the schoolchildren if they believe in God. They chorus "Yeah!" with some gusto. Ginsberg asks what God looks like. A debate starts. Not one kid uses bad language. Off camera, somebody who sounds an awful lot like Bob Neuwirth asks: "Does He play guitar?" *KEEP THIS SCENE*

In a hotel ballroom Ginsberg dances with his old friend Denise Mercedes. His moves make him look like R.E.M.'s Michael Stipe in full party flight, and his enthusiasm for the terpsichorean is obvious. He changes partners and dances with Claudia Carr before reading more of 'Kaddish' over the soundtrack's softly played piano. This indicates that, while the footage may be from any hotel ballroom, the music is certainly from the Sea Crest Motel, on October 29. Ginsberg's reading is beautiful. This is not only a gifted poet, this is a man who clearly loved, and is still mourning, his mother. The piano picks up the tempo. The song is listed in the movie's end credits as 'Hollywood Waltz' but is mercifully not The Eagles' selection of that name. Ginsberg's hirsute appearance and charmingly awkward, yet merry movements suggest a dancing bear. He looks incredibly contented. *KEEP THIS SCENE*

Next, we're in the men's room of a nondescript train station; not the most promising beginning to a movie scene. While washing his hands, Bob Neuwirth spies some coin-operated weighing scales. Not even Neuwirth is hip enough to make this interesting. He and Dylan wait in line to buy tickets. Neuwirth smokes and offers a cigarette to yet another of the movie's many raven-haired beauties, Helena Kallianiotes. After three hours plus of *Renaldo & Clara* it is becoming evident how shy Dylan really is and, equally, how provocative Neuwirth is; a man who wouldn't balk at asking challenging questions of a blank wall or an angry Mafia don. He is fearless. What the neat ticket saleslady must think when confronted by a camera crew, Dylan, Neuwirth, and a brunette beauty in a low-cut blouse is not hard to guess. *LEAVE ON CUTTING ROOM FLOOR*

Suddenly, we're in an unexplained college dormitory hallway; two young men are talking while reading a Rolling Thunder Revue concert flyer when a Dave Myers camera films them in natural light. The two students are asked about their dreams by a voice off camera. The young student on camera cannot remember what he dreamt the previous evening. *LEAVE ON CUTTING ROOM FLOOR*

Dylan and Guam then perform 'Just Like A Woman' (a performance captured at Harvard Square Theatre, on November 20). Dylan's voice is sandpaper harsh; he's been on the road for a while now. Ronee Blakley sings backup; she sounds fine and looks great, admirably filling the role Emmylou Harris had so adeptly played on *Desire*. Scarlet Rivera's electrified violin lends an almost Eastern European tint to the song, effectively bringing to Dylan's music the same kind of swirling, incense-like quality once provided by the Lowery organ parts of The Band's Garth Hudson, coloring and complimenting the music while keeping well out of the way of Dylan's lead vocal melody. T Bone Burnett's guitar has been put through a phase-shifter effect; it was *the* hip sound in 1975, although today it's completely passé. The band then slip straight into 'Knockin' On Heaven's Door,' the coda of which has a McGuinn 12-string part played against Rivera's violin and Mansfield's pedal steel; it is, perhaps, the very definition of musical beauty. McGuinn sings the chorus to 'Knockin' On Heaven's Door' at Dylan's mic. Dylan's lead vocal on the verses is rough and irate sounding, quite a contrast to the trilling McGuinn whose voice is incapable of expressing anger. *KEEP THIS SCENE*

Next, we see Dylan walking off stage and down a hall toward a door marked *private*. *KEEP THIS SCENE*

Cut to Baez's dressing room where an unidentified, bearded man is telling her how wonderful it was to hear her voice upon entering the auditorium. Another man nods in earnest agreement. The scene is straight out of the 1991 backstage documentary *In Bed With Madonna* (known as *Madonna: Truth Or Dare* in more prudish countries). *KEEP THIS SCENE*

Cut to Dylan lying on the middle of a dressing room floor rug, his white shirt partially opened. He looks quite exhausted as he stares at the ceiling. The camera pans around him and down to his riding boots. He's akin to a character form the pages of Victor Hugo or Alexandre Dumas. In fact, Dylan's prone position makes him appear defeated, as if musketeer d'Artagnan has just run him through at the conclusion of an epic sword fight and he is now awaiting death. *LEAVE ON CUTTING ROOM FLOOR*

Back at the Sea Crest Motel, crooner Hal Frazier performs a swinging, jazzy version of the pop song 'In The Morning.' It's a performance criticized and dismissed in just about every discussion or essay about *Renaldo & Clara*. Certainly, as soon as Frazier and his band kick into the intro, it's obvious we're in a different musical realm from 'One More Cup Of Coffee' or 'Romance In Durango.' Frazier's approach is about as far from rock music as it's possible to be. Unlike Dylan, Frazier has a fine, formal, no-doubt coached voice. His task is to deliver an up-tempo, saloon rendition in the Tony Bennett/Frank Sinatra/Johnny Mathis lounge style. That Frazier and his musical crew are *not* bohemians, Beats, or rockers, is possibly the very reason they and this song was chosen by Alk and Dylan to end the film.

The film's critics tend to mock the lyrics of 'In The Morning.' Admittedly, lines such as "Watching rainbows play on sunlight" and "Building castles in the shifting sands," will not be easily confused with the symbol-strewn stanzas of 'Gates Of Eden' or 'Sad-Eyed Lady Of The Lowlands.' For all that, Dylan's appreciation of saloon music, the Great American Songbook, and all kinds of other music, shouldn't be underestimated. Anyone who has enjoyed his eclectic *Theme Time Radio Hour* shows will vouch for that. Moreover, the poetic composer of 'Gates Of Eden' was the same guy who turned up to perform at the Frank Sinatra 80th Birthday Tribute, held at LA's Shrine Auditorium in November 1995, where he sang a respectful, rather moving 'Restless Farewell' in honor of Ol' Blue Eyes. As far back as 1965, Dylan was putting on interviewers and referring to himself as "a song and dance man." Who is to say he was kidding, completely? Perhaps he really does consider himself to be some kind of all-round entertainer; one who sings, writes, and makes movies, too. And let's not forget that in late 2009, Dylan released *Christmas In The Heart*, an album of family-friendly, traditional seasonal favorites. On second thoughts, perhaps we should forget it.

To give the song its due, 'In The Morning' is, in fact, very well-crafted. It was written by Barry Gibb in early 1963 and was originally titled 'In The Morning Of My Life.' The Bee Gees' first released it for the Australian label Festival Records, before they'd returned to Britain and enjoyed their first wave of Beatles-like success. A later version appeared in 1971, as part of the soundtrack to a film called *Melody*. A favorite of the tender gender, the song's lyric contains a subtle message of empowerment. No surprise, then, that it has been recorded by commanding female singers such as Nina Simone, Mary Lynch Gray, Jennifer Warnes, and Lulu, amongst others. Hal Frazier's version is audibly based on Nina Simone's, released on her 1968 RCA album, *Nuff Said!*

This is the very same Hal Frazier who cut the legendary Northern soul classic 'After Closing Time' for Reprise Records. After several early singles in the soul genre, producer Jimmy Bowen became convinced that Frazier was more of a lounge singer than a rhythm & blues man, and by 1972, Frazier was a regular on the Las Vegas circuit, opening for Don Rickles, Joey Bishop, and various other Rat Pack associates. He made frequent appearances on national television in the USA on such institutions as Johnny Carson's *The Tonight Show* and has enjoyed a lengthy and successful career in what the Brits call 'cabaret.' Hal Frazier has nothing to apologize about, and if any of Dylan's fans were as au fait with saloon singing as is the writer of such quasi lounge ballads as 'Million Miles' and 'Make You Feel My Love,' then they would know this.

As Frazier starts to wind his song up, some of the lengthiest, and most absurd, film credits since *Monty Python & the Holy Grail* begin to scroll across the screen. T Bone Burnett as The Inner Voice, Harry Dean Stanton as Lafkezio, and so on. Roberta Flack gets a credit because she was a late substitute for Aretha Franklin who could not make the concert for the inmates of the Clinton Correctional Facility For Women in New Jersey. Ms Flack's screen credit reads Guest Artist, but try and spot her in the film. It should have read Needle In Haystack. *KEEP THIS SCENE*

With that, the four confusing, beguiling, aggravating, and awe-inspiring hours of *Renaldo & Clara* draw to a close. Now the lights are back on, it's time to consider the post-mortems. Author Michael Gray sets the tone for one school of critical thought, arguing that Dylan's "grand failure" bridges a gap in American cultural history between the Beats and the postmodern movement. Paul Williams adored the movie and wrote that it "reinvents film." But these are both Dylan aficionados who have the patience to view a four-hour film several times. Not all of Dylan's devotees were that tolerant. In fact, even some of Dylan's friends took a different view of *Renaldo & Clara*, even if they happened to appear in it. Ronnie Hawkins was one. "I took Kris Kristofferson down to the premier when I was in California. Well, you know Kris, he don't say nothing about anything. He just said, 'Man, that's different.' It *was* different."

David Mansfield was involved from the first day of rehearsals at SIR in New York City, in October 1975, to the last Rolling Thunder gig, in Salt Lake City, in the early summer of 1976. He is able to evaluate *Renaldo & Clara* from both the inside and from a fan's perspective. "Part of my take on it was informed by getting to know Neuwirth and his sort of abstract expressionist view of life: that art is personal and there's no explaining; there is no theory behind it. There is no dividing line behind the disciplines … there are no disciplines. So it fitted in with that kind of creative rationale, in a funny way. It didn't feel like there was some grand intention behind it. It did not feel like we were making a movie with a capital M." When Mansfield finally sat down to watch *Renaldo & Clara* he found himself quite astonished. "I didn't see it until the (1978 Dylan) big band tour [which he played on] was long past. So, just the shock! I couldn't be objective in any way about it. I could see that if one person decided to, they could make a wonderful 90-minute concert film out of it. I had friends who went [to see the film] and found it totally and utterly incomprehensible!"[30]

Scarlet Rivera feels *Renaldo & Clara* wasn't given its due. "The reviews were quite bad and I found that shocking because what all of the critics wanted more than anything … [were] back of the dressing room scenes, insight into what's going on with Dylan in his life, not on stage; so that's what he gave. So I was quite shocked that it was not well received … I thought it was not a representation, but an exploration of our time together with all the different characters we had on stage with us and were on the road with us." [31]

In a 1978 interview, *Rolling Stone's* Jonathan Cott didn't hold back when reminding Dylan that after seeing the film several writers had gone out of their way to call the rookie director "presumptuous, pretentious, and egocentric." In response, Dylan said: "These people probably don't like to eat what I like to eat; they probably don't like the same things I like, or the same people. Look, just one time I'd like to see any one of those assholes try and do what I do." [32]

Variety's Steven Gaydos compared Dylan to Walt Whitman. "I think of Dylan as the Whitman of our time. In the year 2050, when we are all long gone and people are looking at Dylan's work, how are they going to perceive *Renaldo & Clara*? I think they are going to say, 'If Walt Whitman had a movie camera, this is the film he would have made.' He would have made a movie just like *Renaldo & Clara;* it's Dylan's 'I Sing The Body Electric.'" [33]

I sing the body electric, / The armies of those I love engirth me and I engirth them, / They will not let me off till I go with them, respond to them, / And discorrupt them, and charge them full with the charge of the soul.

Was it doubted that those who corrupt their own bodies conceal themselves? / And if those who defile the living are as bad as they who defile the dead? / And if the body does not do fully as much as the soul? / And if the body were not the soul, what is the soul?
Walt Whitman, "I Sing The Body Electric" (first stanza), *Leaves Of Grass* (1855)

Filmmaker and erstwhile Dylan documenter D. A. Pennebaker saw both good and bad in *Renaldo & Clara*. "I sensed that all the way through … what he

[Dylan] had was this wonderful idea happening, and the [Rolling Thunder] tour itself ... full of all kinds of dramatic possibilities in his own life, and the idea of using fictional people. I think *all* of that is terrific. What he never had is a sense of what the story was going to be about. In other words, what he was going to settle for to release. I don't think he [Dylan] should have released two lengths. Those are important decisions, maybe more important than decisions made within the film of what to shoot, what kind of camera work or anything else. What you finally put out there is just like his songs: the song is the song. But in film, he's not bringing that kind of spiritual solvency, that determination of what he knows is right."[34]

L.A. Johnson has no problem with musicians seeking, as Dylan had done, to broaden their creative ambit. "I am fortunate to work with a lot of creative people and I find that musicians, in a way, are less risk adverse [than most]. They're not lawyers. Risk is what they do. They write a song, they speak from their soul; they don't speak from their pocket book, necessarily. I think Bob is a beatnik, he is not a hippy; he comes from the Beat Generation. He comes from a different time and place and I think that is why he liked [cameraman] David Myers, because David was from the Beat Generation in San Francisco and knew [Beat poet Lawrence] Ferlinghetti and all these people who came out of that. I think Bob brought that knowledge of 50s film noir and *cinéma vérité* from French filmmaking. He saw it, understood it, and thought that that was a creative channel for him. Now, whether musicians can do this kind of thing well or not, that is up to the audience, but in terms of Bob's ability to express his creativity, cinematically, with a group of people, I think he had it all going on. He probably would have been better off staying out of the editing room. That's where it all gets confusing and hazy. I think it would be fun for Bob to make another version of the Rolling Thunder tour, take the same footage and go back with a different perspective and re-cut it."[35]

The last thing seen on screen in *Renaldo & Clara* as the credits stop and the film ends is the following statement: "The persons and events in this film are fictitious; their relationship to other persons and events is unintentional."

T Bone Burnett, in 2009: "Sam Shepard was there in the beginning. He was writing some incredible stuff, and then for some reason he wasn't doing it any more. I have never seen *Renaldo & Clara*. Have you ever seen it?"[36]

Question: "Arlo, what were your thoughts when you finally saw *Renaldo & Clara*?" Arlo Guthrie, also speaking in 2009: "I haven't seen the film yet."[37]

CHAPTER 6
CLEARWATER, FLORIDA: THE NBC NETWORK TELEVISION SPECIAL

I t should have been so good; it certainly started that way. Following almost a week of rehearsals at Clearwater's architecturally elaborate Bellevue Biltmore Hotel (attended by innumerable employees, most of whom almost certainly should have been elsewhere changing sheets and restocking mini-bars) and a sprinkling of mid-Florida shows, filming for a Dylan in-concert television show would take place on April 22 1976, in the Bellevue Biltmore's elegant Starlight Ballroom. This was a lovingly planned, meticulously prepared concert shoot, a world away from the filming of the Rolling Thunder show at Hughes Stadium, Fort Collins, Colorado, the following month, where much would be left to chance (not least the weather) but which came together marvelously and miraculously.

The Clearwater show was filmed by a crew under the auspices of Burt Sugarman, executive producer of the then very successful US television show *The Midnight Special* – a rock program featuring bands performing in a concert situation, the length of their set proportionate to their degree of fame. The shoot would be directed by Sugarman's trusted right-hand man, Stan Harris, who had filmed everything from Glen Campbell's wholesome US television specials to David Bowie's 1973 concert film, *Ziggy Stardust And The Spiders From Mars*. Rolling Thunder guitarist Mick Ronson, previously the leader of Bowie's backing band, had worked closely with Harris on the movie and it was he who had advised Dylan that the director might be a suitable choice for this first attempt at a concert special.

Two separate shows were actually filmed on that April day in Florida, one in the afternoon and one in the evening. An initial edit would combine selections from both concerts, although only a keen-eyed observer of clothing nuances and instrument placement would spot the differences (the match cuts don't quite match, to use movie parlance).

The footage begins with a breathtakingly stark introduction; Dylan, alone in the middle of the shot, taking up perhaps a tenth of the screen space, while all around him is darkness. What colors there are seem oddly washed-out, as if something is wrong with the camera or the contrast of the television. He begins playing 'Mr. Tambourine Man' as the camera slowly but inexorably focuses in on his shadowy figure. As the shot gradually lightens, the audience, surrounding Dylan on all sides, becomes visible in what is, without doubt, a bravura opening.

Something will immediately strike many Americans lucky enough to glimpse this never officially released footage. The Starlight Ballroom setup looks *exactly* like the stage of *NBC's Saturday Night Live*, the already popular, television sketch comedy and variety show which had debuted the previous October (and which would soon lose the *NBC's* prefix). On screen, Dylan, in plantation owner's hat atop an Arab *keffiyeh* headdress, and sporting a black toreador jacket with white piping, is seen surrounded by punters above him and behind him – a striking visual that offers a complete contrast with the officially released *Hard Rain* concert footage, but which is no less captivating. Equally striking is the fact that Dylan is so obviously performing for a large number of hotel employees. There is a row of young girls, who surely must be chambermaids, to his right and slightly above him, each of them dressed in identical black outfits with white trim, white aprons, white leggings, and white turned-up caps. At a distance, they might be Dutch schoolchildren; perhaps the owner of the Bellevue Biltmore had a thing for the Netherlands. Other punters were certainly on the set, gratis, as tickets had been given out on April 20, at the RTR concert at the Bayfront Auditorium in St. Petersburg, a mere 12 miles from Clearwater.

T Bone Burnett remembers how oddly seated the Clearwater crowd was. "They built these rafters all around [the ballroom] and there were all these kids sitting in them, with their legs dangling down. The backdrop was all these dangling legs, and we just took one look at it and thought '[surely] this isn't what we're doing.'"[1]

Dylan's version of 'Mr. Tambourine Man' is surprisingly faithful to the 1965 original and his rhythmic harmonica solo, completely in synch with his right-hand strum, is as much a part of the music's beauty as his vocal melody or the vaulting imagery of the lyrics. The entire opening shot is quite magical, in fact; the atmosphere it evokes is incredibly positive and sends out promising intimations of what is to come.

Dylan then delivers 'The Times They Are A-Changin',' an unfussy version that's pretty faithful to the recorded classic. Dylan is singing, *really* singing, in the conventional sense. The gruff, barbed-wire voice of the *Hard Rain* album and the Fort Collins *Hard Rain* television special is yet to come. 'The Times They Are A-Changin' is not quite a match for the preceding 'Mr. Tambourine Man,' however. Despite his fully engaged vocals, there is a quality about it which somehow suggests he is no longer completely at one with the song. 'Mr. Tambourine Man,' by comparison, is delivered with complete conviction and sounds as if it might have been a track off his last album.

The footage, here, isn't quite as dramatic as on the opening song. At times, the camera operator must have been lying on the floor, or at least kneeling quite low, pointing the lens upward and at a three-quarters angle. The resulting shot makes Dylan look like he's singing to the heavens (which may have been the case), with his knees shown in the lower right corner of the screen and his head in the upper left, while he looks towards the upper right. It's a dramatic angle, but one reminiscent of (and perhaps better suited to) 50s Soviet-style documentary. Or perhaps the director was attempting to emulate Alan Lomax's famous color footage of Leadbelly singing 'Pick A Bale O' Cotton,' filmed back in 1945.

Dylan's harmonica solo on 'The Times They Are A-Changin'' isn't the rhythmic chug-along which added such spice to 'Mr. Tambourine Man' – instead, the harp quotes the vocal melody, a rarity for Dylan; it's such a sweet, mellifluous (and familiar) tune, however, that it works perfectly.

At Clearwater, despite (or perhaps because of) the cameras, Dylan is unusually warm in his between-song communications with the audience. That's certainly the case as he announces, loudly and enthusiastically: "I wanna bring out a real special friend of mine, who's been a friend of mine throughout the years; Miss Joan Baez! [applause] ... and she's great!" The crowd claps enthusiastically as Baez walks on from stage left, dressed in chic, pale blue flared trousers and a smart, short-sleeved white shirt, with a white scarf around her neck. Dylan pauses for a moment, looks down at his guitar and strums a chord before continuing to speak. "We wanna dedicate this to all the people in Hibbing, Minnesota [Dylan smiles broadly here, as does Baez, although she stares at Dylan as though he were on day release from an institution for the mentally disturbed], and Duluth, Minnesota."

The Dylan-Baez duet (which back in the early 60s would have been billed as the Baez-Dylan duet), is a potentially historic television moment, and the two of them know it and recognize it by performing the evergreen 'Blowin' In The Wind.' This is a slower, less dramatically affecting version than the official *Hard Rain* television special take, but it is still a noble, powerful effort. Their voices are in near perfect tandem; as near to perfect as Dylan is ever likely to get, anyway. The performance is captured with much more conventional camerawork than at the show's opening; for a few minutes we seem to have happened upon an orthodox concert film.

It is interesting to note the affection and respect Dylan shows Baez during the Clearwater performance. In two other, very different, Dylan film vehicles made 40 years apart, namely *Dont Look Back* and *No Direction Home*, Baez fans could be forgiven for feeling that their heroine had been somewhat slighted. Here, Dylan is contrastingly deferential. It is apparent that he admires Baez personally and is prepared to acknowledge her artistically. He gives her special billing on this initial concert shoot, as he would on the later *Hard Rain* television special, something no other performer received, not even Roger McGuinn. Indeed, she is granted the unique honor of being allowed to perform her own composition, 'Diamonds And Rust,' for the cameras.

By now, Dylan has lost the hat but still has the Arab headgear on. Before they begin the next duet, he speaks again, revealing a puckish sense of humor. "Joan has a habit of changing ... [I] never know what she's gonna do next," he says, and then smiles as he backs out of the head and shoulders shot, to the right. Baez thinks about her riposte for a nanosecond. "Yeah, I remember rehearsing this back in 1965 ... *once!*" There is considerable laughter from the audience. The 'this' Baez refers to is a song not from 1965, in fact, but one from the 1967 album *John Wesley Harding*, 'I Dreamed I Saw St. Augustine.' It's given a vigorous, compelling reading, one matched by the pleasing visuals. Dylan and Baez, almost exactly matched in height, are playing identical model Martin guitars, their necks held at rakish angles to allow the pair access to the same microphone. Baez looks modishly elegant, a bold contrast with Dylan's tipsy Spanish gypsy look.

At the song's conclusion, the members of Guam are visible on stage, Rob Stoner most evidently. The scene then cuts, however, to Baez, alone on stage, halfway through a between-song tribute to Dylan. "By far the most talented ... crazy person I ever worked with," she says, with a smile. Doe she omit the crucial conjunction "and" on purpose? As it is, it's not certain if she thinks Dylan is the most talented *and* most crazy person she's ever worked with or simply the most gifted madman. Whatever the truth, her comments bring applause down from the surrounding audience like drizzle from a Fort Collins rain cloud.

Baez then delivers her heartbreakingly tender 'Diamonds And Rust.' Close-ups reveal a very pretty, very feminine woman in her mid thirties, on the cusp of early middle age. 'Diamonds And Rust' is effectively her version of Dylan's 'Sara,' a clear invocation of the past and of a desperate romance, sung in the presence of the object of affection and with the full knowledge that the audience is in on the whole thing. Her performance flirts with mawkishness but never fully gives in to it. The audience response is overwhelmingly positive, causing Baez to turn temporarily into Sammy Davis, Jr in Vegas ("I've never ... never ... felt so much *love* from an audience before"). Indeed, the crowd applauds 'Diamonds And Rust' more vigorously than they do any of the first four songs of the show. Baez acknowledges this by taking a curtain call, in bullfighter fashion, sweeping her arm gracefully before her and bowing briefly, somehow suggesting both humility and feisty theatricality.

The film edit then dissolves into the next shot, revealing the entire band on stage. Dylan is eager to speak again. "Here's a good friend of mine, now ... we've known each other about twelve hundred years ... Mr Bobby Neuwirth, from Canton, Ohio." This provokes baronial laughter from both Dylan and his old companion. Dylan continues, perhaps in oblique reference to Neuwirth's painting career. "Here's a good friend of mine from Paris, just flown in, Bobby Neuwirth," which elicits further onstage mirth. Neuwirth, whose 60s hip quotient was so vast many felt Dylan had copped his cool act wholesale from the Ohioan, tonight wears a red-checked shirt and matching headband. He gesticulates wildly and jumps around the stage frenziedly, as if he's partaken of the potent coffee Dylan was prone to brew, if not worse.

The ensemble then kicks into 'When I Paint My Masterpiece.' More than one Dylan writer has been harsh about Neuwirth's harmony-singing abilities on this song, but at Clearwater he sings just fine; he and Dylan are both shout-singing the song, loudly and lustily, like a couple of sailors on boozy shore leave. It's a taste of the vocal style that would characterize much of the *Hard Rain* live album captured later that spring. When the band pick up the opening bars it sounds astonishingly like the intro to Larry Williams's 1957 hit 'Bony Maronie,' but it soon settles into its own groove. Dylan walks over to David Mansfield during his fine mandolin solo and mimes turning the tuning pegs on Mansfield's instrument as he's in full flow. The young sidekick simply smiles at Dylan's prank; what else could he do? Neuwirth's harmony, which just as often drops to a unison bark, misses several key phrases, but is there on cue for the chorus. At one point, his wild moves find him several feet from the mic stand when it's time for him to sing.

There are five guitarists on stage at this point (Steven Soles, T Bone Burnett, and Mick Ronson on electrics, Dylan and Neuwirth on acoustics). Two, if not three, of those guitars could be jettisoned and it would unquestionably tighten up the sound. For the most part, they are doubling parts to no real audible benefit, merely thickening the sonic soup. It is also notable how unfashionable the band looks by today's standards; a riot of bell-bottoms, moustaches, lank, unkempt hair, and, in Mick Ronson's case, heavy mascara. All were *du jour* in early 1976 but have dated horribly.

'Like A Rolling Stone' is next. It is only the second appearance of Dylan's searing anthem witnessed on the entire Rolling Thunder tour, and probably a sop to the television crew who were no doubt thrilled to have Dylan essaying what was arguably his most recognizable song on their show. Performed in the key of D, rather than its original C, and given a somewhat light, almost Brazilian carnival flavor, it sounds under-rehearsed and is really not a song for Gary Burke's congas, which are aggravatingly busy and mixed too loud. Dylan is belting out the words but the backing is thin, unimpressive, and debilitated by the absence of Al Kooper's loud, swirling organ hook, or Mike Bloomfield's razor-slice guitar riff – components which so distinguished the song's 1965 recording (and which had been faithfully reproduced by The Hawks, on stage, in 1966). Howie Wyeth, at the piano, or Mansfield on just about anything, might have covered the organ line, and surely the gifted Ronson could have essayed something akin to Bloomfield's part. All in all, it's passionless and underwhelming, closer to the phoned-in version of the song from the 1969 Isle Of Wight Festival than to the blazing original – a recording revered then as much as now. Nonetheless, Dylan's performance certainly *looks* good. At one point, the camera shoots from down low, level with Dylan's right knee. When it points upward for a close-up of the lightly-bearded singer, the glare of the lights and his headgear form a kind of halo, lending Dylan the appearance of Christ in an Italian Renaissance portrait which has mysteriously come to life.

'Isis' was a lynchpin of the Rolling Thunder Revue shows. It is April now; *Desire*, the album from which it is plucked, has been out for four months and is a huge hit in the USA. Audiences would be familiar with its material and, indeed, songs from *Desire* were greeted rapturously everywhere they were played on the second Rolling Thunder. Everywhere, that is, except Clearwater, Florida. Perhaps the less frantic and more focused version captured on *The Bootleg Series Vol. 5: Bob Dylan Live 1975, The Rolling Thunder Revue* would have been the way to go, here, but this is a more uptight 'Isis,' one that certainly doesn't seem to cut the mustard with the Floridian folks. Perhaps they are unable to get past Scarlet Rivera's inability to play exactly in pitch, the band's stop/start rhythms, or Dylan's decision to don a guitar and play along rather than acting out the lyrics, sans acoustic, but with wild, interpretive gesticulations, as he had done, to memorable effect, on many earlier shows. In Toronto, the previous December, for example, 'Isis' had been a total barnburner. T Bone Burnett: "I think that version of 'Isis,' on the first Rolling Thunder Revue, was the most intense rock'n'roll ever got. Led Zeppelin never got so intense, nor did The Rolling Stones. Nobody ever rocked harder or more intensely than he [Dylan] did on that version of 'Isis.'"[2]

Footage from Toronto certainly backs Burnett up, and yet in Clearwater, a mere five months later, the same song is cold, stiff, and hurried. Is this just Dylan being mercurial? Are the band-members wary of being filmed for television? Whatever the reason, the steam is leaking uncontrollably from the boiler, and the set is losing momentum.

The camera now shows Dylan just to the side of center stage, half in shadow, with the band lost entirely in darkness behind him. The stage lights turn blue, a color reminiscent of the glow of an old black and white television glimpsed through an apartment window. It's a nice effect. Dylan then moves center stage to be bathed in this pale, blue light. There is a poignant subtlety to the staging, but the version of 'Just Like A Woman' which it presages is listless. Previous versions on the tour had been more convincing. The a cappella gospel harmonies on the choruses are untidy, here, and add nothing to the song.

"Tonight we have a very special guest with us," announces Dylan at its conclusion. He looks over his right shoulder to make sure the guest has arrived. "We go back a long way … Roger McGuinn!" The leader of The Byrds appears as if recently awoken from a nap and, uncharacteristically, seems incapable of smiling. Again, the Clearwater vibe hardly seems contagious. 'Knockin' On Heaven's Door' is performed in the key of A as opposed to the original G, changing its emotional impact. McGuinn is on camera, fingering interesting chord positions way up the neck of his Rickenbacker 12-string, but, frustratingly, hardly any of it is audible. Nonetheless, he looks extremely West Coast cool in session-player black shirt and nonchalant demeanor. He and Dylan would be the gold and silver medalists at the 1976 Hipster Olympics, without doubt.

Mansfield's choral pedal-steel work dominates the song, sounding, at times, almost like an electric organ. McGuinn comes in close on Dylan's mic to sing the "Mama, take those guns away from me" verse by himself, a generous gesture of respect on Bob's part, then goes back to sing harmony at a mic in the rear, alongside Joan Baez. At the solo, McGuinn plays arpeggios high up the Rickenbacker's neck, while Mansfield's pedal steel echoes him with harmonics. It's a celestial moment right out of a church service; one which is all too brief.

A break follows, into which commercials will later be slotted, then things resume with a quirky, lusty, stab at 'Lay, Lady, Lay.' It is much like the version released on the *Hard Rain* album, only taken at a marginally slower tempo. Slight lyrical modifications (of the "Let's go upstairs" and "Who really cares?" variety) may change the tenor of this once gently seductive ballad, but its new, brittle arrangement adds nothing. By the time Guam and Dylan are halfway through, it is exposed as aimless, the only saving grace being McGuinn's chordal fills after the final chorus under which Ronson essays a lead guitar line. Surely this must have been the beginning of their brief *Thunderbyrd* alliance.

If the Clearwater shoot had been restricted to just 30 minutes, concluding before the turgid electric section put a crimp in the evening, it would have made for a terrific, if somewhat brief, television special.

The Starlight Ballroom of the Bellevue Biltmore Hotel had seen some fine performances, but in the wake of the flaccid 'Like A Rolling Stone,' the players simply lose their mojo. Added to that, the staging of the show begins to seem tame; it's too squeaky clean for an artist of Dylan's iconoclastic stature. The following month's Fort Collins film footage would prove to be a far more moving experience for the viewer; rain storms and glowering skies adding a biblical atmosphere, the huddled Colorado fans enduring like refugees from a war. By comparison, the Clearwater show looks more like a toothpaste commercial.

There can be little doubt that Dylan, Neuwirth, or an editor as adept as Howard Alk, for that matter, would have spotted this when they viewed the rushes. David Mansfield thinks Dylan simply didn't like what he saw. "I don't want to put words in his [Dylan's] mouth, but I imagine it seemed too sort of staged and pedestrian in terms of approach. It was right after rehearsals and things hadn't quite gelled yet. Also, when we were getting back together for the second Rolling Thunder Revue tour, there were quite a few personnel changes. It wasn't like we were going to pick up where we left off."[3]

Dylan certainly did spot the weaknesses in the Bellevue Biltmore Hotel gig when he watched an edit of the Clearwater television show at a local NBC affiliate's studio, later on in the spring '76 Rolling Thunder tour. Indeed, after Dylan had returned from studio, he was seen shaking his head in dismay. Rumor had it that he hated Stan Harris's editing and he also felt the show was too soft, without challenge, and too middle-of-the-road. He also deemed his own attempts at onstage introductions too ostentatious, too 'showbiz.' His bodyguard, Andy Bielanski, was with Dylan when he saw the edit. "He hated that, absolutely hated it," Bielanski is quoted as saying.[4]

Dylan's distaste for the show is understandable. It was literal, where he was mysterious; quite broad in its attempt to reach a large American TV audience, where his was a focused and more specific vision; and a slice of essentially orthodox television, while he was busy deconstructing the music film with *Renaldo & Clara*. Dylan knew the NBC special would have to be done again, elsewhere, and probably on his own dime; but he didn't know where or when. In a few weeks, he would make his decision. One thing was for sure, it wouldn't resemble any accepted television formats, nor would it be easy on the eyes or ears.

CHAPTER 7
HARD RAIN:
BICENTENNIAL
SPRING

everal nights on the fall 1975 Rolling Thunder tour had been recorded for a possible live album. They were: Plymouth, Massachusetts, October 31; Waterbury, Connecticut, November 11; Worcester, Massachusetts, November 19; Cambridge, Massachusetts, November 20; Boston, Massachusetts, November 21 (both shows); and Montreal, Canada, December 4. In addition, it is rumored that both shows at the Niagara Falls Convention Center, on November 15, were also recorded, as was the Night Of The Hurricane benefit show, the tour's December 8 finale at Manhattan's Madison Square Garden. Although reference cassettes were made of these shows and presented to Dylan, he refused to listen to them at any length during the ensuing holidays. It was too soon, and he was too close, emotionally, to the project. He was also focused on the release of his next album, *Desire*. Hitting the racks early in the New Year, Dylan's 17th album swiftly ascended the charts, soon bagging *Billboard's* Number One spot, where it would reside for five weeks. In the UK, *Desire* made it as high as Number Three.

On January 22 1976, a modified version of the Rolling Thunder ensemble convened at SIR studios on Santa Monica Boulevard, in Hollywood. There, they would partake of rehearsals ahead of a second Night Of The Hurricane benefit concert, this time to be staged in Houston, Texas, at the city's cavernous Astrodome. At SIR, percussionist Gary Burke replaced Luther Rix, who was absent with personal problems. Ronee Blakley was otherwise engaged, and Ramblin' Jack Elliott was nowhere to be seen. Texan singer-songwriter, novelist, and humorist Kinky Friedman was a new addition to the troupe.

The Houston Astrodome was a gargantuan, state-of-the-art facility; a domed, multi-sport stadium with an artificial pitch made of Astro Turf which required vacuuming, rather than trimming and watering. The venue was completely air conditioned, had a parking lot for over 15,000 cars, a capacity of 62,000 for football and 55,000 for baseball, and, with typical Texan hyperbole, billed itself as 'The Eighth Wonder of the World.' It had opened in 1965 and was considered a great architectural and technological innovation and a benchmark for future arena construction. Other domed stadiums where soon built in its near image. However, the building's size and the expense of its upkeep eventually worked against it. Professional athletes began to complain that its artificial turf was hard on their knees and ankles; there were even career-ending injuries. After a long decline, the Astrodome doors closed for good in

2004. It still stands at 8400 Kirby Drive, Houston, a monument both to thinking big and to civic folly.

By the time Dylan and his bandmates gathered at SIR to rehearse, the Astrodome already had a reputation as an impersonal, oversized hangar. Although originally scheduled for another impersonal, oversized hangar, the Louisiana Superdome, in New Orleans, the Night Of The Hurricane 2 show was moved to Houston after rapid renegotiations between Dylan's representatives, Rubin Carter's defense fund leader, George Lois, and Houston mayor Fred Hofheinz. A media savvy, erstwhile attorney, Hofheinz recognized that the image of his sprawling, anonymous, city could be at least partially ameliorated by welcoming a Bob Dylan benefit concert to its showcase venue. However, the staging of a large-scale, high profile rock concert at very short notice is, as often as not, a recipe for disaster, as the organizers of the Altamont Festival in 1969 and the Powder Ridge and Phun City Festivals of the following year had found to their cost.

Things got off to a bad start at SIR in Hollywood. The previous summer, Dylan had admirably advised tour manager Louis Kemp that he didn't care if Rolling Thunder turned a profit, just as long as it broke even. Indeed, the main thing he wanted to break was new artistic ground. With the second phase of Rolling Thunder activity, however, the bottom line would exert considerably more influence. Not that there was much evidence of cost-cutting. Dylan had preferred to fly his New York City-based musicians to California for rehearsals, rather than gather them together in Texas. From there, after just two days at SIR, the ensemble would jet down to Huston for the show. It was a sign of the profligacy to come. How such rock star extravagance would benefit anyone at a fundraiser is a question George Lois has no doubt pondered many times.

In LA, Dylan was noticeably more reserved toward his band-members than he had been only a few short weeks earlier, in New England, but that didn't stop the partying starting early. New recruit Kinky Friedman recalls the starriness that would come to characterize the second phase of Rolling Thunder. "The flight out from LA to Houston was great, with Bob, Ringo Starr, Joni Mitchell, and all those people. I also remember one internal flight in Texas, later on the tour … where we did not get first class [seats] and Bob [Dylan], me, and [road manager] Gary Shafner sat in coach. Bob had to sit next to this nice young girl who was so excited, so thrilled, that she kept saying, 'I can't believe it … I can't believe I am sitting next to Bob Dylan!' Bob turned to her and said, 'Pinch yourself.'"[1]

Ticket sales were proving slow in Houston. *Desire* had only just been released and Texas had never been a hotbed of Dylan fanaticism, unlike the urban northeastern corridor that had proved so welcoming the previous fall. In order to boost ticket sales, Stevie Wonder, Stephen Stills, Isaac Hayes, Carlos Santana, and Willie Nelson were added to the Night Of The Hurricane bill. Each would bring their own bands with them, ratcheting up expenses still further. Richie Havens and, as Kinky Friedman notes, Ringo Starr tagged along, too. The tour's original "keeping the egos down" ethos, as proffered by Joan Baez in the *Rock Around The World* Rolling Thunder radio show, broadcast later that spring, was surely untenable in such exulted company. Certainly, Wonder, Stills, and Nelson would only be contented with lengthy sets; there was no suggestion of them making do with guest spots backed by Guam.

The Astrodome concert was, therefore, way too long, making December '75's Toronto marathon seem like a sprint by comparison. The venue was also wholly unsuitable for the purpose. The acoustics in the yawning sports hall were woeful and the much vaunted air conditioning seemed only to intensify the prevailing Texan humidity. In contrast, the onstage vibes were chilly, bordering on frosty. Of the $500,000-plus supposedly raised for Rubin Carter's defense, it is alleged that only a tenth of the total reached his benefit fund, such were the superstar expenses. The Night Of The Hurricane 2 was such a star-studded, over-egged pudding that Roger McGuinn can only recall it with a laugh and a grimace. "The Astrodome, yeah; that's the concert where me and Willie Nelson shared a mic and I didn't know who he was and I don't know if he knew who I was! He was looking at me kinda quizzically, like, 'Who are you? What are you doing on my microphone?'"[2]

The Houston show was also significant in that it was the only Rolling Thunder performance in which Joan Baez did not appear. It would also portend several themes that would play out during the tour's second phase; not least Dylan's escalating mental anguish.

In early 1976, Bob Dylan was in a curious place. On the surface, he seemed to be engaged in a frenzy of positive activity. He had released two albums in a year, and both had been critically lauded and substantial sellers. In addition, the first Rolling Thunder tour was roundly hailed as an artistic success and had won Dylan considerable cachet. Meanwhile, a deal for a major television special had been inked and his first feature film as a director, *Renaldo & Clara*, was waiting to be edited. Beneath it all, however, Dylan's marriage was in trouble and he was apprehensive and agitated. He would spend the days following the Houston Astrodome show wandering around Texas in the company of local pals such as singer Doug Sahm, doing not much of anything. He visited England in March then returned to LA to hang out with The Band at a studio called Shangri-La, in Malibu, alongside the likes of Rolling Stone Ronnie Wood and Eric Clapton. There, they would turn a recording studio party into contributions to Clapton's solo album, *No Reason To Cry*. Dylan even gifted the Englishman a song, 'Sign Language,' which they recorded as a duet. While holed up at Shangri-La, Dylan chose to sleep out in a makeshift tent in the studio grounds rather than return to his own home, which was close by. The ice was cracking loudly beneath his marriage.

Artistically, Dylan was still on the rebound from the early 70s, a period during which he worked very little and had fallen into a kind of stasis, a state of inertia from which he'd been ripped by a revelation, as he later recalled. "I was in Corsica, just sitting in a field overlooking some vineyards; the sky was pink, the sun was going down, and the moon was sapphire; and I recall getting a ride into town with a man with a donkey cart, and I was sitting on this donkey cart, bouncing around on the road there, and that's when it flashed on me that I was gonna go back to America and get serious and do what it is that I do, because by that time people didn't know what it was that I did ... Only the people that see our show know what it is that I do, the rest of the people just have to imagine it."[3]

On April 8, Guam reassembled in Clearwater, Florida, to run through songs for further Rolling Thunder dates and, specifically, for the filming of the now contractually obligated television special. Rehearsals were uncomfortable; Dylan was uncommunicative and would sometimes not speak at all during several hours of band practice. When he did speak, he could be brusque; it was all a long way from the conviviality of October '75.

In her memoirs, Joan Baez recalls the beginning of Rolling Thunder's spring's offensive being inauspicious. "I was feeling impetuous, thinking my status in the show, and the pay scale, should be altered to my benefit. Bob had a thing about wanting me to grow my hair long, the way it was in the beginning. He told me I'd start selling albums again if I let my hair grow. But I had cut it all off between Rolling Thunders, and when I walked into the rehearsal room in Jacksonville [sic], Florida, Bob said, 'What the fuck have you done to your hair?'"[4]

Other members of the tour party noticed that all was not well with their boss. "I think Bob Dylan was going through an awfully tough time and I remember him, during rehearsals in 1976, being a bit of a dark figure," David Mansfield recalls. "He was sometimes harsh with the band. There were some wonderful musical things that happened, yes, but I think that it was different from the lighter, euphoric tone of the first Rolling Thunder tour."[5]

It was during rehearsals in Clearwater that Dylan and crew learned that Bob's old Greenwich Village folk-singing buddy Phil Ochs had hanged himself at his sister's house in Far Rockaway, New York. Dylan and Ochs had enjoyed a fluctuating relationship over the years but, like innumerable Village musicians, Ochs would have loved nothing more than to have been part of Rolling Thunder. His drinking and unbalanced mental state meant he had to be reluctantly passed over.

The gloomy news only added to the sense of ill portent that had already begun to envelop the tour. T Bone Burnett is another tourist who recalls the mood in April 1976 being in stark contrast to the easy-going exhilaration of the previous fall. "It was just a different vibe. We were having death threats every night, because we were in the South and we were springing this 'black murderer' [Rubin Carter] from prison. We had a guy from the NYPD on the road with us and every night he would have something [to deal with]. There would be a death threat, a bomb threat, or something like that. This guy would clear the room to make sure there was no danger. It was a very different vibe by that time."[6]

Rob Stoner concurs with Burnett's sentiment but has a slightly different perspective on the second Rolling Thunder tour. "When the tour cranked up for the second time, we not only had the thrill of working with Bob Dylan, but the thrill of being in a group that had done a hit record [*Desire*]. Of course, the Rolling Thunder Revue was more exciting the first time around, because it was new. Bob's fanbase wasn't as rabid in the South as it was in the Northeast where we had done the first leg of the tour. I could definitely feel that Bob wasn't as into it. The novelty of touring with the Revue had definitely worn off after the first tour, and the ticket sales weren't as good for the second leg. I think the fact that Bob wasn't making a lot of money was starting to get to him."[7]

The negatives were certainly mounting up. A grumpy, uncommunicative bandleader, his marriage in poor shape; troupe members with low morale and ego problems, struggling at rehearsal; the suicide of an old crony; death threats from rednecks; slow ticket sales; it all conspired to make this one of 70s rock's most ill-starred major tours.

What's more, history had started to catch up with the Dylan phenomenon. Whatever sense of magical liberation Dylan's music seemed to embody, even as the aura of the 60s started to fade, would inevitably struggle when it came up against the sheer edifice of the mid-70s music business. By then, the record industry had crystallized into a workforce/job market/lifestyle platform, defined by no less careerist principles than Wall Street, although with a looser dress code and less rigid working hours. Commercial expediency hung over the world of rock music like a rain cloud, and even Bob Dylan wasn't exempt from getting wet. With a lot of money on the line, pressing security issues, and a lot of egos now in regular need of massaging, one thing was sure, the days of jaunty, free-spirited touring in Greyhound buses and motorhomes were over.

Things had moved on in other ways, too. The plight of Hurricane Carter may still have been on Dylan's mind, but musically, he was soon forgotten. Following the second Night Of The Hurricane benefit, the Rolling Thunder troupe would never perform the song 'Hurricane' again, despite it being the lead track on Dylan's new album.

He did introduce some brand new material to the set, however: songs such as 'Seven Days' (another number he had given away, to Ronnie Wood, at the March Shangri-La sessions); and welcomed a clutch of older numbers that hadn't been played on the previous leg of the tour. These included 'It's Alright, Ma (I'm Only Bleeding),' 'Just Like Tom Thumb's Blues,' 'Maggie's Farm,' 'Dink's Song,' 'Rita Mae,' 'One Of Us Must Know (Sooner Or Later),' 'Visions Of Johanna,' and various selections from *Blood On The Tracks*. There were also new covers including Robert Freimark's 'Vincent Van Gogh,' Woody Guthrie's 'Deportee (Plane Wreck At Los Gatos),' and Hank Williams's 'Weary Blues From Waitin'.'

Other original Rolling Thunder tenets had also altered in character. Local heroes were still invited to step up and join the band on stage from show to show, but this was now less a matter of musical conviviality and mutual respect and more about the necessity of selling tickets.

As with the Astrodome show, one notable absentee from the tour party was Ramblin' Jack Elliott. A respected musical figure, Elliott was also well-loved by the troupe (no one interviewed for this book had anything less than kind words for him). He was also a direct link to the US folk music tradition of Woody Guthrie, Cisco Houston, Dock Boggs, and Clarence Ashley. With Ramblin' Jack around, music fans could see Rolling Thunder as a link in a chain which tied American folk history to the present day.

Unfortunately, a figure like Jack Elliott would not put many bums on seats down South. Yes, he could rope a steer, mend a saddle, and fix all the broken down pick-up trucks in Dixie, but he was simply not famous in the Deep South. Dylan had bills to pay, not least the cost of the fall tour's extensive personnel and the expense of shooting *Renaldo & Clara*. The spring tour would continue to play a smattering of smaller venues (although with none of the former spontaneity), but, this time, as Dylan no doubt communicated to Lou Kemp, business was business.

Jack Elliott remembers going to Dylan's house to ask if he was to be invited on the second leg of the tour. "He [Dylan] looked kind of embarrassed and said, 'I don't have anything to do with who gets to go, but I heard a rumor that Joan Baez and Kinky Freidman were coming.' So I left him my phone number and said, 'Well, let me know if anybody makes any decisions,' and I never heard from them. About a month later, I was in San Francisco, in The Grateful Dead's office, and some of the members of the Dead were there. They said, 'Jack, aren't you supposed to be playing the Houston Astrodome today? The Rolling Thunder Revue is starting up.' They had read about it in *Variety*, or something. I found a phone number for the Astrodome and eventually got hold of Bobby Neuwirth. I said, 'Hey Bobby, what's going on?' He said, 'Where are you? We're in Houston and we've got your name up on the marquee.' I wasn't about to jump on a plane at the last minute; I just figured, heck, if they're going to be that disorganized I guess I'm not supposed to go."[8]

In effect, it appears that Kinky Friedman was drafted in to replace Ramblin' Jack. In 1976, Friedman was known not as a droll novelist or as a legitimate candidate for the Texas Governorship, as he is today, but as a wise-cracking country singer with a penchant for provocatively witty humor, much of it based on the novelty of being a proud, urbane, Texan Jew, singing, writing, and performing country & western music. Hence Friedman songs such as 'Ride 'Em, Jewboy,' a caustic yet moving song about the Holocaust, or the Nashville-alienating likes of 'Top Ten Commandments' and 'High On Jesus.' Friedman was already a friend of the tour's chronicler, Larry 'Ratso' Sloman (who even appears in Friedman's novels as a Dr Watson-like character) and was acquainted with tour manager Lou Kemp. Dylan had met Friedman at a gig almost three years earlier, after which they'd chatted and exchanged numbers. The man they call 'the Kinkster' was a contemporary artist releasing records which at least grazed the charts and which were reviewed in the pages of *Rolling Stone*. Ramblin' Jack Elliott, meanwhile, was a slice of living history of most significance to folk enthusiasts, and he recorded sporadically. As the Rolling Thunder Revue progressed between Astrodomes and football stadiums in the spring of 1976, the charts trumped folk history at every turn.

Just as the *The Bootleg Series Vol. 5: Bob Dylan Live 1975, The Rolling Thunder Revue* album would document the previous tour leg (even if it wasn't released until 27 years after the event), there would be also be a live album to archive the second, and final, Rolling Thunder Revue tour. Rather than a historical album, released decades later, this would be very much a product of its time. The album was *Hard Rain*, released on September 13 1976 in the USA, a mere four months after the Thunder had Rolled its last. It would reach Number 17 on the *Billboard* charts. In the UK, it fared even better, making the Number Three spot. What most Dylan fans do not know, and what perhaps even Dylan himself doesn't know, is that some portions of the tracks on *Hard Rain* were re-recorded by a single-minded man in a New York recording studio. What's more, this was an album which almost didn't make it to tape in the first place.

In April, an Enactron truck, belonging to Emmylou Harris's husband, Brian Ahern, and housing a state-of-the-art recording studio, was hired by producer Don DeVito to record a pair of Rolling Thunder shows. Dylan's crew had already taped one Florida show, at Tampa on April 21, but this, as with other shows earlier in the tour, was primarily for reference purposes; with so many musicians on stage, it was often the only way they could gauge their individual contributions and hear what the band actually sounded like.

The first full-scale live recording would take place on May 16, at the Tarrant County Convention Center Arena in Fort Worth, Texas. A second was scheduled for May 23, at Colorado State University in Fort Collins.

Prior to the Fort Worth concert, the Rolling Thunder musicians had been holed up at songwriter Bobby Charles's home, on a bayou near Lake Charles, Louisiana. There, they spent three days and nights enjoying a true Cajun party, the kind that begins with a breakfast of grilled alligator washed down with a cold beer. During this period, Dylan was out of communication with the CBS office in New York City (a not uncommon occurrence in an age before cell phones and the internet) and there were concerns that the first Texas gig, slated for May 8 in Houston, wouldn't be performed at all, with the troupe staying on at Bobby Charles's property for another few days. Perhaps they were deliberately dodging the bad news about Texan ticket sales. The Dallas show, originally scheduled for May 15, had already been scrapped due to scant box office activity and was replaced by an impromptu show at the Gatesville State School for Boys.

Nonetheless, by the time of the May 16 recording, the ensemble had five Lone Star State shows under their belt and was in robust fighting form. A lot of the melody and tenderness that characterized the material played on tour seven months previously had now been replaced by an angry musical attack which seemed to reflect Dylan's state of mind; a siege mentality gripped the stage; appropriately enough since the chosen venues for the recordings were both once Old West frontier forts.

As it transpired, both the Fort Worth and Fort Collins concert recordings would be beset with technical problems. Although the Enactron truck could be parked conveniently right beside the stage at the Tarrant County Arena, engineer Don Meehan remembers having to clamber to the center of the building's domed roof to suspend a stereo microphone in order to adequately pick up the sound of the audience.

Meehan also recalls Dylan and Guam delivering the goods that May evening in Fort Worth. Unfortunately, not everything they played on the night was preserved for posterity. "When we got the tapes back to New York and started mixing, one of the 24-track machines was missing a drum track. We had to bring Howie [Wyeth] into the studio to lay it in."[9] Repeated listening to the Fort Worth recordings reveals that Wyeth's kick drum is absent on the version of 'One Too Many Mornings' and is only the faintest presence on 'Stuck Inside Of Mobile With The Memphis Blues Again.' Might these be the missing drum tracks Meehan mentions? 'Oh, Sister' and 'You're A Big Girl Now' are the best recorded songs, from a technical standpoint, so perhaps these benefit from Wyeth's overdubs. If so, he might have hung around the studio a while longer and replaced those stray kick drum parts.

Although the live recordings created miscellaneous anxieties for Dylan, he was still treating his band with a professionalism bordering on extravagance. Indeed, Don Meehan was amazed at just how well Dylan looked after his people, despite his all too obvious personal problems. After the Fort Worth show, Meehan recalls at least 40 individuals from the Rolling Thunder tour party descending on a Mexican restaurant leased by Dylan for the night. There, they ordered any food or drink they desired; it was a return to the rock star decadence of the *Desire* recording sessions.

While the Rolling Thunder ensemble could put Fort Worth behind them, the Dons DeVito and Meehan could not. When they played back the tapes, they found that not only were drum tracks missing, but several backing vocals, for technical or other reasons, had also not been recorded. This meant a major component of Guam's powerful sound was absent, particularly on the choruses of several songs. To use these recordings as they were, on a live album, would be to completely misrepresent the Rolling Thunder show. To lose the likes of 'Lay, Lady, Lay,' 'Stuck Inside Of Mobile With The Memphis Blues Again,' and 'I Threw It All Away,' was also unthinkable, as these songs had not featured on the fall Rolling Thunder tour dates and epitomized the spring '76 tour's vigor and raucousness.

Don Meehan thinks the problems arose because a number of the backing vocals were not sung close enough to the onstage mics. "The leakage [from other instruments onto the vocal mics] was unbearable; that's the problem with recording live, you've got one shot at it," he explains. His solution was pragmatic, if audacious. "I dubbed the [missing] voices myself. DeVito knew it. I was doing most all of the mixing, all alone, with Lou Waxman running the machines ... I did what I thought should be done. I don't know if anyone else knew it or not. One time, I imitated [60s 'Blue Velvet' crooner] Bobby Vinton on part of a song when he [Vinton] went flat, and no one ever knew it. If you listen very close to the *Hard Rain* [version of] 'Lay, Lady, Lay,' you will hear me sing 'Play upon my big brass band' instead of 'Lay across my big brass bed.' That's what I heard and that's what I sang, since I didn't know the lyrics."

Meehan insists he sang on two or three other *Hard Rain* songs. "It was just so easy for me. I had just come off moonlighting with the top backup group in New York, The Anne Phillips Singers, and could quickly write out a part and sight-sing it in one take."[10] If you take a dictionary and look up the word *chutzpah*, the chances are there's a photo of Don Meehan next to the definition.

Had you been lucky enough to have been sitting next to Messrs Meehan and DeVito in the Enactron truck, on May 16, at the Tarrant County Convention Center, this is what you would have heard on your headphones, and seen on the truck's monitors. I have it on good authority that this is the correct sequence of songs played that evening. Tape traders have since rearranged the running order, but this is the strict sequence of songs as they were essayed on the night.

(A side bar: Some Dylanologists also claim that songwriter Donna Weiss, co-author of Kim Carnes's 1981 smash hit 'Bette Davis Eyes,' was on stage with Guam in Fort Worth. None of the interviewees who were there that evening could confirm this, and no definitive audio or visual proof has yet been presented.)

The show begins with stage lights being dimmed and Guam starting up a one-chord vamp as the unmistakable voice of Bob Neuwirth calls out from the darkness: "Is this Fort Worth? [Loud, affirmative, audience cheers are heard.] Lucky you! It could be Dallas!" The jibe at the neighboring, and rival, city stokes up the audience and with the applause still ringing out, the band breaks into Neuwirth's 'Cindy's Saddle,' delivered with a country feel, rather than the Cajun flavor of the previous tour. At the conclusion, Neuwirth repeats his inquiry and adds a clause. "Is this Fort Worth? 'Cause the name of this movie is *The Last Show In Texas!*" Indeed, Fort Worth would be the last Rolling Thunder gig in the Lone Star State.

They then charge into Earle Scruggs's instrumental classic, 'Flint Hill Special,' transforming one of bluegrass music's great melodies into a Bob Wills-like, country-swing number. David Mansfield's pedal steel mimics all the tuning shifts which Scruggs's banjo had essayed on the original recording; it is an astonishing display of virtuoso technique.

Steven Soles then contributes a song, a co-write with T Bone Burnett called 'Mad Man,' a number which would grace the first album by The Alpha Band, the trio of Soles, Burnett, and Mansfield, which launched soon after Rolling Thunder. Whoever is supposed to be looking after the house sound, or possibly the stage monitors, is clearly enjoying a nice nap, as there is considerable microphone feedback between the songs which must have been excruciating to the audience at high volume through the PA.

Local lad T Bone Burnett takes the center mic next and sings 'The Dogs,' a co-write with John Fleming and The Band's road manager, Jonathan Taplin. Fleming was a musician-painter friend of Burnett's (a dual calling in common with Bob Neuwirth, another of Burnett's pals, expressionist painter and songwriter Larry Poons, and, of course, Bob Dylan) who T Bone describes as "One of the smartest people I have ever known, if not *the* smartest."[11]

'The Dogs' is a song which will also appear on The Alpha Band's debut album. It must have been a thrill for Burnett to play in front of his hometown crowd; every time Neuwirth mentions his name it gets an audible huzzah from a section of the audience.

Rob Stoner was not just a gifted bassist and reliable musical director; he was also an accomplished songwriter whose material had been covered by everyone from Shirley Bassey to Johnny Winter and Jimmy Haymaker. For the Tarrant County crowd, Stoner sings a strong 'Too Good To Be Wasted,' one of his own compositions, during which he takes a solo on his bass, showcasing his chops in the flashy way bass players in 70s fusion bands liked to do.

Following this, Mick Ronson takes the mic to sing his party piece, Roscoe West's 'Is There Life On Mars?' Among Guam's ranks, Ronson had arguably the greatest reputation, thanks to his association with David Bowie and his brief tenure with Mott The Hoople. However, what British glitter-rock would have meant to the denizens of a Texan municipality nicknamed 'Cowtown' is probably best not dwelt upon.

Technical problems continue to make their presence felt during Ronson's spot, with a high frequency rasp bedeviling the PA. The music thus far is fine and varied, but the long between-song gaps are dragging down any sense of momentum. The feeling emanating from the stage is very different from that of Toronto or Montreal, back in the fall. Back then, the audience heard invention and passion pouring from the house PA speakers; now they're mostly getting the sound of clinical professionalism punctuated by feedback.

T Bone Burnett reappears next; he sings 'Here Comes The Blues Again,' a country song by a fellow Texan, Delbert McClinton, which had first been released as a 45 on the Clean label in 1972, credited to Delbert & Glen. No prizes for guessing who Delbert was. Glen was another Texan, Glen Clark, and Burnett was the producer.

Cowtown is certainly being courted by all this country music, and it's starting to work; the crowd is warming to these hipsters up on the stage. The opening set moves toward its close with another of Neuwirth's songs, 'Alabama Dark,' his Cajun-flavored tribute to Hank Williams, which he performs with help from Scarlet Rivera while Mansfield performs the Louisiana fiddle chores. Neuwirth then delivers a song written by the troupe's recent bayou host, Bobby Charles, entitled 'They Had To Move Away.' It's a slow, bluesy number perfect for an intimate venue but rather too leisurely for a large hall such as this.

The opening exchanges having been completed, Joni Mitchell then takes to the stage. She's greeted by a stunned reaction from the crowd; it is as if the late Sam Houston himself had just taken to the boards. With Guam behind her, Mitchell sings 'Black Crow' from her then unreleased *Hejira* album. It's an elegant reading and at its conclusion Mitchell publicly thanks the musicians for having learned it so rapidly earlier that day (with Mick Ronson calling out the tricky chord progressions, no doubt). Guam then exits the stage and Mitchell performs another song from *Hejira*, 'Song For Sharon,' solo. It's a lengthy piece, full of images chasing images, and as such reminiscent of Dylan's solo performances of 'Visions Of Johanna' back on the 1966 World Tour.

The band then stumbles back on stage, having been introduced by Neuwirth. They play a boisterous, rather drunken-sounding version of Johnny Horton's 'The Battle Of New Orleans' which starts off as if Derek & Clive are in the back room at The Docker's Arms, just past closing, before it kicks into a country two-step which would surely have had the late Mr Horton smiling from his perch in Hillbilly Heaven.

Next up is Kinky Friedman. The man who, three decades later, would run for Governor of Texas kicks into 'Rock And Roll Across The USA,' with Guam matching him ridiculous riff for absurd lyric. It goes down a storm with the locals. Friedman then sings 'Dear Abbie,' an original from his *Lasso From El Paso* album (which also boasted his version of Dylan's 'Catfish') – and not to be confused with the similarly titled John Prine number. Friedman's song is a sincere tribute to Abbie Hoffman, political activist and leader of the radical counterculture movement, The Yippies. Hoffman was then a fugitive from justice, having been arrested for what he claimed were trumped-up drugs charges.

Although Friedman had written some marvelous material, his signature song was the satirical 'Asshole From El Paso,' largely penned by Nick 'Chinga' Chavin (sample lyric: "We don't wipe our asses on Old Glory / God and Lone Star beer are things we trust"). It was a parody of Merle Haggard's reactionary 'Okie From Muskogee.' Friedman pulls out this champion novelty number next, and, its provocative, redneck-baiting lyrics notwithstanding, it wins thunderous applause.

The stage then darkens in anticipation of Dylan. He is gradually lit by a single spotlight which fades up as he settles before the center mic. This was one of Jacques Levy's visual tricks which had worked well on the first RTR tour – it is almost the theatrical equivalent of one of Howard Alk's intense close-ups. Dylan's starts in with 'Mr. Tambourine Man,' delivered at an unusually high tempo that robs it of the usual tenderness. It's as if Dylan's right hand wants to play the scrubbed cross-rhythm of 'Tangled Up In Blue' while his mind is dictating the chords and lyrics of 'Mr. Tambourine Man.'

'It Ain't Me, Babe' is next. Although it had been impressively reworked on the first Rolling Thunder tour, here, Dylan delivers a solo acoustic version that is remarkably faithful to his mid-60s renderings of the song. As with 'Mr. Tambourine Man,' it's essayed at a brisk tempo which, this time, suits the song, emphasizing the narrator's dispassion. Dylan ends it to great applause and a shouted: "Thank you ... here's Bobby Neuwirth coming back!"

Backed by the reliable Wyeth and Stoner rhythm section, the Two Bobs then give the crowd their reading of Robert Friemark's 'Vincent Van Gogh,' a summation of the life of the troubled Dutch artist. Friemark knew his subject; he was an abstract painter and an art teacher of Bob Neuwirth's. He had only composed the song informally; Neuwirth and his friend Kris Kristofferson polished it up, adding new lyrics of their own. Rolling Thunder's spring '76 tour party could boast innumerable musician-cum-painters; not least the headline act who might have drawn some vague parallels between himself and the saturnine post-impressionist who'd taken inspiration from the South of France and was troubled by women even as he idealized them. Almost shockingly, the Two Bobs' version is sung in robust, melodic harmony, with Dylan's voice in the upper register, Neuwirth in the lower.

A vigorous, full-pelt blast through Dylan's 'Maggie's Farm' follows, although it was clearly not as convincing as the similarly-styled version taped later at Fort Collins, as it was that take which would eventually grace both the *Hard Rain* television special and the live album of the same name.

'One Too Many Mornings' is next. Before they begin, however, Dylan tunes his white, National Glenwood 98 electric guitar and runs, unconvincingly, over the scale of C minor. There are some who feel this version of 'One Two Many Mornings' is actually better than the Fort Collins take, which would end up on *Hard Rain*. For all that, Dylan's somewhat elementary attempts at basic six-string answering riffs would surely have been better left to Mick Ronson who, for reasons unknown, isn't even on stage at this point.

'Mozambique' follows. Now the band is cooking on all burners. Scarlet Rivera's violin is on its best behavior; her intonation pretty much on the money. Guam shifts gears at the bridge ("Lying next to her by the ocean ..."), slipping into a choppy, eighth-note rhythmic pattern which lasts until the beginning of the next verse. When the bridge is repeated, Mansfield's staccato mandolin chords emphasize this pattern further. It's an effective device; indeed, this is a much more nuanced version than the *Desire* take and proof that a spirited live band can lend a song a particular vividness which no amount of studio graft will necessarily achieve. Dylan has always stated that his recordings are merely 'versions' of songs; whatever happened to have been captured on that particular day, and that they are best judged in their live incarnations.

'Isis' follows; it's very different from the version played on the first RTR tour. At the beginning it sounds like one of the guitarists is reminding himself of the chords and there is some tuning-up before the song kicks in at a slow, country pace. At the end of the third verse, Guam double-up the time signature; it's another brilliant gear change. Dylan punches out the lyrics in a staccato fashion while Wyeth and Stoner adopt a fascinating stop/go rhythm that's closer to Jamaican rocksteady than country or folk-rock. With a "Thank you; see you in a little bit," from Dylan, the first half concludes.

After the crowd has got its breath back, and Levy's simple lighting tricks have reset the stage atmosphere, the second half commences with the unmistakable, pealing intro to the folk-rock-meets-Book Of Ecclesiastes classic, 'Turn! Turn! Turn!' Roger McGuinn instantly transforms Guam into The Byrds with his distinctive, compressed, 12-string Rickenbacker chimes. This is the first song of the evening which the crowd knows by heart and they respond as if locating an oasis in the Sahara. The familiarity doesn't last long, however. McGuinn's 'Jolly Roger' is next – its old English folk guitar riff answered by Mansfield's dexterous violin. With Mansfield and Ronson in very audible support, McGuinn delivers a persuasive reading of his tale of buccaneers on the Spanish Main. It's unlike anything else heard this evening – and you can imagine its co-author, Jacques Levy, grinning with pride from the side of the stage as it's performed.

The Texan crowd has hardly been given a smooth ride, thus far. They've been exposed to glitter-rock, a passionate defense of a Yippie activist, and now a pirate song. They might have felt more at home with McGuinn's next, Southern-tinged, selection, 'Lover Of The Bayou,' on which Rivera takes over on violin. As a result, it instantly sounds like an outtake from *Desire* rather than what it is: a cut from The Byrds' *Untitled* album – the very LP which Joey Gallo had found so lacking. Ronson's guitar kicks in with one wild, breathtaking solo after another; the stage must surely be beginning to levitate.

Belief in such miraculousness would become part of the ethos of the spring Rolling Thunder tour, as fervent rock was increasingly echoed by passionate faith. Mick Ronson had been bought up by Mormon parents back in East

Yorkshire, and still practiced the religion, while Steven Soles and T Bone Burnett were devout Christians. Their evangelism would be highly influential in converting David Mansfield and others on the tour. This begs a question: if these musical believers could kick butt like they did on Rolling Thunder, why on earth is the majority of Caucasian Christian rock so ghastly and anodyne?

McGuinn's set ends with a robust 'Chestnut Mare,' with Mansfield playing some majestic pedal steel which at times sounds like a cathedral organ. On occasion, Wyeth's drums and Stoner's bass can be overly busy, even flashy; not so Ronson and Mansfield. Their playing is exemplary – virtuosic or supportive as necessary. The same is true of Steven Soles's harmony vocals. McGuinn's four-song set is twice as long as the paltry segment he was allowed on the first RTR tour; it's not clear what made Levy and Dylan change their minds in this regard.

Joan Baez is up next. She begins her set with a daring a cappella version of the Aretha Franklin hit 'Do Right Woman, Do Right Man.' It's a complete contrast to McGuinn's preceding, ensemble-backed performances and the Tarrant Arena loves it, although, as with her fall '75 versions of 'Swing Low, Sweet Chariot,' it's hard not to regard this performance as being first and foremost a party piece, a dazzling trick. Not so her next selection, a song by Hermanos Cantoral called 'El Preso Número Nueve' ('Prisoner Number Nine'), which Baez had had recorded on her Spanish language album *Gracias A La Vida*, released almost two years previously. As so many of its songs were political in nature (Baez, of Mexican stock, had long been a critic of US foreign policy in Latin America), and sung in Spanish, the album received little airplay in the USA but was a bestseller in many Central and South American countries.

Readings of Dylan's 'Forever Young' and her 1971 US Top Ten version of The Band's 'The Night They Drove Old Dixie Down' follow. Curiously, the hit-starved Cowtown crowd fails to embrace the latter with any obvious enthusiasm. 'Sweeter For Me' is next – a Baez original from her only album of self-penned compositions, *Gulf Winds*, much of which had been written on the previous RTR tour. It is a poignant, painful song about the loss of a love, one which anyone on this evening's bill would have been happy to have written.

With Guam behind her every step of the way, Baez then sings Martha & The Vandellas' 'Dancing In The Street.' It is a no doubt heartfelt, well-intentioned version, but it doesn't really work. Wyeth's complex drumming is way off – it needs a Motown stomp beat – and even the usually reliable Ronson delivers a solo that sounds like a scale exercise from a guitarist's instruction manual. What's more, the ensemble stretches the song out for over seven minutes, and while it is no doubt a blast for the musicians it must surely have had some of the punters looking at their watches.

There is still more Joan Baez to come, however, as she ends her set with a warm and tender 'Diamonds & Rust,' a song that, for all her later denials, was surely about Dylan. Its inclusion on any Rolling Thunder date was bound to send out a frisson of intrigue and start tongues wagging.

By this stage, Fort Worth has sat through more than two hours of music. When Levy fades the stage lights to black again, Baez remains on stage and other figures are seen, two of whom come forward and set up a microphone. There is another figure visible but there is not enough light to properly identify anyone.

When the lights do come up, they reveal Dylan and Baez together at the stage-front microphone. To considerable crowd excitement, they immediately embark on 'Blowin' In The Wind,' delivered with a new, staccato vocal phrasing that works well. Dylan's close harmonies are further proof, after his earlier reading of 'Vincent Van Gogh,' that he *can* sing a consistent, orthodox part when he wants to.

'Railroad Boy' is next, a traditional folk song of lost love and suicide better known to British and Irish folk fans as 'The Butcher Boy.' It's another beautifully rendered duet, with Baez playing the high pitched riff on her guitar. She then begins Woody Guthrie's 'Deportee (Plane Wreck At Los Gatos),' with Dylan joining her only on the choruses. He seems to be trying to match Baez in pitch at times, making his voice sound pinched. He relaxes on the line "The sky plane caught fire over Los Gatos canyon," and sounds much more convincing, and is much easier on the ear, as a result. The duo's phrasing is not as tight as it was on 'Blowin' In The Wind,' making some of the verses sound muddled, the words difficult to make out.

The final duet is 'I Pity The Poor Immigrant,' with Guam much in evidence, transforming the austere *John Wesley Harding* track into an unlikely but wonderfully effective samba. Baez even shakes some maracas while Dylan audibly lays into his National Glenwood 98. It's one of the most successful remakes of the entire Rolling Thunder experience.

It's instructive to hear Dylan stumble through some sub-Elmore James slide licks before the ensuing 'Shelter From The Storm' sparks to life. You can hear the blues effect he is *trying* to achieve by playing bottle neck; clearly it's not a technique he has mastered. With Baez hardly off the stage, Dylan is back to barking out the lyrics rather than *singing* them. Yet, his phrasing is fantastic, unique; the definition of dynamic. He brings the lyrics alive and ignites the emotion within them, granting the words a power they don't have on the page. Dylan's approach is curiously reminiscent of the way Sinatra sings the occasionally mundane lyrics on his classic 1955 Capitol album, *In The Wee Small Hours.*

The next three songs from the Fort Worth performance would all make the cut for the *Hard Rain* album released later in the year. A harshly rendered 'I Threw It All Away' finds Dylan sounding less than believable on the ingenuous bridge lyric ("Love is all there is, it makes the world go 'round") – hardly surprising, with his marriage falling apart. Where the *Nashville Skyline* original was soft and autumnally hazy, the *Hard Rain* take is as tough as a scouring pad.

'Stuck Inside Of Mobile With The Memphis Blues Again' is another song presaged by Dylan noodling unnecessarily on guitar, this time causing the band to make their entry slightly out of time. Whichever of the Dons it was, DeVito or Meehan, who decided to edit out much of Dylan's aggravating, between-song guitar extemporization for the versions that appeared on *Hard Rain*, that man made a wise judgment. Despite this inauspicious beginning, it's a bravura version of the *Blonde On Blonde* classic; the band's playing is infectious and it's hard not to smile as Dylan alternates between softly sung verses and gruffly shouted choruses, with a stentorian Bob Neuwirth backing him up on the latter. This is how The Shadows Of Knight might have played the song.

'Oh, Sister' follows. It is perfectly audible that Dylan is a big star who is not in a warm, approachable mood. The sound of his National guitar is crude and right out front in the house mix, even though its tone is almost as unpalatable as that of Chuck Berry's Gibson ES-355 in the movie *Hail! Hail! Rock'n'Roll.* All the while, Mick Ronson, one of rock's true six-string virtuosos, is idling backstage. By the same token, no one has pointed out that David Mansfield's well-tempered fiddle intonation might have worked better than Scarlet Rivera's overly expressive pitch approximations; that the drum heads have been tuned so tightly that it sounds like a kit comprising only piccolo snares; and that the five onstage guitarists are effectively doing little more than duplicating one another. And yet, somehow, the whole unwieldy package works; an oblique, hymnal supplication to a woman, or God, or both.

If 'Oh, Sister' is worthwhile, against the odds, then its successor, the perhaps not entirely unrelated 'You're A Big Girl Now' is positively sublime. Guam plays it soft and slow. Either someone is playing vibes or David Mansfield is capable of the greatest pedal-steel harmonics ever heard. It is almost certainly the latter. If you removed the acoustic guitars and turned up the piano, you could easily imagine it as a Frank Sinatra song. It's 3am, closing time, and the narrator is desperately talking to his girl in a dimly-lit corner booth, while a bartender slowly puts chairs up on tables and prepares to sweep the floor. Lyrics like "Love is so simple, to quote a phrase / You've known it all the time, I'm learnin' it these days" would have been perfect for Ol' Blue Eyes' laconic, world weary style.

'You're Gonna Make Me Lonesome When You Go' is another *Blood On The Tracks* nugget given a stylistic makeover. Performed at a canter, it's a swinging, honky-tonk country romp. Dylan's singing (not shouting) is positively euphoric, as if he's really relishing the prospect of incipient solitude; which, indeed, he may have been. His National guitar is down in the house mix, now, and this helps warm up the overall band sound considerably. David Mansfield recalls such stylistic reinventions of Dylan's songs being a hallmark of the spring '76 tour. "Sometimes we'd totally throw the arrangement out the window. Something which might have been a waltz might become a blues shuffle." [12]

"We're gonna do this tonight as a special request," announces Dylan by way of introduction to 'Lay, Lady, Lay.' "We're gonna send it out to you. You can send it back." Meehan and DeVito might not have captured the vigorous chorus backing vocals on tape, but they are certainly present in the house PA. Although Dylan had begun to rewrite some of his recent songs' lyrics, concentrating on narrative momentum and scene-setting, in light of Jacques Levy's directorial lessons, 'Lay, Lady, Lay' is apparently made over to purely bawdy effect – its "Forget this dance ... let's go upstairs" and "Let's take a chance ... who really cares" couplets somewhat undermining the song's former grace and mystery.

Curiously, perhaps, Dylan then chooses to break the flow by introducing T Bone Burnett to the lead mic, where the local boy delivers another song he co-wrote with John Fleming, 'Silver Mantis.' It's a daring move, as T Bone, despite having pockets of support out in the audience, was then a new face and most fans were there to see the veteran Dylan. What's more, it's getting late; the crowd has been seated for three hours and they must be hungry for the hits. Levy and Dylan evidently knew what they were doing, however, as Burnett delivers an achingly tender and understated 'Silver Mantis' with a tenor to soprano backing vocal (could it be Donna Weiss?) closely shadowing his lead vocal. 'Silver Mantis' would appear on The Alpha Band's second album, *Spark In The Dark*, in 1977, an album which would be 'directed' by Bob Neuwirth and produced by Steven Soles. The song clocks in at over eight minutes at the Tarrant County Arena and gets a generous round of applause, which is some achievement considering how eager the Dylan fans must've been for more Bob.

The surprises are not over, however. Dylan returns to centre stage to play a rarely aired song, 'Going, Going, Gone,' from 1974's *Planet Waves*. It's a staggering version, the verses, delivered with the stop/start rhythm at which Stoner and Wyeth excel, giving way to a new, smoother, rhythmic backing on the chorus which lifts the song brilliantly every time it's deployed. Dylan's voice is flat at times, but he's singing from the heart so it doesn't detract form the performance. It would have been criminal to have passed this over for the *Hard Rain* live album were it not for two fatal flaws – at 3:20 and again at 4:50 – where Dylan takes guitar solos that could be diplomatically termed rudimentary. At these points, he is, wisely, mixed down in the house PA while Rivera's dramatic violin flourishes are brought up to cover Dylan's fumbling. David Mansfield has pointed out that Dylan's knowledge of musical scales, and their exact relationship to the guitar fretboard, was not great at the time of Rolling Thunder. Yet, the main problem with Dylan's cubist approach to guitar soloing is one of timing, or lack thereof. He always seems to enter a musical phrase too early or too late. It's a shame he never took any tips from the likes of Ronson, Mansfield, or McGuinn; each is a gifted instrumentalist with great timing and feel in his solos and among the finest technicians the 1976 rock scene had to offer.

Dylan again dips into *Blood On The Tracks* for the next number, 'Idiot Wind.' It's another song which benefits from Mansfield's swooning pedal steel. This young David is a musical Goliath; he could play a bathtub and make it sound sweet. Dylan has rewritten the song's lyrics; perhaps in deference to McGuinn and Levy he omits the original line, "Visions of your chestnut mare," replacing it with "Visions of your flaming town … ." Playing the song at this point in the set actually smacks of Jacques Levy. It's everything a theater director would love: dramatic, almost to the point of melodrama, full of wild imagery and complete with unexpected twists and turns. With its anthemic chorus, 'Idiot Wind' would be a climactic song in anyone's set. Wyeth and Stoner are on their best behavior on this song; there is no over-elaborate riffing, no willful rhythms; just a locked-in tightness that is purely in service of the singer and the song.

Stoner, watching Dylan's gestures like a hawk, helps guide Guam, and all of the Tarrant County Convention Centre Arena, wherever this wind may blow them.

After that, the subsequent 'Knockin' On Heaven's Door' seems almost like an afterthought; it's certainly not the majestic Rolling Thunder hymn it once was. Perhaps the musicians are as exhausted as the audience. As ever, the breakdown, with the drums and bass dropping out and McGuinn's Rickenbacker chimes shimmering into Mansfield's pedal-steel harmonics, is the celestially hued highlight. They elongate it, here, allowing Rivera's violin to enter delicately before the bass and drums rejoin the fray, bringing along the rest of the posse for the ride home.

The final song of the evening is 'Gotta Travel On,' a folk hymn to hobo restlessness written by Paul Clayton, the musician, folklorist, and Dylan fan and who had tragically committed suicide in March 1967. Clayton collected songs from southwestern Virginia, as did A.P. Carter before him, thereby helping save the region's cultural heritage from the rampant homogenization of burger chains and their ilk. On the spring '76 tour, 'Gotta Travel On' fulfilled the same function that 'This Land Is Your Land' had the previous fall – a grand, communal finale every bit as spirit-lifting and affecting as Woody Guthrie's warhorse. 'Gotta Travel On' had been a big hit for Billy Grammer back in 1959 and was covered by everyone from The Weavers, Bill Monroe, and The Kingston Trio to Timi Yuro, The Seekers, Chet Atkins, Boxcar Willie, Jerry Lee Lewis, Bill Monroe, and Harry Belafonte. Even Lawrence Welk had a crack at it. Its credentials were undeniable.

As 'This Land Is Your Land' had been on the fall dates, this evening's all-hands-on-deck denouement is marshaled by Joan Baez. She announces who will sing each coming verse with schoolmarm authority but can do nothing to halt a pervading sense of onstage chaos. It sounds like the entire company – and perhaps some of the caterers – are all playing along at once; each one of them is apparently having a stone-cold blast. Somewhere in middle, Mick Ronson discovers his amp goes up to 11. Texans love *more*, whether that means bigger or louder, and the place duly goes nuts. They cheer for over two minutes before an announcement issues forth from the PA: "The band of the Rolling Thunder Revue, we thank you; you've been a great audience, good night." And with the house lights up and blazing brightly, Levy signals everyone off the stage. The evening is over.

Four songs from Fort Worth would make it onto the *Hard Rain* album. The remaining five would be cherry-picked from the outdoor show at Colorado State University's Hughes Stadium, in Fort Collins, on May 23.

Heavy rain had been falling in northern Colorado for days by the time the troupe arrived at Fort Collins. This, the penultimate show of the second and final Rolling Thunder Revue tour, might have been imperiled by the weather if it hadn't already been earmarked for filming, a substitute for the Clearwater footage which Dylan had nixed. A thick television contract meant cancellation was out of the question.

Against glowering skies, squalls of rain, and plummeting temperatures, Dylan and the band would deliver a performance that was as desperate and, in places, raggedly glorious as anything on the entire Rolling Thunder adventure.

The opening track on *Hard Rain*, 'Maggie's Farm,' was actually the fourth song Dylan and the band played at Fort Collins and was early evidence of the show's tattered brilliance. Stoner's bass is all over the song, as if Dylan were paying him by the note. It would be distracting, unfettered noodling but for Dylan's curiously timed intro and subsequent rough-toned riffing, which all but obliterates it. Against this, T Bone Burnett's guitar plays a repetitive, melodic pattern, sporadically sifted through his beloved phase shifter, while Ronson plays a riff that almost doubles Dylan's at the introduction of each new musical phrase. Unlike his bandleader, Ronson plays perfectly in time. Dylan's guitar tone is nasty but it adds to the song, somehow. At one point, he is audibly laughing as he riffs away unapologetically.

'One Too Many Mornings' was the next Fort Collins offering, and also the second song on *Hard Rain*. It's distinguished by a fine pedal-steel part from David Mansfield, its swooping elegance all the more remarkable when you consider the trying circumstances under which it was performed. "For me, the Colorado *Hard Rain* [show] was pretty hellish difficult," confirms Mansfield. "I remember playing steel guitar and I was so cold in my jeans and whatever I was wearing, that my foot was shaking on the volume pedal and I couldn't get a smooth tone. Thankfully, there are such wonderful things as volume limiters so it wasn't discernible but it was a really harsh environment. Physically it was *cold!*"[13]

When Mansfield solos on the pedal steel (panned hard left on stereo speakers), between 1:38 and 2:16, Dylan is also picking, but his guitar is buried way down low in the mix. Was that engineer Don Meehan's choice? In contrast, at 2:57, Bob lets go with a few well-intended riffs which do help move the song along and which are more proudly placed in the mix. In Meehan's unpublished autobiography, he claims that he and Don DeVito started mixing *Hard Rain* tracks at Glen Glenn Sound studios, in Los Angeles, before scrapping them and starting afresh in New York City.

The sixth track on *Hard Rain* is 'Shelter From The Storm,' which ties in a dead heat with 'A Hard Rains A-Gonna Fall' for the most ironically titled song to be wheeled out before the sodden Fort Collins crowd. On it, Dylan returns to his shout-singing approach, but the fulsome arrangement seems to actually require it. The Stoner-Wyeth rhythm section is back to its economic best while Dylan punctuates the verses with the most wicked-toned, undisciplined slide guitar since Hound Dog Taylor and Brewer Phillips dueled away the nights at Chicago's Checkerboard Lounge. In contrast, Burnett injects a fine reggae riff, tinted with a hint of phase shifter, which dovetails with Dylan's six-string (Burnett is panned left on the *Hard Rain* album mix).

If Allen Ginsberg was the most tragically underused personnel member on the first Rolling Thunder sojourn (and likewise in *Renaldo & Clara*), then surely Mick Ronson is the most wasted virtuoso on this second RTR tour. While Dylan and Burnett are essentially playing interlocking parts, no one is taking the lead and there are several places in the song with gaping, Mick Ronson-shaped spaces but no Mick Ronson.

'You're A Big Girl Now' follows; it's a rough diamond, heaven-sent to Fort Collins, although the packaging is torn by the time it arrives. Dylan plays acoustic guitar but still contrives to make it sound harsh and metallic, while Steven Soles plays a much more mellifluous-sounding acoustic part, and Scarlet Rivera's violin slots in behind Dylan. The rhythm section, with Gary Burke now playing drums, stays manfully with Dylan's 'unique' timing. Indeed, Stoner is at his best here, following Dylan like a bloodhound, while Howie Wyeth's piano is understated and drenched in melancholy, emphasizing Dylan's anguish on the "Like a corkscrew to my heart" line. It's a minor masterpiece, the very definition of the old country & western epithet "ragged but right."

The best is saved for last, however. 'Idiot Wind' is a great song for a bad day *anywhere*, but is surely the perfect riposte to a bad day in the rain, with your wife watching you searchingly (as Sara Dylan was) as you prove that you're no more, and no less, human than the poor souls freezing out on the saturated bleachers of Hughes Stadium.

Wearing matching Arab headgear, percussionist Gary Burke and drummer

Howie Wyeth play with perfect synergy, Burke's rhythms circling Wyeth's solid beat like hornets around a hive as they propel Guam on a valedictory ride. Dylan's vocal is the passionate side of forceful and utterly compelling. Listen to him, at 5:11, delivering the line "It was gravity which pulled us down and destiny which broke us apart," and then again at 5:23 – "You tamed the lion in my cage but it just wasn't enough to change my heart" – and know just why Van Morrison thinks Dylan is an outstanding singer. At 6:01, Mansfield finds those heavenly harmonics on the pedal steel, again, locating a higher, even more blissful tone at 6:17. In contrast, Dylan's guitar is more distorted than Johnny Ramone's ever was (although it's still a cleaner sound than Hound Dog Taylor's).

David Mansfield recalls this song being typical of a kind of onstage unburdening process which Dylan was going through toward the conclusion of Rolling Thunder. "I wouldn't want to put words in his mouth, but it seemed to me like Bob had found a cathartic way to let out a lot of his rage. His performances were almost electrically charged and vitriolic at times. On 'Idiot Wind' it just seemed like there was this almost harsh, adversarial tone, even against nature itself. It was so different to play in that weather ... it was out of tune, out of time. ... There were moments of inspiration and there were other times where it sounded like it was coming unhinged. There were some things where the passion was just so intense that I didn't mind any out-of-tune playing at all."[14]

The most unhinged thing on 'Idiot Wind' is Dylan's vocal, and the song is all the better for it. Nothing from the Grand Coulee Dam to the Capitol could match the power coming off a skinny Minnesotan on that wet, tempestuous afternoon in Colorado.

CHAPTER 8

FORT COLLINS, COLORADO: THE HARD RAIN TELEVISION SPECIAL

I n its review of the *Hard Rain* telecast, broadcast by NBC Television on September 14 1976, *The New York Times* memorably described Dylan being "enigmatic as a fox." However enigmatic, he certainly didn't look happy, although his appearance was positively biblical, and neither innocuously or accidentally so.

In his prime, or rather during one of his periodic primes, Dylan has always looked the part, an actor aware of his own presence. His onstage appearance, and the visual message he thereby sends to his audience, has always gone hand in glove with the resonance and, yes, enigma of his music. In those periods of his career when Dylan is really *on*, he is no less an iconic figure than James Dean in his rebellious red windbreaker, or the young Cassius Clay entering the ring wide-eyed with expectation. By the same token, when Dylan isn't playing, writing, or performing well, his look suffers accordingly and he is equally capable of delivering ill-considered glitz and gloss in place of substance.

Whenever the cameras close in on Dylan during the NBC special, he has the appearance of a rather concerned, almost sinister, and somewhat underfed, Old Testament prophet. One fan even likened Dylan's *Hard Rain* image to that of Christ, which is perhaps going a bit far. Indeed, *which* Christ would he resemble? Surely not a muscular Michelangelo Jesus, or the King James Version of the Son of God who has a rock'n'roll image, but one that's closer to that of the hirsute John Lennon crossing Abbey Road in his white Tommy Nutter suit than it is to Bob; and, anyway, The Bible clearly describes Jesus as looking Ethiopian.

This Dylan looks like he's been on the road too long. By the time this show was filmed, on May 23 1976 at the Fort Collins, Colorado football palace known formally as Hughes Stadium (home of the mighty Colorado State Rams and a short drive off Interstate 25), Dylan probably wanted to be anywhere but on a stage. Sara Dylan had flown in to join the troupe in Fort Collins and perhaps Dylan felt hemmed-in having his beloved wife around. He couldn't even partake of the many tour temptations still at hand.

The *Hard Rain* broadcast rejigs the set order followed by the band that day, presumably at Dylan's request, although it might have been a network decision. Only half the Hughes Stadium set was actually broadcast. The following songs were left on the cutting room floor: 'Mr. Tambourine Man,' 'It Ain't Me, Babe,' 'Vincent Van Gogh,' 'Isis,' 'Oh Sister,' 'I Want You,' 'Tangled Up In Blue,' 'You're A Big Girl Now,' 'You're Gonna Make Me Lonesome When You Go,' 'Lay, Lady, Lay,' 'Silver Mantis' (sung by T Bone Burnett), 'Going Going Gone,' and 'Gotta

Travel On' (Paul Clayton's folk standard, sung as the ensemble finale). With delicious, Dylanesque willfulness, only one song from *Desire*, his most recent album, and a US Number One, makes it to the broadcast set.

Shot through the drizzle on a grim, gray, afternoon, *Hard Rain* is a curious film in many ways. No formal director is credited; perhaps there was no one formally directing it, or perhaps there was some debate about who would get the credit. In *The Bob Dylan Encyclopedia*, author Michael Gray says of *Hard Rain*: "Filmed and edited by Howard Alk, this was magnificent television, using the small screen imaginatively." Yet, while Alk was definitely among the camera operatives, the television footage wasn't edited using his signature style; there is no cutting from conversation to musical performance and back again to underscore some over-arching point, for example. The bottom line is, *Hard Rain could* have been directed by Alk, but his documentary style, as evinced by *American Revolution 2* and *The Murder Of Fred Hampton*, certainly isn't evident here. The end credits offer no clues.

If indeed it is Howard Alk's work, then *Hard Rain* is surely his finest moment as an editor or cameraman, or both. His signature shot (as seen repeatedly in *Renaldo & Clara*) is the close-up of the center stage microphone – a static frame which resists following the singer as he or she moves. In *Hard Rain*, Dylan enters just such a static frame and appears in dramatically tight close-up. As he sings, he is seemingly emotionally charged, wide-eyed, and open-mouthed. This is how the *Renaldo & Clara* footage might have looked, had it not been brutalized by jump cuts. So, there is evidence for and against the hand of Howard Alk in *Hard Rain*.

Cinematography would've been quite a chore at Hughes Stadium on that damp day in May. Throughout the film, cameras are seen sheathed in plastic against the rain. A large Persian carpet covers much of center stage; it had been used on previous shows, but was it also there to withstand dampness and the threat of electric shock?

In addition to the carpet, the stage was given a new, eye-catching backdrop: a white sheet upon which Dylan and Neuwirth painted various images such as a figure-eight (or is it an infinity symbol?), a Star Of David, a man with a very red face, what appears to be one of the Three Wise Men with a quiver of arrows at his back, a bottle opener, a man playing a clarinet (clearly in Dylan's painterly style, recognizable to anyone who has seen the jackets of *Music From Big Pink* or *Self Portrait*), a green fish, a figure looking uncannily like Bruce Springsteen in a sleeveless shirt, a skeleton key, and a winged beast with a large heart which seems to be the mythological creature called, ahem, a griffin.

Among the musicians, headgear seems important, worn, perhaps, as a symbol of status or rank. As shown on the *Hard Rain* album jacket, Dylan sports a desert Arab's headdress, a *keffiyeh*. It's a white cloth hat worn as protection against the blazing sun and the dust of desert storms; it is particularly popular in Persian Gulf states such as Kuwait. A thin circle of rope, an *agal*, is sometimes seen around the wearer's forehead; it keeps the *keffiyeh* from moving around.

Although bassist Rob Stoner defies peer pressure by performing bare-headed, at Fort Collins, percussionist Gary Burke, drummer/pianist Howie Wyeth, and guitarists T Bone Burnett, Steven Soles, and Roger McGuinn all opt for the Bedouin headgear, while Kinky Friedman, Ramblin' Jack Elliott, Mick Ronson, and Bob Neuwirth remember they are in cowboy country and sensibly opt for Stetsons. For the record, Joan Baez wears a red turban and a lot of rouge on her cheeks while Scarlet Rivera sports a long blue scarf.

The Fort Collins shoot may have been emotionally and physically uncomfortable but at least there were some old friends behind a few of the cameras and, as T Bone Burnett recalls, one of them was the aforementioned Howard Alk. "Some of the guys who had been filming on the first leg of the tour came back [at Fort Collins], like Howard Alk and Larry Johnson, and filmed some more. That [footage] got put together for ABC TV. The story goes that when it finally was sent to New York City, for the network to look at, the head of the company saw the footage and said, 'I can tell you one thing; he is no Cary Grant' [laughter]. There, on some executive's TV screen, was this guy with a rag tied round his head! By that time, the '76 tour had become Rag Rock."

Burnett can also reveal the provenance of the Arab headgear. "Just before Dylan left on the second leg of the tour, he was putting a brick wall round his house and all the bricklayers had those rags 'round their heads to stop them getting concrete and various bits of plaster or whatever in their hair. Dylan went out there to help these guys and out of that we got the babushka headdress, or whatever hell it's called, and then he just kept it on for the road."[1]

As would be the case in Martin Scorsese's 1978 movie of The Band's farewell show, *The Last Waltz*, the first song shown in *Hard Rain* is actually the last song of the concert. Its title may have been the reason it was placed at the beginning, but, taken at a slow, slow tempo, 'A Hard Rain's A-Gonna Fall,' is as powerful an opening gambit as can be imagined.

The Dylan-Baez duet 'Blowin' In The Wind' is up next; it's contrastingly rapid, almost like a samba coming off some Rio de Janeiro dance floor at 3am. For once, Dylan and Baez enunciate as one voice, and they seem to treble their lung power by doing so. This is the uncommon sound of Dylan consciously following a properly rehearsed vocal pattern. He has moments during this acoustic segment with Baez where he almost seems to be enjoying himself, although he never really loosens up fully. He does allow himself a brief smile at the end of 'Blowin' In The Wind' as he points at the cameraman (could it be Howard Alk, perhaps?) in the press pit. Having already scrapped one attempt at filming a television special, at Clearwater, Florida, the previous month, perhaps the furrowed brow that Dylan more typically wears in *Hard Rain* is simply a reflection of his anxiety about getting a decent film in the can.

Next up is 'Railroad Boy,' the American West's reworking of an old Dublin folk song, 'The Butcher Boy.' In fact, this tune was also known as 'The Gosport Tragedy,' 'The Miller's Tale,' and 'London Town,' and had many other variants depending on the country or town in which it was sung. By the time Buell Kazee recorded 'The Butcher's Boy' on January 16 1928, it was widely known by all of the above titles. It was Kazee's version which Harry Smith curated for his 1952 *Anthology Of American Folk Music* collection, which is probably where Dylan first heard it. Bob's friend Bonnie Beecher recorded him performing it in May 1961, as 'The Railroad Boy,' on what is now known as the *Minneapolis Party Tape*. The song was part of Baez's musical history, too. Their familiarity with this old musical friend may be why Dylan almost, *almost*, looks like he's having some fun here. He plays an emphatic rhythm on his sunburst J25 Gibson acoustic as Baez picks a primitive but effective lead line on her Martin 00-18 which answers the vocals on the verse. On the last line, "And tell the world I died for love," they hold the word "world" for a good ten seconds. The effect is quite astonishing; astonishing almost to the point of sinking the song entirely.

Woody Guthrie's 'Deportee (Plane Wreck At Los Gatos)' is an oft-covered folk song about the tragic plane crash, on January 29 1948, near Los Gatos Canyon, 20 miles west of Coalinga, California, in which 32 people died. Newspaper reports only gave the names of the pilot and crew; the remaining 27 dead, being merely illegal Mexican immigrants, were referred to only as "deportees." The song started out as a poem by Woody Guthrie; in 1958 a schoolteacher named Martin Hoffman added a tune and Pete Seeger began playing it in concert. In *Hard Rain* it is performed in folksy 6/8 time and filmed as one long, close-range shot of Dylan and Baez together at the mic. Dylan is playing a guitar in standard tuning while Baez has a capo at the fifth fret, so their fingering is different (while Dylan makes a G chord, Baez must make a D, and so on), This allows their two acoustics to ring off each other harmonically, creating sweet-sounding overtones. The close-up reveals that Baez is wearing a wedding band.

'I Pity The Poor Immigrant' is next. This is one of the most bizarre song re-arrangements of the entire Rolling Thunder tour. Initially, it sounds like they are playing the intro to Charlie Pride's 1970 country & western smash 'Is Anybody Going To San Antone?' It's actually a surprise when Dylan sings the first line and it isn't Pride's classic. The swaying, full band re-arrangement features repeated stop/start passages. Baez plays maracas – really plays them – adding swaying rhythm to these sections. Visually, she's reminiscent of Jerome Green shaking wild percussion behind his boss, Bo Diddley, although Green was not known to perform in heavy facial makeup and a red turban.

The footage continues to show Dylan's concern about the ensemble's performance. He keeps turning around to make sure all the stops and starts are accomplished as scheduled. *Hard Rain* would also offer the first audio-visual evidence of Dylan as lead guitar player. While his timing is sometimes questionable, his ideas as a picker are usually well-designed. His guitar-playing certainly adds something to the songs, although it's anyone's guess if what he plays is what he originally intended.

'Shelter From The Storm' is the first of two selections from *Blood On The Tracks*. Suitably, by this point, Dylan is getting a bit wet. If the electric instruments are ignored, the damp setting is starting to look like something out of The Old Testament. When the cameras turn on the sodden, yet enthusiastic crowd, it takes relatively little imagination to believe that under his *keffiyeh*, Dylan is thinking his friend Christ is in real trouble with the Romans this time.

Bob plays slide on his white National solid body, the very make and model which David Lindley was then popularizing through his work with Jackson Browne. Dylan's model appears to be from the late 50s. His slide playing works well with T Bone Burnett's reggae riff played through a phase-shifter pedal. There is a push-and-pull rhythm interchange between the guitars which defines the song as much as Dylan's gruff, declaratory vocal. His Bobness is both visibly and audibly biting off the words and spitting them back out, never taking in more than he can chew, although he has the power to bite heads off with this material.

Next, it's back to the 60s for 'Maggie's Farm.' Dylan plays a lead line in the high register, and the concentration on his face is quite something. Not for Bob the intense look of the guitar superhero, nor the warm, childlike stare at the fretboard so common amongst puzzled beginners and those classical guitarists who view their instrument as an extension of their souls. No, Dylan looks at his axe with some irritation as if to say "why can't this guitar do what I want it to do?" Mick Ronson plays a quite different, low-range answering riff and at the end, when they go into a vamp on the chords, Ronson throws in some lovely Chuck Berry/Carl Hogan riffs to keep it interesting right up to the final chord. Ronson should have worked with Dylan again, it was an opportunity missed.

David Mansfield's aching pedal steel amplifies the existential angst at the core of a measured 'One Too Many Mornings,' his lazy chordal slides painting the emotional picture even before Dylan's lyrics describe it. Mansfield, in common with Roger McGuinn, gets little screen time during *Hard Rain*, yet Mansfield plays, on one or other instrument, throughout most of the set. It's as if someone in the editing booth was afraid of showing us such an innocent young face in the company of ne'er-do-wells like the chain-smoking Neuwirth, the rock god Ronson, and the frowning shepherd of the flock in the ragged headgear.

As the performance goes on, the cameras capture the audience hunkering against the incessant drizzle; they look a crowd of misbegotten refugees. It's if Dylan and his band are emergency aid workers and the Fort Collins masses residents of a squatter camp, waiting for them to distribute UN food parcels.

Desire is finally mined for a song, 'Mozambique.' The country which the song so insouciantly celebrated was going through violent civil unrest at the time of this filming. After the likes of 'George Jackson,' and 'Hurricane,' most Dylan fans who saw the title 'Mozambique' on the jacket of *Desire* would have thought it likely to be a song about the recent civil war in that country – a Cold War in microcosm in which the Soviet Union deployed Cuban soldiers to back the country's Marxist-Leninist rebels and the USA had the CIA train the opposing forces. The reality was a light and somewhat superficial song about having fun and romance in a country which was drastically short of both.

'Mozambique' was the sixth song in the original, unedited Fort Collins performance and is a played slightly faster than the *Desire* version. Rob Stoner finally succumbs and dons a *keffiyeh*, perhaps he's getting rained on, or perhaps he wants to make it clear that he's on the boss's team. The album version harmony was sung, of course, by Emmylou Harris and here it sounds like it could be Ronee Blakely, although the mystery female vocalist is never shown. It could be Joan Baez but it seems odd that she would not be shown.

A slow, aching, partially rewritten 'Idiot Wind' is the penultimate song on the broadcast. Steven Soles plays acoustic guitar with a heavily bandaged first finger on the left hand and a plastic yellow duck, a child's toy, stuck at the top of his guitar neck by the tuning pegs. Soles, whose stage movements recall both Ginsberg and Michael Stipe, provides attractively strident harmonies on the chorus while Stoner plays a busy bass line which leads the entire band through the melodic changes without ever crossing the line into 'lead bass' showboating territory. Stoner is shown moving to the rhythm he is helping to lay down; he looks good, he could teach some of the others a thing or two about onstage bopping. As on 'One Too Many Mornings,' Mansfield's pedal steel resists all country & western cliché as it teases out every last emotional nuance.

A curious note: at several points during 'Idiot Wind,' bassist Rob Stoner can be seen to stop playing, yet the sound of his instrument continues. Further to this, at other points, Stoner is making shapes on the neck of his fretboard which do not correspond with what is heard on the soundtrack. Is this further evidence of Don Meehan's after-the-event overdubbing? Where, when, or by whom such overdubs or corrections were actually made is not known. But they happened.

'Knockin' On Heaven's Door' is the last song of the broadcast, and finally McGuinn takes the center stage with Dylan. If Bob was so keen to get him on board for this tour, why is McGuinn kept in the background so much; has he fallen out of favor with the court? The ex-Byrd has the same look of concern as Dylan, perhaps they both fear imminent electric shock. The song and the performance have a mood which perfectly matches the portentous afternoon sky and they close out the proceedings with a sense of pre-ordained doom. You can do that when your songs so freely quote, reference, rewrite, and reflect the themes of The Bible.

As the credits start to roll (see next page), McGuinn steps forward to the mic to sing his customary verse, the one that begins "Mama, take these guns off of me." However, instead of the usual line, he sings "Mama, take these purse strings off of me." Did Dylan write those lines, or is McGuinn making a point?

Throughout it all, the only comments Dylan gives the crowd are two simple words, "Joan Baez," spoken matter-of-factly at the end of 'I Pity The Poor Immigrant.' Like the man said, enigmatic as a fox.

The US *Hard Rain* Television Special credits

Hard Rain
Starring: Bob Dylan
Special Guest: Joan Baez
With: Gary Burke, T Bone Burnett, David Mansfield, Scarlet Rivera, Steven Soles, Rob Stoner, Howie Wyeth, Bob Neuwirth, Kinky Friedman, Allen Ginsberg, Roger McGuinn, Mick Ronson
Stage Director: Jacques Levy
Special Inspiration: Bobby Charles
Produced by TVTV in association with Streaming Eagle Productions, Inc.
Production: Wendy Appel, David Axelrod, Steve Conant, Hudson Marquez, Allen Rucker, Michael Shamberg, Megan Williams
Cameramen: Howard Alk, Paul Goldsmith, L.A. Johnson, David Myers, Ron Sheldon
Music produced by Don DeVito
Recording and mixing engineer Don Meehan
Supervising engineer: John Godfrey
Thanks to: Arthur Rimbaud, Joel Bernstein, Gerry Bakall, Jeff Raven, Robert Johnson, Michael Ahern, Peter Orlovsky, Vince Humphrey, Gloria Ashley, and Woody Guthrie
Concert Sound: Arthur Rosato
Audience Courtesy of Gary Shafner
Perseverance Award: Louis Kemp
This program was made for Bob Gilbert
Mechanic: Dominic Placco
The Man In The Blanket Was Played By Victor Maymudes
Muscle And Movers Supplied By Andy, Steve, Lou, Danny, and Barry
Head Gear By Denise Mercedes and Anne Waldman
Backup Choir: Naomi, Beatrice, and Sarah D
Edited by Gangbusters c1975 Streaming Eagle Productions, Inc.
Brought to you in its entirely [sic] by Craig Corporation, makers of PowerPlay Car Stereos and Series 500 Audio Components. Craig ... When You're Serious About Music.

CHAPTER 9
THE JAPANESE
HARD RAIN
TELEVISION SPECIAL

T
he television network Tokyo 12 Channel (today known as TV Tokyo) first broadcast the Fort Collins *Hard Rain* television special on March 20 1977. There is no question that this dampest of concert films was shown to Japanese viewers in higher quality, and with more visual detail and clarity, than in its US counterpart.

In the mid 70s, US television was still in the Dark Ages as far as its transmission set up was concerned. Its NTSC analog broadcast system had enjoyed no major upgrading since color was first made available back in the 50s. Japanese media companies, however, had been encouraged by their government to improve upon NTSC's 525 line picture (in a 4:30 aspect ratio) formula and, since the coming of color to Japanese television in the early 60s, they had been providing enhanced picture fidelity even within the 525 line parameter. Whatever the technical details, *Hard Rain* certainly looked a whole lot better on Tokyo 12 Channel than it did on NBC Television's US transmission.

Contents-wise, the Japanese *Hard Rain* concert was effectively identical to the US version, save for one omitted song, the Dylan-Baez duet 'Railroad Boy.' While that might be a minor irritant to the Dylan completist, there are other constituents of the Tokyo 12 Channel broadcast which may become somewhat more infuriating, particularly to any Western viewer not blessed with at least a working knowledge of the Japanese language or its *Kanji* pictograms.

In order to introduce Bob Dylan to the uninitiated Japanese viewer who has somehow stumbled upon Bob-san's Rolling Thunder concert special while channel surfing, a bright red sash appears across the screen at key moments in the broadcast, a backdrop on which Japanese script spells out biographical information about the star of the show. This bold crimson stripe not only obscures much of the onstage action but inevitably distracts any non-Japanese speaker who not only misses crucial elements of the performance but who is tantalized by not knowing what the words are saying about Dylan.

Text appears elsewhere on the film. As each song is performed, a translation of key song lyrics is superimposed on the screen, although on these occasions without the bright red background, which means that the onstage action can at least be viewed. The subtitles are more intrusive as they identify each musician, their name spelt out in *Kanji* script superimposed across the torso as they are located in the center of the screen. In addition, at three distinct points, translated Dylan quotes appear, obliterating part of the screen while keeping the oriental Bob neophyte au fait with the importance of the man's art and the depth of his passion.

Noted Japanese rock music scholar Tomoki Tanikawa believes that the *Hard Rain* broadcast helped stoke national interest in Dylan, something which would swell over the following year and lead to Dylan's first ever Japanese shows in 1978. Indeed, a repeat of *Hard Rain* was broadcast on Tokyo 12 Channel on Monday, February 13 1978, just one week before Dylan's hotly anticipated Tokyo debut.

Here is a list, salvaged from the vaults of TVTV (Top Value Television – the San Francisco production company who shot the *Hard Rain* show in partnership with NBC), detailing every song filmed at Fort Collins on that rainy day in May 1976. Those songs which made the broadcast edit of the Japanese *Hard Rain* special are shown in **bold type**.

'Asshole From El Paso' [Kinky Friedman]
'Dear Abbie' [Kinky Friedman]
'Sold American' [Kinky Friedman]
'Mr. Tambourine Man'
'It Ain't Me, Babe'
'Vincent Van Gogh' [Dylan and Bob Neuwirth]
'Maggie's Farm'
'One Too Many Mornings'
'Mozambique'
'Isis'
'Blowin' In The Wind'
'Railroad Boy' [Dylan and Joan Baez]
'Deportee (Plane Wreck At Los Gatos)' [Dylan and Joan Baez]
'I Pity The Poor Immigrant' [Dylan and Joan Baez]
'Shelter From The Storm'
'Oh, Sister'
'I Want You'
'Tangled Up In Blue'
'You're A Big Girl Now'
'You're Gonna Make Me Lonesome When You Go'
'Lay, Lady, Lay'
'Silver Mantis' [T Bone Burnett]

'Going, Going, Gone'
'Idiot Wind'
'Knockin' On Heaven's Door'
'Gotta Travel On' [The Rolling Thunder ensemble]
'A Hard Rain's A-Gonna Fall'

Here follows a translation, by Kiyoko and Takashi Yoshida, of the various Japanese texts, in sequence, as they were superimposed on the *Hard Rain* footage for the enlightenment of the Asian audience. The timings to the left refer to the chronological placement of the individual interjections as they appear, if the viewer is watching the Japanese *Hard Rain* DVD from the very beginning (00:00).

00:00: *Bob Dylan Live Concert Special*

00:03: *Hard Rain*

00:10: "This is footage of a concert given by Bob Dylan, whose massive influence on the young generation was felt throughout the 1960s and 70s. The concert took place in the Great Hughes Stadium in Colorado, Massachusetts [sic], on May 23 1976 – the last day of the Rolling Thunder tour."
[This text appears over the opening shot of Dylan leading the band into 'A Hard Rains A-Gonna Fall' – actually, of course, the encore at Fort Collins. The information is erroneous; Rolling Thunder was a long way from Massachusetts – in several ways – by now, and the Salt Lake City show, on May 25, was actually the last ever RTR performance.]

00:28: "Bob Dylan"
[This surely superfluous identification appears over a close-up of Dylan singing 'A Hard Rains A-Gonna Fall.' He is wearing a classic blue American work shirt, leather jacket, and Arab headdress. Directly behind Dylan in the shot is Gary Burke, working out some major stress on his congas.]

01:05: "Bob Neuwirth"
[Neuwirth appears in white cowboy hat, tinted aviator shades, and the world's longest cigarette; surely a Virginia Slims 120.]

02:29: "Jack Elliot [sic], Kinky Friedman"
[This unlikely duo is shown marching to the microphone, arm-in-arm, with Friedman looking indescribably foolish in his primary colors and Ramblin' Jack looking more than a bit puzzled, as well he might, considering how Friedman had effectively taken his place in the Rolling Thunder troupe. Ramblin' Jack explains his unlikely presence at the Colorado show: "I happened to be in Colorado, so I went to see the show. It was in a football field outdoors in the rain … beautiful day though, rain or shine, as it was nice to see them all. I was standing in the front and Bobby Neuwirth saw me on the field and he reached down and grabbed my hand and pulled me on to the stage. I ended up singing a song with them all and after the song was over I retired to the backstage and saw some of my good old friends. There was different sort of vibe, they didn't seem to be the same happy-go-lucky group that I remember from the first tour in 1975."[1]

03:23: "Roger McGuinn, Joan Baez"
[Baez is singing earnestly on 'A Hard Rain's A-Gonna Fall' while McGuinn stands to her right looking decidedly concerned about all the electric current powering the equipment on an obviously damp stage.]

03:29: "Howie Wyeth"
[The late Wyeth, who in his last few years would concentrate on playing piano with jazz bands, is shown here drumming for all he is worth.]

04:03: "Bob Dylan was born on May 24 1941 in Duluth, Minnesota. In 1962, he released his first record, *Bob Dylan*, as a folk singer with CBS Records. Over the next 15 years he released 21 albums. He devoted his life to his music and was inspirational to the young generation. The songs that really represent his work are 'Blowin' In The Wind' (1963) and 'Hard Rain' (1963), and it was these songs that gave him the title 'protest folk singer.' Since then, he has continued to exert an influence on all musical genres including rock as well as folk."
[This text appears superimposed over shots of the rain-drenched, long haired, crowd. In his weighty tome *The Bob Dylan Encyclopedia*, Michael Gray writes: "By the late 1980s, young people coming to the film afresh tended to remark on the awfulness of the 1970s clothes and all that hair."]

05:39: "'Blowin' In The Wind' (1963)"

[The lyrics to Bob's evergreen anthem appear superimposed directly over the footage of Dylan and Baez duetting, with no red sash backdrop.]

09:02: "'Deportee' (1961)"
[Another acoustic duet with Joan Baez; again, the lyrics appear onscreen, although not the full title: 'Deportee (Plane Wreck At Los Gatos).']

10:24: "This is one of 1,000 songs written for repressed peoples composed by the songwriter Woody Guthrie (1912–1967). John Steinbeck referred to Guthrie as 'the true spirit of America.'"
[This quote appears while Dylan and Baez continue to sing Guthrie's tragic tale.]

12:35:
"Woody Guthrie was my last idol
Since I met him he became my first idol
And because of this he was
He was also my last.

Usually idols that you can't see can be scary
If we become emotionally battered
We lose all sense of hope

But it was different with Woody.
He didn't scare me.
He didn't take away my hope."
[Although there is no credit line for this, which appears on screen during the Dylan-Baez duet, it is, of course, from '11 Outlined Epitaphs,' Dylan's Beat-like poem found on the jacket of his 1964 album, *The Times They Are A-Changin'*.]

12:56: "'Poor Immigrants' (1961)"
[Apparently no one told these Pacific Rim cats that the song is actually called 'I Pity The Poor Immigrant.' The contracted title appears over some great footage of Dylan holding a sunburst Fender Telecaster.]

13:00: "One year before this song was released, on July 29 1966, Bob Dylan had a motorcycle accident at the Woodstock festival and didn't appear publicly for

the next seven years, a self-imposed seclusion which deepened the air of mystery surrounding the star."
[The Woodstock Festival actually took place in August 1969, of course, and Dylan was nowhere near it. If the Japanese Dylan fanatic wasn't distracted enough by the samba arrangement of 'I Pity The Poor Immigrant,' this oversight would surely be a jaw-dropper.]

17:26: "'Shelter From The Storm' (1975)"
[The title appears as Dylan plays slide on his beautiful, white National guitar. This instrument might have been purchased for peanuts in the mid 70s; National 'Map' guitars were breathtakingly unhip, back then. This is a Val-Pro model; they were sold through the US store Montgomery Ward. If Dylan still owns it, he could flog it to a National enthusiast such as David Lindley or The White Stripes' Jack White and make himself an easy $5,000.]

17.37: "Finally ending the long period of darkness, on the 3 January 1974 Bob began a tour of the United States. It was his first tour in eight years. After that, Dylan upped the ante creatively and released his *Before The Flood* album (1974) followed by the album that includes this song, *Blood On The Tracks*, which cemented his comeback and heralded a prolific period of creative activity."
[Although this may not be watertight discographic history, they get the gist of it. Dylan is back, out of retirement, and firing on all cylinders.]

19:07: "Steven Soles"
[He is shown in close-up, looking like an evil Arabic horseman in an Errol Flynn desert drama. The smart money says he never dressed like this around the house.]

19:10: "In October 1975, the single 'Hurricane' was released as a proclamation of the innocence of the black boxer, Hurricane Carter."
[For some reason, this information appears superimposed over footage of 'Shelter From The Storm.' Perhaps the Japanese editors wanted this text in *somewhere*, and felt it logical to mention the word "Hurricane" during a song with "Shelter" in the title.]

22:00: "Gary Burke"
[The percussionist is shown grinning and looking like Neil Young's maniacal

younger brother in Arab headdress and red blazer; Dylan's old friend Greenwich Village buddy Victor Maymudes is visible over Burke's shoulder.]

22:27: "In October 1975, Bob formed a community with Joan Baez, Allen Ginsberg, et al and departed for the Rolling Thunder Revue tour. Stars such as Joni Mitchell, Gordon Lightfoot, et al made special guest appearances throughout the tour."
[This appears over footage of Dylan and Rob Stoner rocking out at the end of 'Shelter From The Storm.']

22:50: "'Maggie's Farm' (1965)"
[The song is performed.]

26:01: "Mick Ronson, T Bone Burnett"
[Both are in the same shot as they perform 'Maggie's Farm.' They will never be mistaken for twins. With Dylan entering the frame, the trio provides three very different visual definitions of the word "cool."]

27:45: "'One Too Many Mornings' (1964)"
[The song is performed.]

29:34: "Scarlet Rivera"
[Correctly identified playing on 'One Too Many Mornings,' she has either been off stage, inaudible, or simply out of the cameras' sightlines before now. In a blue scarf, red poncho, and swinging a lengthy ponytail, she takes both Burnett and Mick Ronson's place, musically speaking. Ronson can be seen behind the amps, surveying the stage while enjoying a cigarette.]

29:40: "'I use language as my weapon of protest; I just have to spit it out!' (Bob Dylan)"
[This quote is attributed to Dylan, where the earlier quote was not. It is possible these two lines are also from *11 Outlined Epitaphs* but that something has been severely lost in translation.]

31:36: "'Mozambique' (1975)"
[Title appears on screen over a shot of Rivera, Dylan, and Stoner. Stoner and

Dylan are both tapping their feet in rhythm, but not in time with each other.]

34.57: "David Mansfield"
[The cherubic Mansfield appears in a white cowboy hat and sky blue denim jacket; he looks uncharacteristically upset. Perhaps the technophile Roger McGuinn has reminded him that they are standing next to high voltage electrical wiring that is being lashed by rain.]

35:24: "'Idiot Wind' (1975)"

46:05: "'Poets don't necessarily have to write poems. There are poets that work at gasoline stands. I don't call myself a poet. Let's say I'm a street performer.' (Bob Dylan)"
[This quote is from scriptwriter-to-be Nora Ephron and Susan Edmiston's August 1965 interview with Dylan, shortly after his historic Forest Hills 'electric' concert. It appears as the show is concluding. The band is performing 'Knockin' On Heaven's Door' as the credits roll from the NBC program, only to do battle with Tokyo Channel 12's superimposed end titles. This final Dylan quotation appears on screen just as a tired-looking Roger McGuinn steps to the microphone for his verse. He sings: "Mama, take this 12-string off of me / I can't play it anymore / You can turn it back into a tree."]

At this point, the Japanese broadcast fades to black, meaning most Japanese viewers not only missed the passed-over 'Railroad Boy' duet, but also 13 further seconds of 'Knockin' On Heaven's Door.' Perhaps Craig Car Stereo is not as influential in Japan as they are in the USA. The Dylan quote is not entirely accurate. It should read: "You don't necessarily have to write to be a poet. Some people work in gas stations and they're poets. I don't call myself a poet because I don't like the word. I'm a trapeze artist."

The Tokyo Channel 12 broadcast was the first time the Land of the Rising Sun had ever really witnessed the live Bob Dylan phenomenon, putting a performing face to the enigmatic figure they had previously only read about, or listened to on record. It would set the stage for Dylan's later successes in the Far East and was, in many ways, a cultural landmark, signposting the imminent Japanese love affair with Western rock'n'roll.

After The Thunder

The gypsy-circus era of Dylan's wild mercury career began sometime in the summer of 1975, on the streets and in the folk music taverns of his adopted hometown, New York City. If a specific moment has to be chosen as the beginning of this phase, then it would have to be July 3, the date Dylan leapt on stage at the Other End, in Greenwich Village, at the invitation of his friend and sometime mentor, Ramblin' Jack Elliott.

This part of the career of popular music's greatest living lyricist began with all the enthusiasm of youth and all the idealism of the very best of the 60s. Rolling Thunder certainly began that way in Plymouth, Massachusetts, the most liberal state in the Union. It ended on May 25 1976, at Salt Lake City's cavernous Salt Palace, in Utah, the most Republican state in the Union. It was a show, before a half-full auditorium, of which even Dylan's most devoted acolytes have yet to find a decent recording, and one which many of its participants admitted was emotionally dispirited if, sporadically, musically exciting. Save for his fascinating appearance at The Band's Last Waltz, the Salt Palace show would be Bob Dylan's last onstage performance until he embarked on a world tour, beginning in Tokyo, Japan, on February 20 1978.

Between the Other End and the Salt Palace, Dylan had appeared on television to celebrate the life of his friend John Hammond, toured the initial Rolling Thunder Revue through New England, planned (if that is the word) and then filmed his first motion picture, organized a triumphant Madison Square Garden show honoring the incarcerated Rubin 'Hurricane' Carter, released the Number One album *Desire*, completed a second, stressful, RTR tour of the American South, filmed one abortive and one successful *Hard Rain* television special, and on the seventh day he rested. In fact, he spent the remainder of the calendar year 1976 attending concerts by fellow icons such as Eric Clapton and Bob Marley, as well as beginning the lengthy editing, re-editing, and re-editing again of the *Renaldo & Clara* footage in a Santa Monica studio/hideaway alongside his close friend and associate Howard Alk.

Dylan's marriage was by now crumbling and it was understandably taking its emotional toll. Although it would be easy to conclude that he was physically hiding away from life, working away in a darkened room, for Dylan there would be no respite from emotional travails in his professional toil. On an almost daily basis, he was staring at footage shot by seasoned professionals of his own musician friends acting amateurishly in scenes which dealt with the fragility of human relationships in general and, more specifically, the traps, trials, and tribulations forced upon any soul who dares enter the bear pit of sexual relations. There would be no respite; the months of editing and re-editing would eventually stretch on throughout 1977, concluding in early December.

Further toll had also been taken. The time and money spent on *Renaldo & Clara*, not to mention its lack of US box office earnings, coupled with the hefty divorce settlement granted to Sara, would oblige Dylan to tour the world in 1978 in order to put his bank account once more in the black. A 60s icon – indeed a 20th century icon, according to *Time* magazine – was now being forced to perform a lengthy tour not to promote his latest mind-blowing, world-reshaping art but to preserve the lifestyle to which he had grown accustomed over the previous decade, paying bills so painfully related to his personal mistakes.

Neither youthful enthusiasm nor 60s idealism were identifiably present in the now deeply emotionally scarred troubadour. Separation from his wife had been a severe body blow. As he later stated: "Nobody in my family gets divorced." He felt he had let himself and his family down, and the divorce clearly left him feeling, to use a wonderful Britishism, *gutted*. In addition, his career and position as rock's top dog would look increasingly imperiled after the critical drubbings given to his next two albums, 1978's *Street Legal* and the following year's *Live At Budokan*. T Bone Burnett had been right in his summation; Dylan was once again Homer, with no (obvious) direction home, courageously continuing with his life's great journey until his battered ship sailed into safe waters again.

Typically for a man who is anything but typical, Bob Dylan would find his way forward through evangelical Christianity, the last safe harbor on earth where any of his acolytes would have once dreamed their hero would willingly drop anchor. However, the clues were there all along. References to The Bible had appeared in his lyrics since 1963's *The Freewheelin' Bob Dylan;* religious figures featured in its Beat poetry-like liner notes. His print interviews had long contained theological asides, and the backdrop painted by Dylan and Bob Neuwirth for the Fort Collins Rolling Thunder concert included religious imagery. Dylan could certainly *look* Christ-like at times, whether in the Jerry Schatzberg photo in which he brandished a small wooden cross, as used on the rear jacket of *Greatest Hits, Vol. 2*, or garbed in Middle Eastern headgear at the *Hard Rain* concert in Fort Collins.

Dylan's gypsy-circus era was as much a product of its time as his earlier balladeering, surrealistic rock'n'roll, or later gospel rock were of theirs. The Rolling Thunder Revue and all its by-products, whether movie, television special, or live album, were the last major gasp of the aforementioned 60s idealism in Bob Dylan's career, a free-spirited valediction before the music business began its relentless drive toward corporate thinking and endless marketing. Rolling Thunder was of a time, to use the words of Bob Neuwirth, spoken so eloquently in the *No Direction Home* documentary, "when art was not necessarily dollar-driven." After Rolling Thunder, not only was the wider music industry increasingly "dollar-driven," so was Dylan. This groundbreaking artist had some serious bills to pay.

His fans would now get the their first glimpse of the former troubadour hero cashing in and becoming the artist who would later license 'The Times They Are A-Changin'' to advertising campaigns for the accountancy agency Coopers & Lybrand (who had allegedly looked the other way while notorious media baron Robert Maxwell was busying himself with fraudulent activities) and the (presumably Maxwell-free) Bank Of Montreal. Dylan and his band would go on to play the occasional highly lucrative private corporate party, to say nothing of Dylan's later awkward appearance in a television advertisement for the Victoria's Secret lingerie brand.

Fading 60s idealism met the market-driven future head-on in the mid 70s and, as writer David Sheppard points out: "The two legs of Rolling Thunder seem to straddle the divide; initial optimism, spontaneity, and not-for-profit romanticism eventually ceding to self-indulgence, ego, and the dictates of the dollar." Rolling Thunder started out as Allen Ginsberg lived his life; with bohemian impulsiveness and Dada-styled reasoning. That it ended in the concrete barns that call themselves basketball arenas meant the goose was laying an egg far more golden for the money changers than for the Allen Ginsbergs of this world.

Bob Dylan and his merry backing band, Guam, provided a spectacle in late 1975 that is impossible to fully appreciate today, unless you happened to have been there. Here was one of rock's most iconic figures, its most enigmatic jester, and a man marinated in mystique and known to be shy even around familiar faces, showing up at short notice in relatively small towns, playing small theatres with a rag-tag crew of musicians. Would the likes of Jagger, Springsteen, or Madonna have ever risked such a venture? (Admittedly Paul McCartney's newly formed Wings had done something vaguely similar in the early 70s, showing up to play ad hoc shows at British University student unions.)

Rolling Thunder and its spin-offs gave a platform not only to rock stars but to important American voices such as Ramblin' Jack Elliott, Allen Ginsberg, and Kinky Friedman. It also spotlighted new talent in the shape of David Mansfield, Ronee Blakley, and T Bone Burnett, all of whom ended up working in film as much as in music. Moreover, it gave Bob Dylan reason to be excited about playing live again after the numbing repetition of his 1974 tour with The Band. The Rolling Thunder Revue, *Desire*, *Renaldo & Clara*, the television special and album, and the various other sidelights of this period of Dylan's career all added up to a traveling, amorphous Beat Hotel where the residents came and went seemingly at the will of the hotel's inscrutable manager, a Mr R.A. Zimmerman of Minnesota.

As with his so-called protest era, his wild mercury 60s, or the country music of his Nashville period, Dylan would never make art like this again. Rock'n'roll hadn't previously witnessed anything quite like the two Rolling Thunder tours or the astounding, confounding music and motion picture they spawned. It was all proof, if any were needed, of Bob Dylan's unique creative restlessness and peerless pioneering spirit. Equally certain: there has been nothing remotely akin to any of it since Dylan's circus folded its big top and rolled away.

ROLLING THUNDER
APPENDICES

Endnotes

1. The World Of John Hammond

1 *Bob Dylan 1966–78: After The Crash* DVD

2. Desire And Rolling Thunder

1 Author's interview, March 13 2009
2 *Bob Dylan 1975–1981: Rolling Thunder And The Gospel Years* DVD
3 Author's interview, February 11 2008
4 Author's interview, December 4 2008
5 Author's interview, August 25 2009
6 Author's interview, November 5 2009
7 Author's interview, October 30 2008
8 Author's interview, December 3 2008
9 *Rolling Stone*, August 28 1975
10 Author's interview, October 30 2008
11 Author's interview, March 3 2009
12 Author's interview, March 3 2009
13 Jacques Levy as quoted in *Bob Dylan 1966–1978: After The Crash* DVD
14 Derek Barker interview with Levy, December 12 1999, reprinted in *Isis* fanzine, issue 90, May 2001
15 *People*, December 22 1975
16 Meehan, *Dancing With Pigs*
17 *Bob Dylan- 1975–1981: Rolling Thunder And The Gospel Years* DVD
18 Sloman, *On The Road With Bob Dylan*
19 *Creem*, April 1976
20 Sloman, *On The Road With Bob Dylan*

21 *Creem*, April 1976
22 *Mojo*, August 2009
23 Meehan, *Dancing With Pigs*
24 Eliot, *The Sacred Wood: Essays On Poetry And Criticism*
25 Author's interview, May 21 2009
26 Meehan, *Dancing With Pigs*
27 Rob Stoner as quoted in *Bob Dylan 1966–1978: After The Crash* DVD
28 Author's interview, April 3 2009
29 Author's interview, April 3 2009
30 Author's interview, April 3 2009
31 Rob Stoner as quoted in *Bob Dylan 1966–1978: After The Crash* DVD
32 Author's interview, November 5 2008
33 Rob Stoner as quoted in *Bob Dylan 1966–1978: After The Crash* DVD
34 Author's interview, December 3 2008
35 Author's interview, November 7 2009
36 Author's interview, March 16 2009
37 Author's interview, May 21 2009
38 *Melody Maker*, October 23 1976
39 Author's interview, November 19 2008
40 Author's interview, December 3 2008
41 Author's interview, December 3 2008
42 *Seattle Weekly*, August 21 2007
43 Author's interview, November 5 2008
44 Author's interview, March 3 2009

4. Main Title Theme: The Backdrop To Renaldo & Clara

1 *Biograph* liner notes, 1985
2 Transcript, by John Hinchey, of Ginsberg's talk at Swarthmore College, Swarthmore, Pennsylvania, November 4 1978, quoted in Gray, *The Bob Dylan Encyclopedia*
3 Miles, *Ginsberg: A Biography*
4 Author's interview, April 21 2009
5 Shepard *The Rolling Thunder Logbook*
6 *Bob Dylan: 1975–1981: Rolling Thunder And The Gospel Years* DVD
7 *Rolling Stone*, January 26 1978
8 *Bob Dylan: 1975–1981: Rolling Thunder And The Gospel Years* DVD
9 *Bob Dylan; 1975–1981: Rolling Thunder And The Gospel Years* DVD
10 Brunette, *Shoot The Piano Player*
11 Dylan, *Chronicles: Volume One*
12 Baez, *And A Voice To Sing With: A Memoir*
13 Author's interview, December 18 2008
14 *Rolling Stone*, January 26 1978
15 Lee, *Like A Bullet Of Light: The Films Of Bob Dylan*
16 *Rolling Thunder Newsletter*, November 12 1975
17 Mel Howard quoted by John Hall in *The Telegraph* Number 46, summer 1993
18 *1966 And All That: D. A. Pennebaker, Film Maker,* reprinted in Gray & Bauldie, *All Across The Telegraph: A Bob Dylan Handbook*
19 Lee, *Like A Bullet Of Light: The Films Of Bob Dylan*
20 Heylin, *Dylan Behind The Shades, Take Two*
21 Author's interview, December 18 2008
22 *Rolling Stone*, November 16 1978

5. Renaldo & Clara: The Four-Hour Dream

1 Author's interview, October 30 2008
2 Author's interview, March 3 2009
3 Author's interview, December 12 2008
4 Author's interview, March 3 2009
5 Author's interview, November 19 2009
6 Author's interview, November 19 2008
7 Author's interview, December 12 2008
8 Author's interview, March 3 2009
9 Author's interview, July 22 2009
10 Author's interview, May 21 2009
11 Author's interview, April 21 2009
12 Author's interview, October 30 2008
13 Gray & Bauldie, *All Across The Telegraph: A Bob Dylan Handbook*
14 Ginsberg, *Collected Poems 1947–1980*
15 Author's interview, February 10 2009
16 Baez, *And A Voice To Sing With: A Memoir*
17 Author's interview, November 5 2008
18 *Rock Around The World* syndicated radio broadcast, April 25 1976
19 Author's interview, December 4 2008

20 *Rock Around The World* syndicated radio broadcast, April 25 1976
21 Author's interview, November 5 2008
22 Author's interview, December 3 2008
23 Author's interview, February 10 2009
24 Author's interview, December 12 2008
25 Shepard, *The Rolling Thunder Logbook*
26 Author's interview, March 3 2009
27 Shelton, *No Direction Home*
28 *Rolling Stone*, November 16 1978
29 Author's interview, April 21 2009
30 Author's interview March 13 2009
31 *Bob Dylan: 1975–1981: Rolling Thunder And The Gospel Years* DVD
32 *Rolling Stone*, November 16 1978
33 Author's interview, December 18 2009
34 *1966 And All That: D. A. Pennebaker, Film Maker*, reprinted in Gray & Bauldie, *All Across The Telegraph: A Bob Dylan Handbook*
35 Author's interview, December 12 2009
36 Author's interview, May 21 2009
37 Author's interview, February 10 2009

6. Clearwater, Florida: The NBC Network Television Special

1 Author's interview, May 21, 2009
2 Author's interview, December 3, 2008
3 Author's interview, November 5, 2008
4 Farinaccio, *Nothing To Turn Off: The Films And Video Of Bob Dylan*

7. Hard Rain: Bicentennial Spring

1 Author's interview, October 19 2009
2 Author's interview, October 30 2008
3 Bauldie, *Diary of A Bobcat* / Sloman, *On The Road With Bob Dylan*
4 Baez, *And A Voice To Sing With: A Memoir*
5 Author's interview, November 5 2008
6 Author's interview, December 3 2008
7 *Bob Dylan 1966 To 1978: After The Crash* DVD
8 Author's interview, December 4 2008
9 Author's interview, April 9 2008
10 Author's interview, April 3 2009
11 Author's interview, October 19 2009
12 Author's interview, November 5 2008
13 Author's interview, November 5 2008
14 Author's interview, November 5 2008

8. Fort Collins, Colorado: The Hard Rain Television Special

1 Author's interview, May 21 2009

9. The Japanese Hard Rain Television Special

1 Author's interview, December 4 2008

Bob Dylan Discography

Albums

Desire (Columbia 1976)

Hard Rain (Columbia 1976)

Masterpieces (Columbia 1978)
Originally released in Australasia and Japan only; released worldwide in 1991.
Contains the 1976 single B-side 'Rita Mae.'

4 Songs From Renaldo And Clara, A Film By Bob Dylan (Columbia 1978)
Promotional EP containing RTR versions of 'People Get Ready,' 'Never Let Me
Go,' 'It Ain't Me, Babe,' and 'Isis.'

Biograph (Columbia 1985)
Contains the previously unreleased *Desire* outtake 'Abandoned Love,' and 'Isis'
and 'Romance In Durango,' recorded live in Montreal, December 4 1975.

The Bootleg Series, Volumes 1-3: Rare & Unreleased 1961-1991 (Columbia 1991)
Contains *Desire* outtakes 'Golden Loom' and 'Catfish,' and 'Seven Days'
recorded live in Tampa, April 21 1976.

Bob Dylan Live 1961–2000: Thirty-Nine Years Of Great Concert Performances
(Columbia 2001)
Contains 'It Ain't Me, Babe' from the original soundtrack to *Renaldo & Clara*.

Bob Dylan Live 1961–2000: Thirty-Nine Years Of Great Concert Performances (SME
Records 2001)
This Japanese release contains 'It Ain't Me, Babe' from the original soundtrack
to *Renaldo & Clara* and 'Shelter From The Storm,' from *Hard Rain*.

The Bootleg Series Vol. 5: Bob Dylan Live 1975, The Rolling Thunder Revue (Sony
2002)

Joan Baez *Rare, Live & Classic* (Vanguard 1993)
A career-spanning boxed set, this contains her duet with Dylan on 'Blowin' In The Wind,' recorded live at Fort Worth, Texas, May 16 1976.

Singles
'Hurricane (Part 1)' / 'Hurricane (Part 2)' (Columbia 1975)
'Mozambique' / 'Oh, Sister' (Columbia 1976)
'Stuck Inside Of Mobile With The Memphis Blues Again' / 'Rita Mae' (Columbia 1976)

DVD
Promotional DVD EP given away with initial copies of *The Bootleg Series, Vol. 5: Bob Dylan Live 1975, The Rolling Thunder Revue (Sony 2002)*
Includes live footage of 'Tangled Up In Blue' and 'Isis' and also an audio-only version of 'Isis.'

General Discography

According to T Bone Burnett, the Rolling Thunder Revue was "a master class in writing, theater, performance, psychology, and stage-directing. There were writers everywhere; songwriters, playwrights, poets – *serious* poets. ... Everyone was constantly playing songs for each other. We would sit around and play in circles, throwing ideas back and forth. We would talk about poetry and read poetry; and we'd talk about film – there were filmmakers there. It was the complete classroom ... Every possible bit of the arts was there, with the exception of sculpture."

If the Rolling Thunder tours, particularly the first one, were indeed arts master classes, it should come as no surprise that the musicians came away inspired in ways unlikely to have been provoked by more typical rock'n'roll environments. The following discography is a subjective list of the acts which grew directly out of Rolling Thunder and those particularly inspired by it, although it commences with two albums without which the RTR might never have happened in the first place. Not every Rolling Thunder participant's post-tour LP is listed – that would be a book in itself – but here are those albums which are germane to the story, and also those which feature two key RTR players or more.

John Herald

John Herald (Paramount 1973)

Herald was a member of the groundbreaking New York City bluegrass band The Greenbriar Boys, the act which Robert Shelton, the respected *New York Times* critic, went to see on September 29 1961, at Gerde's Folk City, and whose review of the evening eloquently praised the 20-year-old opening act, Bob Dylan (and hardly mentioned the headlining Greenbriar Boys at all).

Although Dylan later called Herald "the country Stevie Wonder," such effusive praise failed to slow his professional decline, a decline so precipitous that four years before his tragic 2005 suicide, Herald could be found playing out-of-the-way Scottish gigs with local alt.country acts which were almost certainly oblivious of his pedigree.

After a distinguished career in bluegrass, Herald's first solo album was recorded in 1972, before he moved to the West Coast. It was during its making that four key Rolling Thunder players first met: Dylan's old chum Bob Neuwirth, pianist/drummer Howie Wyeth, bassist Rob Stoner, and guitarist/organist/singer Steven Soles.

The album is also home to a song called 'Ramblin' Jack'. Sadly, the record now sounds dated and twee, if not completely without charm. The three live tracks, "directed by Bob Neuwirth" and recorded at Max's Kansas City, in Manhattan, audibly reflect the spirit of the October 23 1975 Gerde's Folk City hootenanny, which Dylan presided over and which is captured, in part, in *Renaldo & Clara*.

Bob Neuwirth

Bob Neuwirth (Asylum 1974)

In *Chronicles: Volume One*, Dylan describes Bob Neuwirth as "a renaissance man leaping in and out of things … [he] had talent but he wasn't ambitious." Bob Neuwirth is, perhaps regrettably, best known for being a companion of the famous, most notably Dylan but also Janis Joplin, Kris Kristofferson, Patti Smith, and Jim Morrison. Yet, he was (and is) also a fine painter, a provocative songwriter, and an important filmmaker/cinematographer. He had written songs during the 60s but felt he had "nothing to say," so he didn't push this aspect of his career. Instead he became Dylan's wingman. By 1974, he and David Geffen agreed that Neuwirth finally had something to say, and duly signed Akron's finest to a recording contract.

With every SoCal singer-songwriter, scenester, and session man on board, it is a jumbled album, but it is important not only because it contains flashes of greatness (including the songs 'Just Because I'm Here Don't Mean I'm Home' and the oft-covered 'Mercedes Benz') but because to help promote it, Geffen had Neuwirth belatedly booked into Greenwich Village's the Other End for a one-week residency in mid July. It was during this week that several of the future Rolling Thunder tourists would first meet and play together, Dylan included. With Roger McGuinn in the audience and Ramblin' Jack Elliott popping by, this week of album promotion would prove to be ground zero for the Rolling Thunder Revue.

The Alpha Band
The Alpha Band (Arista 1976)
Spark In The Dark (Arista 1977)
The Statue Makers Of Hollywood (Arista 1978)
The Alpha band was perhaps the most promising Rolling Thunder offshoot, and also the most disappointing. The band comprised T Bone Burnett, Steven Soles, and David Mansfield; in other words, a marvelous, inventive songwriter, a fine, expressive singer, and a gifted multi-instrumentalist. The Dylan/RTR connection is further enhanced by Bob Neuwirth co-writing songs on the first two albums. His "directed by" credit also reappears on *Spark In The Dark*. The third album of this trilogy features Rob Stoner's bass, while one Cindy Bullens (who was dismissed by one of the musicians in this paragraph as being "with Rolling Thunder for maybe one gig, for maybe five minutes"), sings harmony on both *Spark In The Dark* and *The Statue Makers Of Hollywood*.

For all their credentials, The Alpha Band's albums are extremely hit-and-miss. The debut holds up best, although arguably their finest song, 'Silver Mantis' was saved for *Spark In The Dark*. It's a song that appeared in Burnett's solo set well into the early 80s, and was, of course, one of his featured numbers on Rolling Thunder. *The Statue Makers Of Hollywood* was a complete misstep from this trio of Christians, as the religious proselytizing was simply too heavy a cross for a heathen audience to bear. Tracks such as 'Tick Tock' and 'Perverse Generation,' while musically polished, will remind the listener of Dylan's *Saved* album: sincere in expression of belief, yes, but sincerely flawed, too.

All three Alpha Band albums are now collected on one Evangeline CD; a curate's egg if ever there was one.

T Bone Burnett
Truth Decay (Takoma 1980)
Now this is the stuff to build a career on. Instructed by legendary LA record mogul Denny Bruce to make an album "like Buddy Holly would make in Las Cruces, if he was alive in the last year of the 70s," J. Henry Burnett did exactly that. With David Mansfield, Steven Soles, and many of The Alpha Band's co-conspirators on board, *Truth Decay*, both in its rollicking lyrical observations and in its gut-level roots-rock intensity, often resembles the Rolling Thunder band at its hard-hitting best. Indeed, it's an album which truly reflects the bright light of Rolling Thunder era Dylan and one that surely warrants a 30th anniversary boxed set edition.

Roger McGuinn
Out Of The Nest (Head 1995)
Cardiff Rose (Columbia 1976)
Thunderbyrd (Columbia 1977)
Few have benefited more from Dylan than the ex-leader of The Byrds. That said, Dylan is gracious enough to admit that The Byrds continued a process started by Peter Paul & Mary; that of making Dylan's songs palatable to the American masses. *Out Of The Nest* is a bootleg CD, captured at McGuinn's July 12 1975 show at My Father's Place, in Roslyn, New York, a village on the north shore of Long Island. It was a former bowling alley converted into a hip, 400-capacity nightclub and its diminutive size was indicative of McGuinn's waning mid-70s appeal. He was there to promote his third solo album, *Roger McGuinn & Band*, an album which failed to dent the American Top 100. Of the 20 songs on *Out Of The Nest*, 13 are Byrds songs and only three are from *Roger McGuinn & Band*.

McGuinn distinguishes himself on the Rolling Thunder tours and, as he told writer Jud Cost (in liner notes to the CD reissue of *Cardiff Rose*): "Mick Ronson and I spent a lot of time bending the elbow." They also plotted to work together. First up was McGuinn's most memorable solo release, *Cardiff Rose*, produced by Mick Ronson, who also played guitar and piano. The album also boasted David Mansfield as multi-tasking instrumentalist, Rob Stoner on bass, and Howie Wyeth on drums. That was five key Rolling Thunder musicians playing together again; it worked a treat. The erstwhile leader of The Byrds is leading something new here; music with a harder edge. The musicians sound like they've been playing together for a long time – which they had, courtesy of Rolling Thunder. Almost every track works, from the opening 'Take Me Away,' a direct evocation of the first Rolling Thunder tour, to 'Jolly Roger,' McGuinn's hilarious comparison of the RTR tour bus, Phydeaux, to a pirate ship. There's also his version of Dylan's 'Up To Me' (a leftover from *Blood On The Tracks*), a terrific cover of the folk standard 'Pretty Polly,' itself a much-jammed RTR backstage standard, and the concluding 'Dreamland,' a Joni Mitchell contribution gifted to McGuinn one night as Phydeaux motored through the New England darkness.

Thunderbyrd was originally to feature Mick Ronson on lead guitar and vocals and McGuinn on his trusty 12-string and vocals. Don DeVito, producer of *Desire*, was also brought on board. Somehow, rehearsals never quite gelled. It could have been great, with McGuinn and Ronson a fascinating guitar duo, but ultimately *Thunderbyrd* would featured nothing from Ronson and only three names from Dylan's Rolling Thunder era; McGuinn, DeVito, and lyricist Jacques Levy. The latter co-wrote 'It's Gone, Dixie Highway,' 'I'm Not Lonely Anymore,' and the startlingly inventive 'Russian Hill,' a criminally unheralded classic which McGuinn still occasionally performs in his acoustic, career-spanning show. *Thunderbyrd* is not a bad album in its own right, but it's a comedown after the dizzying artistic heights scaled on *Cardiff Rose*.

Mick Ronson

Play, Don't Worry (RCA 1975)
While it's impossible to imagine either Bob Dylan or Bob Neuwirth listening to this and particularly enjoying it, *Play, Don't Worry* must be declared a minor, late classic of the UK's glam-rock era. The original LP featured nine tracks, with no Rolling Thunder connection other than Ronson. Gifted guitarist and producer as he was, it seems unlikely that this LP was enough on it own to have merited Ronson being invited onto Rolling Thunder. More probably, it was his work with the band Pure Prairie League on their 1972 album, *Bustin' Out*, that gave Bob Neuwirth the idea that the Limey should tag along on the RTR – especially given that a song from the album called 'Amie,' an undeniably catchy country-rock tune, was a hit US single in the fall of 1975.

The CD reissue of *Play, Don't Worry* contains nine extra tracks, six of which have a notable Rolling Thunder influence and musical direction. After the fall 1975 RTR tour concluded, Ronson entered Sundragon Studios in New York

City to record some demos with David Mansfield, Rob Stoner, Howie Wyeth, and Steven Soles in tow. Sundragon was chosen as it was inexpensive and Soles often recorded there. David Mansfield told me about six Sundragon recordings which found their way onto the CD reissue of *Play, Don't Worry*. "The bonus tracks are mostly from the Sundragon sessions, a funky little studio in Manhattan ... they were just demos. On those six tunes, the rhythm section is always Rob Stoner and Howie Wyeth. I'm playing a lot of pedal steel, always through a Maestro phase shifter, which was what I used all during Rolling Thunder. 'Stone Love' is *really* familiar-sounding, same thing with 'I'd Rather Be Me.' These are just Mick, Howie, Rob, and I. Maybe they were songs Mick contributed to the abortive *Thunderbyrd*, maybe we rehearsed them on the RTR.

"'Is There Life On Mars' [was] written by my good friend Bob Barnes, aka Roscoe West. I don't know who the background singers are but I'm sure Steve Soles is one of them. This was the very song Mick played for his featured spot in the RTR show, although I do remember he did a song by my friend Nan O'Byrne, entitled 'Street Angel,' a few times. 'Pain In The City,' I don't remember ... I'm not on it but Mickey Raphael is playing harmonica. I can tell that it's Stoner on bass and Howie on drums, though. 'The Dogs' is a T Bone [Burnett] song, we used to play it now and then in the Guam set, and we recorded it as The Alpha Band, with a very similar arrangement. '28 Days' is a jam that I'm not on and don't remember ... must be Mick, Rob, and Howie."

Topaz

Topaz (Columbia 1977)
Produced by Don DeVito this is, like McGuinn's *Thunderbyrd* album, an extremely slick, polished-sounding record. Although Rob Stoner is on bass and vocals, the album's artistic vision seems to have been dictated to him by a CBS A&R man. Stoner's alleged hero is Gene Vincent, but there's no evidence at all of Sweet Gene's influence here.

Due to its AOR sheen, *Topaz* sounds almost shamefully geared for US FM radio and is, therefore, completely devoid of any Rolling Thunder influence or attitude. It's a fine example of why punk rock had to happen. Despite the presence of Mick Ronson, Howie Wyeth, and Luther Rix (to say nothing of Don DeVito), you would never in a million years guess these participants had something to do with *Desire* or *Hard Rain*. *Topaz* proves David Mansfield was correct when he said (of the aborted initial *Thunderbyrd* project), that the writing styles of McGuinn, Ronson, and Rob Stoner were "too disparate to ever really gel."

Kinky Friedman

Lasso From El Paso (Epic 1976)

He could've been a contender. Now established as Bill Clinton's favorite mystery novelist, a pundit on Bill O'Reilly's reactionary Fox television show, and a man who won 12 per cent of the vote in the 2006 Texas gubernatorial race, Kinky Friedman is not a man to be dismissed lightly. Dylan has long contended that if Kinky had recorded earlier, he would've had a better chance at a successful singing career. As it was, Friedman's satirical country & western debut, *Sold American*, appeared in 1973, when his generation of singers were already well into their careers. As Friedman has pointed out, he spent much of the 60s picketing segregated Austin restaurants and working for the Peace Corps, so it was non-musical time well spent.

Lasso From El Paso is his third solo album, although it kicks off with a new take on the title track from his debut – a live RTR version on which Friedman is introduced to the crowd by Bob Neuwirth and backed by Guam. This recording dates from the *Hard Rain* television shoot in Fort Collins, Colorado, with Friedman ostensibly filling the shoes so ably worn by Ramblin' Jack Elliott on the tour's earlier leg.

There are other RTR/Dylan connections. Although the album is cursed by a very 70s predilection for amassing superstars in the studio, this is not the usual case of quantity over quality and the musicians certainly make an impact. T Bone Burnett, Roger McGuinn, Mick Ronson, Steve Soles, Howie Wyeth, Gary Burke, and Ronnie Hawkins all appear on it – Hawkins contributing an amusing song unblushingly called 'Kinky.' Who knew The Hawk was a good songwriter? Dylan's oft-covered 'Catfish' is essayed here in fine fashion, the equal of Guam's version on Rolling Thunder and better than Joe Cocker's bizarre misreading (exactly how much baseball Cocker was exposed to, growing up alongside the Sheffield steel mills, is not known).

Lasso From El Paso is not an album to play for your children, your bank manager, or the vicar when he comes to tea. To say it is simultaneously childishly vulgar and challengingly adult-themed is to say the Pope wears sparkly clothes and speaks Latin.

Scarlet Rivera

Scarlet Rivera (Warner Bros 1977)
Scarlet Fever (Warner Bros 1978)

Scarlet Rivera should have been one of the main benefactors of the Rolling Thunder/*Desire*/*Renaldo & Clara*/*Hard Rain*-era period, as she is so heavily featured in every move Dylan made during his post-*Blood On The Tracks* creative whirl. When she dismounted at the end of Rolling Thunder's dusty trail, she, unsurprisingly, received innumerable offers of session work. Thanks to her hard-won high profile, and through the managerial auspices of Mary Martin (the same Mary Martin who in 1965 was the secretary in Albert Grossman's office and who had advised that The Hawks would be the perfect backing band for Bob Dylan), Rivera landed a solo contract with Warner/Reprise Records.

Looking undeniably alluring on the covers of both albums, young Scarlet would have been a logical star for Warners to market in the unlikely event that the desiccated world of jazz fusion had been capable of birthing *any* sex symbol whatsoever. Ms Rivera's two solo albums were certainly fusion-based, somewhat arty, and in no way musically related to anything Dylan would ever do. Some 30 years down the line, they sound technically accomplished, musically complex, and conceptually deft. They're certainly exhausting to any listener brought up on 'Louie Louie,' 'Light My Fire,' or even 'Like A Rolling Stone.' Rivera is accompanied on her debut by Gary Burke, the percussionist who replaced Luther Rix for the second Rolling Thunder tour, and who later played with Joe Jackson. Burke performs admirably on percussion, drums, and vibes on these two albums. Rivera makes the fatal mistake of having her manager not only produce the recordings but, for the second album, help with the songwriting. Dylan detectives will note the presence of keyboard player Paul Griffin on *Scarlet Fever*.

In 2010, these two albums are best regarded as music made by musicians for other musicians. The lengthy structure of the melodies, the challenging time changes, and the frequent soloing suggest a jazz-rock Schubert. File next to Frank Zappa's similarly inclined excursions, The Mahavishnu Orchestra, and Larry Coryell's Eleventh House. Weep not for Scarlet Rivera as she plays on today, as passionate as she was when backing Dylan at the *World Of John Hammond* show, one windy night in Chicago.

Index

75, 78–82, 86–95, 118,
120,
128–129, 138, 146,
148–149, 161–162, 166,
170, 179, 182–183,
200–201, 205–206, 213,
217–218, 222, 227,
239–241
McLean, Don, 62
Meehan, Don, 43, 48,
52–56, 194–195,
203–204, 207–208,
217–218
Melody film, 171
Melville, Herman, 144
'Mercedes Benz,' 64, 239
Mercedes, Denise (*see also*
Felieu, Denise), 60, 128,
168, 218
'Mexico City Blues' (poem),
160
Meyer, Russ, 144
'Michael, Row The Boat
Ashore,' 74
Midler, Bette, 27, 29, 56, 58
Midnight Cowboy movie, 118
Midnight Special, The
television show, 176
Miles, Barry, 99–100, 138,
168
'Miller's Tale, The,' 214
'Million Miles,' 172
Minghella, Anthony, 109
Minneapolis Party Tape
album, 214
'Mr. Tambourine Man,' 73,
176–177, 198–199, 211,
221
Mitchell, Joni, 65, 71–72,
82, 87–91, 128, 138,
148, 186, 197, 225, 241
Moby Dick book, 144
'Money Blues,' 50, 52, 54
Monroe, Bill, 206
*Monty Python & The Holy
Grail* movie, 174
Moore, Davey, 47
Moorehead, Agnes, 114
Morrison, Jim, 32, 238
Morrison, Van, 209

Mothers Of Invention, The,
60
Mott The Hoople, 197
'Mozambique,' 37, 49, 55,
199, 216, 221, 226, 237
Murch, Walter, 109
*Murder Of Fred Hampton,
The* movie, 116, 212
Murphy, Willie, & The Bees,
56
Music From Big Pink album,
212
Myers, David, 117, 130,
133–134, 145, 169, 173

N
Nash, Graham, 63
Nashville movie, 64
Nashville Skyline album, 203
NBC's Saturday Night Live
television show, 177
Nauyaks, Fred, 40
'Need A New Sun Rising
Every Day,' 64, 142
Neil, Fred, 151
Nelson, Willie, 156, 188
Neuwirth, Bob, 28, 30–36,
54, 57–58, 60–65,
67–68, 71–73, 98, 104,
128–129, 131, 136,
139–140, 146–147,
150–151, 155, 168, 172,
180, 183, 196, 199, 203,
205, 212–213, 216, 218,
221–222, 230, 241
'Never Let Me Go,' 69, 167
New Riders Of The Purple
Sage, 69
Night Of The Hurricane
benefit show, 76, 113
Night Of The Hurricane 2,
188, 191
'Night They Drove Old Dixie
Down, The,' 71, 201
*No Direction Home: Bob
Dylan* movie/DVD, 115,
139, 230
No Reason To Cry album,
189
'Norwegian Wood,' 51

Nuff Said album, 171
'Nurse's Song,'139

O
O'Byrne, Nan, 242
Ochs, Phil, 36, 114, 131, 190
'Oh Brother,' 50
Oh! Calcutta! (theatrical
revue), 36
Oh Mercy album, 149
'Oh Sister,' 23, 49–50, 54,
73, 203–204, 211, 221,
237
'Okie From Muskogee,' 198
Oliver, James, 40
'On Reading Dylan's Writing'
(poem), 159
On The Road book, 160
'One More Cup Of Coffee,'
26, 30, 37, 49, 55, 74,
157, 170, 225
'One Of Us Must Know
(Sooner Or Later),' 191
'One Too Many Mornings,'
156, 194, 199, 207,
216–217, 221
Oppel, Peter, 125
Oppenheim, David, 26, 37–38
Orbach, Jerry, 45, 47, 49
Orbach, Martam, 45, 49
Orlovsky, Peter, 60, 128,
138, 218
Other End, the (folk club, *see
also* Bitter End, the),
27–34, 37, 57–58, 71,
131, 152–153, 228, 239
Out Of The Nest album, 240
Outlaw Josey Wales, The
movie, 119

P
Paralysed album, 33
Parker, Eleanor, 114
'Pastures Of Plenty,' 70
Pat Garrett & Billy The Kid
movie, 50, 117–118,
120–122
'Patty's Gone To Laredo,' 166
Paxton, Tom, 27
Pearl album, 64

'Perverse Generation,' 239
Peckinpah, Sam, 50,
118–119, 121–122
Peer Gynt play, 36
Pennebaker, D.A., 98,
116–117, 122, 146, 173
'People Get Ready,' 140
Peter Paul & Mary, 25, 27,
240
Phillips, Brewer, 208
Phydeaux (tour-bus), 60, 65,
78, 85–86, 92, 241
'Pick A Bale O' Cotton,' 178
Pickens, Slim, 119, 122
Pink Floyd The Wall movie,
116
Planet Waves album, 205
Play Don't Worry album, 64,
241
'Please Come To Boston,'
70–71
Poons, Larry, 196
Porco, Mike, 36, 59, 131, 152
'Postcard To D___' (poem),
159
Preminger, Otto, 119
'Pretty Boy Floyd,' 30
Pride, Charlie, 215
Prine, John, 198
Profaci, Joseph, 46
Proof Through The Night
album, 62
Pure Prairie League, 241
'Put Down Your Cigarette
Rag (Don't Smoke),' 85

Q
Quo Vardis movie, 78

R
'Race Among The Ruins,' 72
Raeben, Norman, 37, 51,
104, 123–124, 126, 161
'Railroad Boy, The' (*see also*
'Butcher Boy, The'), 202,
214, 220–221
'Rainy Day People,' 72
Ramblin' Boys, The album, 66
'Ramblin' Jack,' 65
Ramone, Johnny, 209

Acknowledgements

Books
Joan Baez *And A Voice To Sing With: A Memoir* (Summit Books 1987)
Derek Barker (ed) *Isis: A Bob Dylan Anthology* (Helter Skelter 2004)
Derek Barker (ed) *Bob Dylan Anthology Volume 2: 20 Years Of Isis* (Chrome Dreams 2005)
John Bauldie (ed) *Wanted Man: In Search Of Bob Dylan* (Citadel Underground 1991)
Olof Bjorner *Olof's Files: A Bob Dylan Performance Guide, Volume 2, 1970–1977* (Hardinge Simpole 2003)
Mark Blake (ed) *Dylan: Visions, Portraits, And Back Pages* (DK 2005)
Tim Brookes *Guitar: An American Life* (Grove Press 2005)
Doug Boyd *Rolling Thunder* (Delta 1974)
Peter Brunette (ed) *Shoot The Piano Player: François Truffaut, Director* (Rutgers 1993)
Jonathan Cott (ed) *Dylan On Dylan: The Essential Interviews* (Hodder & Stoughton 2006)
Sydney R. Davies *Walking The London Scene: Five Walks In The Footsteps Of The Beat Generation* (Grimsay Press 2006)
Kevin J.H. Dettmar (ed) *The Cambridge Companion To Bob Dylan* (Cambridge University Press 2009)
Glen Dundas, *Tangled: A Recording History Of Bob Dylan* (SMA Services 2004)
Vince Farinaccio *Nothing To Turn Off: The Films And Video Of Bob Dylan* (Vincent Farinaccio private printing 2007)
John Gibbens *The Nightingale's Code: A Poetic Study Of Bob Dylan* (Touched Press 2001)
Robert Graves *The White Goddess* (Faber and Faber 1948)
Michael Gray & John Bauldie (eds) *All Across The Telegraph: A Bob Dylan Handbook* (Futura 1987)
Michael Gray *Song & Dance Man III: The Art Of Bob Dylan* (Continuum 2000)
Michael Gray *The Bob Dylan Encyclopedia* (Continuum 2008)
Clinton Heylin *Bob Dylan: Behind The Shades – The Biography –Take Two* (Penguin 2001)
Clinton Heylin *Bob Dylan: The Recording Sessions 1960–1994* (St. Martin's Griffin 1995)
Brian Hinton *Bob Dylan Album File & Complete Discography* (Cassell Illustrated 2006)
C.P.Lee *Like A Bullet of Light: The Films Of Bob Dylan* (Helter Skelter 2000)
Barry Miles *Ginsberg: A Biography* (Penguin 1990)

Keith Negus *Bob Dylan* (Indiana University Press 2008)
John Nogowski *Bob Dylan: A Descriptive, Critical Discography And Filmography* (McFarland 2008)
Sam Shepard *Rolling Thunder Logbook* (Sanctuary 2004)
Larry "Ratso" Sloman *On The Road With Bob Dylan* (Helter Skelter 2005)
Howard Sounes *Down The Highway: The Life Of Bob Dylan* (Doubleday 2001)
Paul Williams *Bob Dylan: Performing Artist 1974–1986: The Middle Years* (Omnibus 1994)
Paul Williams *Bob Dylan: Watching The River Flow, Observations On His Art-In-Progress: 1966–1995* (Omnibus 1996)

Magazines
These are in addition to those cited in the endnotes.
The Big Issue November 23–29 2009 No.874, Dylan interview by Bill Flanagan
Creem April 1976, Lester Bangs *Bob Dylan's Dalliance With Mafia Chic*
Rolling Stone December 4 1975, Larry Sloman *Bob Dylan And Friends On The Bus – Like A Rolling Thunder*

DVDs
Bob Dylan 1966-1978: After The Crash (Chrome Dreams 2005)
Bob Dylan 1975-1981: Rolling Thunder And The Gospel Years (Music Video Distribution/Wienerworld 2006)
Down The Tracks: The Music The Influenced Bob Dylan (Eagle Vision 2008)
Les Enfants Du Paradis (Second Sight 2005)
Federico Fellini's 8½ (Nouveaux Pictures 2001)
Shoot The Piano Player! (Criterion, 2005)
The Woman In White (Scooter Movies, 2008)

Picture Credits
The pictures in this book came from the following sources, and the publishers are grateful for their help.

Jacket © Bob Gruen/bobgruen.com; **2** © Bob Gruen/bobgruen.com; **6** Blank Archives/Getty Images (map and flyer); © Bob Gruen/bobgruen.com (curtain); **7–12** © Bob Gruen/bobgruen.com; **13** ©1974 Elsa Dorfman all rights reserved/elsadorfman.com (Dylan and Ginsberg); © Bob Gruen/bobgruen.com; **14** © Bob Gruen/bobgruen.com (live shot); Blank Archives/Getty Images (poster and 45); **15–16** © Bob Gruen/bobgruen.com.

Author's Thanks

Proud author Sid Griffin is proud of many things. He is proud of this book, to be sure, but proud also of the many old friends and the many new faces who gave of their time and of their talents to make *Shelter From The Storm* what it is. First off let me thank my interview subjects, for without them much of any book of this nature would be conjecture. Please take a bow T Bone Burnett ("I'd like to thank the Academy…"), Roger McGuinn, Ramblin' Jack Elliott, Louis Kemp, Kinky Friedman, Ronnie "The Hawk" Hawkins, Arlo Guthrie, Larry "Ratso" Sloman, Barry Miles, David Mansfield, Don Meehan, and Steven Gaydos. A special thank-you goes out to the late L.A. Johnson, who took time out from his LincVolt automobile project with Neil Young to give me a lengthy and quite amazing interview. Larry Johnson was a true talent, was one of a kind, and he will be missed greatly.

As stated, old friends pitched in too, none more so than ex-Long Ryders bass player, singer, and songwriter Tom Stevens. Without my old Long Ryder buddy from Indiana helping with the research and then acting as a Greek Chorus to many of my ideas, this book would have been the size of a comic and about as valuable. Thanks, Tom. Also invaluable were Bill Wasserzieher in Long Beach, Derek Barker at ISIS, Domenic Priore in Hollywood, Stratton Owen Hammon, wherever he lays his hat, Greg Sowders of Warner-Chappell in LA, Jeff Rosen in New York, and painter/musician/songwriter extraordinaire Bob Neuwirth.

To my beloved Coal Porters band: Carly Frey, Dick Smith, Andrew Stafford, and my rock-solid Scottish compadre Neil Bob Herd: may God bless and keep you always. To my sister, the amazing Eleanor, I can only say my writing books is little brother's attempt to catch up. And most of all thank you to my family: Dr Rhiannon Owen (the very pride of the NHS) and my much-loved, gorgeous children, Esther Mae Griffin and her younger brother Noah Greenberry Griffin. Now you know why Daddy has no day job.

Since the publication of *Million Dollar Bash*, a noticeable number of people, upon seeing the Author's Thanks therein, have approached me and shyly asked if my mother did live to see its publication. She did: she held the book in her arms and told me how proud she was of me. *Million Dollar Bash* was very well-received, yes, but that was the greatest compliment I got by far. And I repeat that moment in my mind frequently.

"I think, now, that Rolling Thunder was a reference to an American Indian chief, but Bob, being multi-faceted, probably knew it as a slam to the Vietnam war, which had Operation Rolling Thunder, a hideous napalm bombing campaign. You know, there were a lot of meanings: we were rolling down the road and making a lotta noise, as well."
Roger McGuinn, 2008

Other books in this series:

MILLION DOLLAR
BASH: BOB DYLAN,
THE BAND, AND THE
BASEMENT TAPES
by Sid Griffin

HOT BURRITOS:
THH TRUE STORY OF
THE FLYING BURRITO
BROTHERS
by John Einarson with
Chris Hillman

BOWIE IN BERLIN:
A NEW CAREER IN A
NEW TOWN
by Thomas Jerome
Seabrook

THE
AUTOBIOGRAPHY:
YES, KING CRIMSON,
EARTHWORKS, AND
MORE
by Bill Bruford

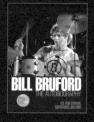

BEATLES FOR SALE:
HOW EVERYTHING
THEY TOUCHED
TURNED TO GOLD
by John Blaney

TO LIVE IS TO DIE:
THE LIFE AND DEATH
OF METALLICA'S CLIFF
BURTON
by Joel McIver

MILLION DOLLAR
LES PAUL: IN SEARCH
OF THE MOST
VALUABLE GUITAR IN
THE WORLD
by Tony Bacon

THE IMPOSSIBLE
DREAM: THE STORY
OF SCOTT WALKER
AND THE WALKER
BROTHERS
by Anthony Reynolds

Autumn 2010:

JACK BRUCE:
COMPOSING
HIMSELF: THE
AUTHORISED
BIOGRAPHY
by Harry Shapiro

A WIZARD, A TRUE
STAR: TODD
RUNDGREN IN THE
STUDIO
by Paul Myers

RETURN OF THE
KING: ELVIS PRESLEY'S
GREAT COMEBACK
by Gillian G. Gaar

SEASONS THEY
CHANGE: THE STORY
OF ACID AND
PSYCHEDELIC FOLK
by Jeanette Leech

FOREVER CHANGES:
ARTHUR LEE AND THE
BOOK OF LOVE
by John Einarson